A FLYFISHER'S WORLD

BOOKS BY NICK LYONS

THE SEASONABLE ANGLER

JONES VERY: SELECTED POEMS (editor)

FISHERMAN'S BOUNTY (editor)

THE SONY VISION

LOCKED JAWS

FISHING WIDOWS

TWO FISH TALES

BRIGHT RIVERS

CONFESSIONS OF A FLY FISHING ADDICT

TROUT RIVER (text for photographs by Larry Madison)

SPRING CREEK

A FLYFISHER'S WORLD

A FLYFISHER'S WORLD

Nick Lyons

DRAWINGS BY MARI LYONS

THE ATLANTIC MONTHLY PRESS · NEW YORK

The essays in this book originally appeared in *The Riverwatch,* the *New
York Times, Field & Stream,* and, chiefly, in my "Seasonable Angler"
column in *Fly Fisherman.* My warm thanks to Edward McGlinn (*The
Riverwatch*), Duncan Barnes and Slaton White (*Field & Stream*), and to
my longtime and valued editors at *Fly Fisherman,* John Randolph and
Philip Hanyok, for first publishing all this work. I remain grateful to Carl
Navarre for wanting to publish a second book of mine and to Bonnie
Thompson, the finest of copy editors.

Published simultaneously in Canada
Printed in the United States of America

First edition

Library of Congress Cataloging-in-Publication Data

Lyons, Nick.
    A flyfisher's world / Nick Lyons; drawings by Mari Lyons. — 1st ed.
        p.   cm.
    ISBN 0-87113-628-7
    1. Fly fishing—United States—Anecdotes.   2. Fishers—United
States—Biography.   3. Lyons, Nick.   I. Title.
SH463.L96   1996
799.1′2—dc20   95-39206
    [B]

Design by Liz Driesbach

The Atlantic Monthly Press
841 Broadway
New York, NY 10003

10 9 8 7 6 5 4 3 2 1

FOR **TONY**— UP TO HIS GILLS IN FISH BOOKS

"The take instantly validates our efforts,
conferring a measure of definitiveness and closure to
to an enterprise otherwise riddled with uncertainty
and inconclusiveness. Few things in life,
I think, have this to offer."

—TED LEESON, *The Habit of Rivers*

CONTENTS

INTRODUCTION *xiii*

PART ONE
Various Beginnings and Revelations

1 Au Sable Apocalypse *3*
2 A Fisherman's Childhood in Brooklyn *8*
3 Green Trout *15*
4 Another Season Begins *21*

PART TWO
Some Fish I've Chased

5 The Generous Bluegill *29*
6 Small Fish *37*
7 Little Wolves of the Weeds *42*
8 Largemouth Magic *48*
9 Riverbass *56*
10 First Blues on a Fly *62*
11 Selective Blues—and Striped Bass *68*
12 Civilization and the Blues at East Hampton *74*
13 World of the Silver Kings *78*
14 French Pike *84*
15 Brookie *90*
16 The Snobbish Brown Trout *96*

PART THREE
How We Do It—and with What and Whom and When . . .

17 How We Do It *103*
18 Fly Fishing for Anything, Any Way *109*
19 Gadgets and Gizmos *115*

20 A Fine Madness *119*
21 Space Age Stuff *125*
22 In a Barrel *130*
23 The Journals of Clyde Fish *135*
24 Honey Holes *140*
25 Sizing Up New Rivers *145*
26 Water Watching *152*
27 The Mystery Hatch *157*
28 Local Genius *163*
29 Country Hardware Store *169*
30 When *175*
31 In the Car *180*
32 Records *186*
33 Dog-Day Redemption *191*
34 On a Small Creek *197*
35 Enough *202*
36 Day of Rest *207*
37 Seasons End *212*

PART FOUR
Fishing in the Head (Mostly)

38 Fishing Backward *219*
39 The Collector's Hook *224*
40 Crowds *230*
41 Mean Streams *235*
42 Midspring Afternoon Dreams *240*
43 What I Did Last Summer *246*
44 Rhythms *251*
45 The Antic Angler *257*
46 Humanity: A to Zern *263*
47 A Fierce Pursuit but Not a Circus *268*
48 A Parliament of Skills *273*
49 The *Things* of Fly Fishing *278*
50 Fly Fishing in Bed *283*

INTRODUCTION

I am struck, as I move deeply into my sixties, by how much I still love to fly fish and to write about fly fishing, how grateful I am for the simple fun and happy intensity this passion has given me since that day, many years ago, when I saw a trout rise and had some brand of apocalyptic vision on Michigan's Au Sable River.

I had fished since before memory—with worm, frog, doughball, and spinning lure—but fly fishing, requiring such a galaxy of disciplines, was different; and from that day, despite all the complexities of my personal life and the much greater complexities of a world in volatile flux, fly fishing has always been in my head: quirky, maverick, green thoughts that shaped themselves into the kind of personal essays I've collected in this book. They came while I was strap-hanging in a New York subway almost as often as when I was on a river, while I was in business conferences, reading a book, waiting for a doctor, and even, a year ago, as I lay in a hospital bed, as I returned from a sour brush with death.

I have not deluded myself all these years into thinking that fly fishing was a religion, a "way of life," an activity more important than a thousand other human activities—neither growing a family, putting together a life in classrooms and offices, nor wars, tragic events in Bosnia or Africa or Russia or Asia, nor high art. It is merely a lovely, useless activity that, somehow, has become an axial line in my life, an anchor. I wanted desperately to write when I was young, and fishing, somehow, became a magnet for most of what I have had to say on *any* subject; I have found it one of the happiest parts of my life to write about this activity, to dream and imagine and recollect and theorize about fly fishing. It did not take me long, in my twenties, to discover that I was not Joyce, neither was I Faulkner. Tolstoy and Dickens were vaster than I knew, Kafka wiser; even a local columnist I thought thin had his special craft. In fly fishing I found a plot of land that was mine—small but not contemptible, capable of yielding a strange and amusing fruit or two, mostly beneath the world's notice, but always and inescapably my lot and something satisfying to write about. That it gave enough people pleasure to read what I'd done helped me to write more, and I am grateful to them as much as I am to rivers and fly rods.

This summer, in the West, as I've collected these essays, mostly of the past half-dozen years, I've noticed that more and more seem to be looking backward or to theory. Three-quarters of my life is behind me and so are most of my "firsts"—with tarpon, bluefish, pike, and other species but also, probably, with places. I've never been much of an explorer. I've always preferred intimacy to the exotic. Increasingly, I lean toward memory and reflection—perhaps because I am no longer bursting with energy, as I was in my manic youth. My fires are banked now: less flashy but probably hotter and certainly more concentrated. I fish more wisely; I have a keener sense of where fish will be and when they'll be up. I probably fall in less—and certainly I have reported on my pratfalls enough for this trip.

What's left?

Always to connect and to distill. Always to understand a bit more. The urgency of our senior years, if we rise to the challenge, is the urgency to find some "blessed rage for order," a desire to put things in their places. I doubt very much if "the best is yet to come," but we have more history than we had forty, twenty, or even ten years ago and that history can be very satisfying. We do not have to catch as many fish or fish quite so long and so hard each day; less counts for more. And as we extrude our history, the way spiders extrude their silky strands, we provide the traps in which to capture our future.

I fished a spring creek I knew well last week and came to a bend I'd fished fifty times before. It was a one- or two-fish bend, below a large lake-like expanse of the river, and it was a big-fish bend; I had twice hooked outsized browns here—one that ran me up to the lake and broke off in tangled roots, the other that I'd caught a year ago, twenty-seven inches' worth, on a hopper. I knew exactly where to position myself and where to look for fish. There was some nervous water in the small eddy and I thought I must have spooked the fish on my approach. So I sat down calmly, as I do more and more frequently, and changed my leader tippet from 6X to 5X. I checked the Surgeon's Knot I now use, tied on my favorite imitation of a Pale Morning Dun, the obvious *plat du jour* after two hours of proof, checked that knot too, turned back to the eddy, and made a crisp, low twenty-five-foot cast.

The fish took instantly and rocketed upstream. It swept past the willow roots at the outward bend, furrowed just beneath the surface, and then made a gigantic leap. Just as I thought. It was one of the alligators this river held—a truly gigantic brown—and I leaped from my seat as the fish leaped, prepared to chase it.

Then the fish leaped again. But this time its zeal sent it high on the bank, where it wriggled in some rose brambles and then flopped back into the river, my PMD in its lip.

That excitement—the odd admixture of the known and the new, of old skills leading me into deeper, unpredictable waters, of the electric rise and the hilarious, unimagined escape—keeps me coming back, and always will.

I am grateful to such moments—as I am grateful that, on a grizzly day in Michigan, forty years ago, I had my life nudged in a totally different direction simply by a trout's rise.

—NICK LYONS
Ennis, Montana
Summer 1995

PART ONE

Various beginnings and revelations

AU SABLE APOCALYPSE

Soon after we were married, my wife and I moved
to Michigan—I to start graduate studies in Ann Arbor, Mari
to study art at the Cranbrook Academy. We first lived in
Pontiac—in the kitchen area of a huge, decaying mansion
where it got so cold that first winter that a cup of coffee left
on the table overnight froze solid. When our first son was
born, we moved to Ann Arbor. Marrying, fathering, studying
were each full-time occupations, and for more than a year I
fished not at all. Soon afterward we had a second child, and

for a while I was so preoccupied that I even stopped *thinking* about fishing.

But you cannot hide fire in the straw. When I passed my oral exams, I begged for a rest, and we all headed upcountry to the Au Sable River. I owned a white glass fly rod then and knew just enough about using it to avoid threading the line through the keeper ring. I practiced casting on basketball courts and ponds, and I had caught bluegills—though never a trout—on a fly. I had to face it: I was lousy with a fly rod and didn't think I could catch a fish with one. Mostly, I used a Mitchell spinning reel and a C. P. Swing—the ultimate in simplicity and killing power—for all occasions.

We found a cheap motel near Grayling, had a noisy family dinner, and in the morning I sneaked out about 5 A.M. and fished with my spinning outfit. It was late in April and quite cold. The water was a bit discolored, but clearing. I cast my spinner in against the famous "sweepers," into the heads of big bend pools, and by 8 A.M. had taken five or six good browns. It had been a very pleasant morning and I'd enjoyed this new river very much, and it felt terrific being on the water again.

We had a leisurely breakfast, and I asked Mari what she would like to do. I'd taken some fish and wasn't in any particular fever to fish again—at least not for a few more hours. I could be generous.

There really wasn't much to do on a drizzly late-April day in Grayling with two infants, so we ended up taking a drive. It ended (as have so many since) on a bridge over a beautiful river. It was still chilly, so Mari stayed in the car with the kids. I said I'd be back in a few minutes.

The water had cleared a bit. It was a gorgeous section of the Au Sable, with deadfalls, overhanging willows, bright runs and riffles. You could see the bottom now, and I thought I saw several auburn shapes upstream by a large boulder. I can't swear to it, though. I often imagine fish.

Farther upstream, a fly fisher was wading out from the right bank, stripping line from his reel, watching the route of the current along the far bank. He had on a large streamer, and moments later he was casting it with great authority against the bank and fishing it downstream toward me. It was a pleasant, rhythmic sight, and I must have lost my sense of time before I heard Mari call out from our car parked beyond the bridge.

I thought she might be upset, but when I got to the car, she laughed and said I'd looked as if I was enjoying myself, the children were asleep, and she'd gotten into a good book, so why didn't I take out my rod and fish, which is what we'd come upstate to do.

In the trunk of the car, I saw the white fly rod lying to one side without a case, its Pflueger Medalist reel fastened to the handle. And I knew I had a plastic box full of flies in my canvas tackle bag. Why not? I'd caught some trout, the angler above the bridge looked as though he knew what he was doing, and the sight of the water already had made me itchy to get into my hip boots. So I rigged up, kissed Mari good-bye, skipped to the bridge to watch the fly fisher for a moment, then headed downstream a hundred yards.

For a half hour, I flailed away crudely, slapping the water behind me, ending my casts with big, flopping loops halfway to where I wanted them to be. Though I waded upstream, I remember casting across and downstream with a streamer, imitating the spin-fishing techniques I knew so well. But my casts were hopelessly short, and the harder I cast, the shorter they fell. The movements of the current that I had exploited well with my spinning rod now perplexed me as it ramrod-ded the bulky fly line and sent my fly scuttling in odd directions. I did not feel my fly was any threat whatsoever to trout.

Above me, I saw the fly fisher take two trout and release them. Then, at the bridge, he changed the spool on his reel, tied on a new fly, and began to fish upstream. I now was close enough to see that his fly floated. And I also was observant enough to notice there were now some pale yellowish flies coming up out of the water, a few fluttering just above it while others rode the current downstream.

I felt my hands tremble.

Clipping off my streamer, I rummaged through my fly box for a yellow fly. The best I could find was a battered Lady Beaverkill with a gray and yellow egg sac. I tied this onto the heavy leader I had been using. Leaving the river, I climbed back onto the bridge just in time to witness an event I had not seen before: a trout take a dry fly. My eye picked up the yellow fly the other angler had cast, and I watched it float a dozen feet, smoothly, pertly bounding up and down on the surface. Then, dramatically, it disappeared in a boil much like bluegills made when they took my flies. It was a decent brown, about 13 inches, and he soon had it in his net, then returned it to the river.

Now my whole body started to tremble. Is that all there was to it? I fiercely wanted to try this, and when the angler waved to me that he was leaving the river, I scooted down the bank, took up a position near where he had been, and again began flailing away. Nothing. My casts slapped the water, and the fly dragged as soon as it landed. It was hopeless and, worse, frustrating beyond measure.

Finally, I breathed deeply, brought in my line and decided simply to watch. There were still a few flies floating about and an occasional rise. A bit below me and near the far bank, a series of rises caught my attention. They always were within a four-foot circle, and when I inched downriver, I could see a big brown lolling just beneath the surface.

There had been some sun, but it now was gone and the drizzle had started again. I was tempted to go back to the car and get my spinning rod, which would make short work of this trout, but instead I kept inching downstream until I was parallel to the fish. Then I crept toward it as far as I dared, then a little more, and cold water came over the tops of my hip boots. That didn't matter. I looked at the bedraggled Lady Beaverkill and my thick leader and decided I needed a lighter connection. I found some 4-pound-test spinning line and tied it on with three or four overhand knots, since that knot and the clinch knot were all I knew.

On my fourth cast, the fish came a foot upstream and took the fly at the surface in a rush. I struck—and the knot broke.

It was a remarkable moment—electric, vivid, unforgettable—and eventually it changed my life.

I fished for an hour after that, using the heavy leader, fishing myself into a fast and hopeless frenzy. Of course, I raised nothing. By this time, the rain was quite hard, the water roiled, and after I had seen no flies or rises for ten minutes, I headed back to the car, soaked and shivering.

"You should have seen that fish come up," I started to say as I neared the car, then I stopped. The children were howling, and Mari—who had been alone with them in the car for hours—was crying bitterly.

It rained throughout our four-hour trip back to Ann Arbor, which was one of stony silences punctuated by muffled crying and the howls of infants, who could feel the tension. I had visions of a marriage slipping pertly downstream. I also kept seeing that trout rising and taking my Lady Beaverkill, and I dreamed of other trout in a world of which I had been given the briefest glimpse.

We soon moved back East and never again lived in places where coffee froze at night, or near enough, in my mind, to rivers. But now, years later, I have the same wife, and we've made our fish truces, and four children, who have grown and mostly do not fish, and I am still trying to get a full look at that world I glimpsed one rainy day on the Au Sable when a trout rose—with astonishing power and grace—to my fly, and changed my life forever.

A FISHERMAN'S CHILDHOOD IN BROOKLYN

Bedford Avenue in Brooklyn was sterile ground for a budding sportsman. We had the Dodgers and our own intense half-court basketball games at Wingate Field; we had stickball in the street, with the manhole in front of Ira's house as homeplate, bike rides to Bensonhurst and Bushwick, stoop ball, tough touch football on the fenced-in cement field near P.S. 193; but there was no water closer than Steeplechase Pier at Coney Island—and the fishing there could only be rated as poor.

I had started to fish at my grandfather's hotel, the Laurel House, in an obscure corner of the Catskills, before memory. Then, fatherless, I continued to fish in a sump called Ice Pond during all those grim years from four to eight at a frightening boarding school in Peekskill, where my growing passion for fishing surely buoyed my spirits and possibly saved my life. When my mother and my stepfather brought me to Brooklyn, I was ten, and the first thing I noticed was all the cement. The place was lousy with gray. There was no fishing, not anywhere.

Summer camp, on Lake Ellis in the foothills of the Berkshires, helped. I caught bullhead there, perch and several varieties of panfish, and my first bass. On a picnic to Bull's Bridge on the Housatonic, I saw a magnificent trout rise to an unseen insect and though I did not fish for trout for some years, that image never left me: the fish, nearly two feet long, starting as a shadow, turning into the shape of a fish— sleek and spotted—that slipped downstream with the current and then angled up so gently that its white mouth barely opened and there was only a slight bending down of the surface and then that neat spreading circle sliding downstream. At Steeplechase Pier, on cold November or February days, we used two-ounce sinkers, frozen spearing, and thick glass rods to catch skate, mackerel, fluke, flounder, hacklehead, occasional snappers, and whiting. They were not pretty fish, this grab bag of the seas, and the fun of it was all contained in that little tug forty-five feet below and then the sight of a wriggling thing as we hoisted it upward, reeling like mad.

Every afternoon during my early teens I worked for a gardener who tended lawns and backyards in the neighborhood. He was a high school math teacher and I usually got to his house first, around three o'clock, readied the tools, and then sat atop the bags of mulch and pungent fertilizer in the carryall he attached to his car, waiting for him to arrive. With the little money I earned I bought my first spinning reel, various lines, hooks, and lures, my first fly rod (made of white glass), and bait for my saltwater sojourns; and I subscribed to four outdoor magazines. In the mid- to late 1940s,

I could not wait each month to get the magazines, my windows on the great outside world of angling. Lee Wulff, Joe Brooks, Ted Trueblood, A. J. McClane, H. G. Tapply, and Ed Zern became household names to me, though no one in my house fished or hunted and my stepfather thought it pretty stupid; I fished with those men from the Keys to Newfoundland, from the Beaverkill to the Deschutes. With Lee Wulff I jumped off a bridge over the Battenkill to see whether you'd die if you went underwater in waders, and I got just a little better (what with my three thumbs) at tackle tinkering by reading Tap Tapply—and I fell madly in love with Ted Trueblood's West.

Eventually I found books. Ray Bergman's *Trout* was first— as it has been for many thousands of other trout fishermen. I was looking for some logic to it all—the history I now became aware of, the never-ending stream of tackle, the conflicting techniques, the practical lore of a thousand kinds without which one cannot really be a complete angler. *Trout* included a measure of everything one went to ''The Word'' for. Bergman's patient, steady, thoughtful voice made good sense out of the mysteries of the craft and the greater mysteries of why a trout—under various circumstances—behaves as it does. His early experiences, decades earlier, paralleled those I was having—with their inescapable movement from ''crude'' to ''more refined,'' from unknowing to knowing. His instinctive dislike of hordes of people and of those ''who are not in accord with the true spirit of nature'' defined my own growing uneasiness with such people. I might, by circumstance, live in the heart of a gray city but my ancestors must have been Tapplys or Bergmans—with at least one Leatherstocking in the batch.

Even before I tied my first fly onto a leader, Bergman gave me eyes to see what was in rivers—and he gave form and focus to my eventual love of fly fishing. He introduced me to wet flies, streamers, nymphs, and dries, and how they should be used; he described water I'd seen and was only just beginning to understand from my worming and spinning; he led me, also, to think as much about what respect I owed my fellow fishermen and my quarry as what a trout sees and how to play it more deftly once hooked.

All this was in stony Brooklyn, far from rivers of any stripe—though by now I had in fact discovered that with some vigorous travel I could find flowing water only several hours away. From the age of thirteen on, and without ever missing an Opening Day or half a dozen trips each April and May, Mort and then Bernie and Don and I would take wearying treks north. We were all drawn to moving water—and we all still are, nearly fifty years later. The fishing was not very good, based on what I've experienced since: mostly stocked fish with a few holdovers, all caught rather unceremoniously in a passage of water between two city reservoirs, on worms first, then spinning lures. But we loved it. And we learned great lessons on those hard-fishing waters. Those days stolen from the gray city streets meant worlds to me then—and we had nights and Opening Day mornings that were as full of excitement as anything I've known since. A 15-inch holdover brown—with a bright orange belly and a bit of a kype—was a prize not soon forgotten.

To fish those Westchester and Dutchess County rivers we needed bait, and the best, always, had been worms. Working for a gardener, I was in a position of great privilege: in an afternoon of hard spade work I could always slip ten or twenty choice garden worms into the Prince Albert tobacco can I kept in my back pocket; neither my boss nor my clients cared. But better, I knew the lawns that had automatic sprinklers or owners who were conscientious users of the hose—and I had scouted out the lawns filled with little mud mounds with a hole in the center of each, the telltale mark of nightcrawlers. With flashlight and coffee can I could, whether it had rained or not, always count on collecting three or four dozen nightcrawlers on any spring night. Once the light had flashed across their shining backs, I'd turn it away, bend and grab quickly for the spot where the long worm entered the earth, then tease it out, like Arthur the great sword from the stone. When Mort and I worked in tandem, we'd keep an eye out for suspicious homeowners or the police and whisper loudly when we had some success— whispers sometimes punctuated with "A double!," which meant we'd gotten two at one thrust, joined at the neck, in their act.

Those days and the words of the sport I read in book and magazine led me to dream of fishing in states far-flung; I felt linked by my passion for fishing to every other fisherman in every other part of this diverse country—from the catfisherman in Missouri to steelheaders in Oregon to a bream fisherman on a bayou in Louisiana. I even ordered from some of the two dozen mail-order catalogs I got each spring lures and hooks that could be used only in such places. Ted Trueblood and A. J. McClane were my eyes and ears, and my soul, long before I knew anything about them other than what appeared in their articles; they gave me skills and techniques and made me a westerner and southerner long before I ever fished such waters. They gave me an ethic, too—one that has only grown stronger, more a part of me, over the many years.

Slowly, then, our worlds broadened. To summer camp and Sheepshead Bay and the Croton watershed rivers we added the great Catskill rivers, the huge St. Lawrence (for smallmouth bass and pike, with Mort's father), then (in college) rivers in Pennsylvania, Connecticut, and Vermont. At first we took trains or buses; later we hitchhiked, barnstorming through the East, pursuing faint rumors and glimmers of promising water, gleaned from stocking reports that Bernie got from the New York State Conservation Department or from magazine articles or from hearsay. The great Sportsman's Show—filled with hundreds of irresistible displays of lures, rods, reels, and lodges—came to Madison Square Garden every winter and we never missed it. It too gave us new dreams. We collected every travel brochure in the place and studied them harder than algebra or civics. We even traced the great landlocked salmon and outsized trout from the Maine and Canada exhibits to a place called, ungraciously, Reservoir 3, in Westchester County—which proved, for us, only a very good lake in which to catch big crappies.

Then, in 1955, the summer I got out of the army, I bought a black 1946 Ford convertible with twin silver exhaust pipes. It was my first car and it gave me the West. I loaded it with fishing tackle and headed across America for the first time. It was a miraculous trip, filled with revelations: after the cities and eastern mountain ranges, the day-long flatness of the prairie and my first sight of the snow-tipped Rockies, looming in the distance for hours before I reached them. I went north, then south, crisscrossing the Continental Divide: to the Madison, the Henry's Fork, the Big Hole, then down to the great Gunnison in Colorado. I went up again to Silver Creek and the Big Lost River in Idaho, and found some unnamed spring creeks whose trout were mammoth—and, for me, uncatchable. I had never seen such water—so much of it and so wild, fecund. Eventually I wandered through Oregon, camped in the shadow of Mount Shasta, and then, on the way back, got vapor lock in the desert and had to be towed thirty miles. I had seen more water than I could fish in ten lifetimes, more fish of greater size than I'd seen in my entire childhood. If I stayed an extra day or two in a dry desert town waiting for my car to be fixed, it did nothing to blur the miracle of cold water.

Back in the Rockies I remembered a lake an army friend had said held "big ones." It did. I caught eight or ten truly huge trout, packed them carefully in ice, and raced back to Brooklyn. Don still remembers the day I arrived on East 24th Street in my 1946 Ford convertible and stopped in the middle of the street, where he was playing stickball, to show him my fish. He had never seen such trout. No one had. We talked for hours in my backyard, the tiny patch of gray summer grass surrounded by cement appearing even smaller—by a lot—than I remembered it. I had stopped working for the gardener when he paid me one dollar to cut my own grass and charged my parents ten dollars for the job; I had long skinned the yard of any nightcrawlers, and it was untended and dry now.

I told Don and Mort everything I had seen. They looked at the trout, my bona fides, and nodded. I swore I'd go back; I swore I could learn how to fish for those elusive spring creek trout in Idaho. There was a vast world beyond Brooklyn. We'd seen nothing.

I knew I would always be a visitor to such places and I knew too that I would treat them with perhaps even more respect than those who lived there did—for the sad rivers of my childhood were auguries of what could happen to rivers anywhere. I was shocked, years later, to see some local fishermen beach a rubber raft above Varney Bridge on the Madison and display a full limit of huge trout, laid out like frozen meat slabs in an ice chest; the limit was ten or fifteen in those days. It was during the stonefly hatch and they had caught their fish on live stoneflies. There were four of them in that little boat, jammed in like city subway riders, cackling. They boasted that they had time before dark to float from McAtee down again and take another limit each.

But by then I knew that rivers belong to those who love them, and that these men were no friends of this river.

That afternoon in the backyard in Brooklyn I knew I would go west again, and south and north, too. Suddenly there was a whole country full of rivers and lakes to fish—or fish again.

And so I have.

And so I will.

GREEN TROUT

Green trout. I cannot imagine why we called them
that. One Opening Day of the trout season more than forty
years ago, I had told a game warden that I'd caught five
"green trout." He'd asked to see them and I had proudly
produced the stringer. I was fourteen that year and had come
upcountry alone on the milk train, which arrived at Brewster
about eight o'clock. I had fished all that day, fruitlessly,
in freezing squalls, and had in midafternoon found a pod of

fish that readily took my nightcrawlers suspended beneath a red-and-white plastic bobber. I'd happily taken five, and I had shown them to the warden with the easy stupid pride of a buffoon.

Fortunately, those "green trout," which were bright spawning smallmouths, survived when I slipped them gingerly off the stringer as the warden grimly watched. The last one just made it.

The green trout that Bernie had mentioned came later, and they were true trout, but I couldn't remember where we had been fishing, or why they were green. He had called from California, where he's lived for years; he calls every year or so, now that we've hooked up again, and we talk vaguely about getting together, perhaps in the Rockies, and then one of us mentions the old days, those halcyon days in our teens, and a hundred trips come tumbling back in my memory. For those were great years when, intently, we learned the basic skills of trout fishing and an ethic; we fished hard and explored whatever waters we could reach by train, foot, or thumb, and talked about what we'd learned as if our lives depended upon learning everything about trout and their world.

When he called, Bernie asked me if I remembered a certain night when we were hitchhiking upstate and had gotten picked up by an oil truck. I did. We'd left after classes on a Friday, taken a subway as far as it would go, then gotten out on the road about ten o'clock and hitched. The driver of the oil truck had been mildly nuts. He talked loudly, disjointedly, and gesticulated with his hands while holding the wheel lightly with his elbows. And the huge truck careened through the darkness, near midnight, toward some river in which Bernie and I had later caught green trout.

I remembered the ride. We had been scared silly. We sat high in the cab of the truck, the three of us jammed close, with all our gear on our laps, and this fellow raged on and on, for an hour, his hands flailing the air, and drove along twisting back roads at sixty or seventy miles an hour. Bernie and I were catatonic. We stared straight ahead at the cave the lights cut in the dark and gripped the dashboard until our fingers ached. When he let us out we could not speak; later, relieved, we could not help laughing at our good luck.

Could it have been the Berkshires, the Catskills, or the Adirondacks? The Hoosic River or the upper East Branch, the Ausable, or the Esopus?

Bernie and I had fished them all in our teens, and dozens of others.

"We got about ten trout each," he remembered.

"I remember," I said.

"And you called them 'green trout' because they were greener than any fish we'd ever seen. I remember those fish. I still haven't seen any greener."

"I remember."

"It must have been from the vegetation in the water. But I've tried for a week to remember what river that was and I can't."

Neither could I.

When he got off the phone, I began to think about how deeply we fly fishermen live in our memories, how important they are to us. So much of our knowledge comes in to us this way. We recall the particular movement of a particular brown trout in a particular lie some twenty years earlier. It was just off the edge of the rock and came at once to a Grey Fox Variant pitched five feet above it. But the water was a foot higher that day than it is today, and that was May, not June. What fly to use? Where to cast it? Will the fish be closer to the main current? Every gesture of our assault on a trout comes from memory applied. If fishing is a form of meditation, it is meditation mingled thickly with memory and action. Sometimes our response is so fast that we call it instinct, and sometimes we must consciously and carefully think through a fishing problem at hand, applying what we remember to help solve a situation that seems perfectly new.

Sometimes we remember "through a glass darkly," inexactly, imperfectly. Some of it is there but it's aslant, incomplete. Or we remember the image of something but not its name, or its name—Indian paintbrush, Engelmann spruce, larkspur, fringed gentian—but not the image, not exactly.

My intense fishing life has always been lived with astonishing clarity in my brain. I always believed I could remember every trout, from the first one I'd gigged at age five from a small mountain stream to big ones caught or lost on #18 Pale Morning Duns. I remember my first on a fly, on Michigan's Au Sable, the first my son Paul got on a fly, on the Madison with Mike Lilly, my first salmon (after three days of not catching any, while everyone else did), a thousand unexceptional fish on three dozen different rivers, the sight of old Sparse taking one and Doug Swisher taking ten and Sandy taking a fat three-pound brown (very silvery and footballish) from a small spring creek, and one I lost on the Kennet, and a dozen I finally caught on that lovely chalkstream, and small and big ones that eluded me, and one the size of a pike that took me up three bends and then summarily broke me off in some tangled roots, and a six-inch cutthroat in the upper Taylor's Fork that had exquisite black and green coloration, and a tortuga from Craig's Tortuga Pond, and one Justin and I fussed with under the Raynolds Pass Bridge on a rainy night and finally hooked and lost, and a couple that busted up from the boiling water in the Ausable for a Hairwing Royal Coachman and another that merely flashed for a muddler on one of the braids of the lower Madison, and a big hybrid in Henry's Lake that fooled with me for a half hour, then had enough of the game and busted me off on some lily stalks, little brook trout on the Green in Massachusetts and sleek cutthroats from a river on the Colorado-Wyoming border, and three I took from the Shoshone, just off the road, where we stopped our first time West, little trout and trout whose size blasted my whole body with shivers. I can see the braided currents of a thousand runs, the faint, green water of a ledge pool, a feeding lane on a large western river in October, the flat surface of a thin pondlike pool pocked with a dozen feeding fish, the farrago of currents where three channels met and turned, pocket water below a cliff on the Schoharie, where Art Flick took four in four casts on a Grey Fox Variant, and a run on the Battenkill where he did the same thing, and a New England brook, overhung with willows, dappled with sunlight, the brookies rising everywhere.

My head is filled with such images—thousands upon thousands of them—and I treasure them and they are more vivid than any trout I might have been stupid enough to kill, stuff, and hang on the wall near my desk.

But I cannot remember those green trout, or the river in which we caught them.

And that carries with it the thought that some day I will forget so much more—and that fills me with terror. For my fly fishing memories are the balm of my brain; they save me from the buffetings of gray city streets, the loss of rivers and friends and the betrayal of friends, my own fallings-off, and the thousand other arrows a middle-aged man, finally, gets stuck in his pride with. The phrase "I still have my memories" is no lark; sometimes I want to cry out, "I *am* my memories."

And so Bernie's call, with its augury of memories sinking, like Poe's "City in the Sea," slightly but steadily into some silence and blindness and deadness, rattled me for a moment. I didn't like the sound of all that emptiness.

Yet the call also gave me some resolve to find new memories, to fish more, to fill my remembrances with more runs and riffles and bright brown trout.

The green trout, apparently, are gone. I'll never find them again. But they weren't the biggest or most interesting trout I've caught, and quite possibly not worth remembering.

Maybe what all this fuss and rumination are about is that I'd like to go back, and of course can't, to those intense, rich, carefree days, when I had nothing better to do but barnstorm for trout, when every day we learned something new, with a brave eagerness. Maybe I would like to go back to a time when Bernie and I could be quite content to sit, petrified, a loon at the wheel, hurtling in an oil truck in the middle of the night to a river we've both forgotten.

4

ANOTHER SEASON
BEGINS

The best time to go fishing, said a very wise man, is when you can. So the best time to open a new season must be as soon as you can but under no circumstances later than the first week in May, unless kept from doing so by storm, tax audit, or a broken casting arm.

In my salad days I opened each trout season as soon as it was legal to do so: 12:01 at night, April Fools'. These were desperate, night-long marathons from which I returned bleary-eyed, beat, absurdly proud of my heavy creel. Now I am wiser. I wait until the mayflies start hatching or the weather reaches 65° three or four days in a row, or I simply can't wait any longer.

What I've lost in passion by avoiding the intensity of Opening Day I've gained in health. The last time I opened the season at 12:01, nearly two decades ago, I almost died of hypothermia, exhaustion, and (since all I caught in fifteen hours of that madness was a seven-foot length of weed) boredom. Last week I opened another season, a safe month after the lunatics, after two weeks of preparing my boxes of flies with meticulous care, with the greatest of expectations.

I headed up the West Side Highway with my young friend Justin Askins, a fellow teacher and happy enthusiast, and never looked back. The city and the long gray winter vanished. My eyes filled with maple and birch budding everywhere, the wedding white of the cherry trees along the Hudson. In Riverdale we saw pink magnolias and then delicate pale-green willows along the marshes near the Saw Mill River.

We were heading for the Amawalk, which flows for several miles between two reservoirs an hour out of the city, and I told Justin about the years when they'd closed it to all fishing and how fine a head of trout it boasted for three years after that. ''Thirty-five? You really got thirty-five trout there in one afternoon?'' he asked, his voice rising, and I said the fishing had been awfully good for a few years, back then. I had a secret way to get to the lower end, which might be a good place for us to start—if the river was still there, if it hadn't been rerouted or dammed, if oil hadn't spilled into it again or acid rain or road salts killed the insects, or three housing projects hadn't been built on its banks, or it wasn't too crowded. You never knew these days. But if the Amawalk didn't work, we'd head up to the East Branch of the Croton River.

It was a glorious day, the third warm one after a month of torrents, and we were happy as pigs in mud to be out, and in no rush. My fly boxes were carefully packed with every fly I could possibly need and I'd bought new waders that wouldn't leak. Justin was getting a bit overenthusiastic but he'd settle down and we'd make a sensible, civilized day of it.

There were nine cars parked at my secret back entrance to the Amawalk so we drove to Route 35 and over to the Wood Street pool, where we found eight more. But we got out at the little bridge and looked down into flowing water for the first time this year. The water, from all the rain, was tawny, high, braided with swirling leaves and twigs. Up at the East Branch we got the same message: the warm weather hadn't been around long enough to clear the water or, probably, get the fish rising, but cars and fishermen were hatching like mad.

Well, it was time to do what we'd come to do, so we put on waders and vests and rigged our fly rods; I checked my four carefully packed fly boxes and then we walked to the old stone bridge beneath which I'd fished a hundred times. Once, disastrously, I'd stopped there on Father's Day when my four children were small, saw and could not resist a large rising trout, waded in after it in my Sunday shoes and suit, hooked the thing—and then lost it and nearly my whole family. A guy with a bandanna around his forehead was fishing nymphs upstream below a little white Styrofoam strike indicator; it looked like a lousy, clumsy way to fly fish but he caught two rainbow trout while we watched.

Justin got very excited. Me, too.

We fished hard for two hours, with dry flies, then streamers, then nymphs, caught nothing, then drove to the lower section of the East Branch, at Brewster. Once, I told Justin, you could walk from the lower to the upper section and see only trees; now there was a full-rigged shopping center, a used-car lot, a dozen places to eat, and a slew of other commercial buildings. It was the lower section that Mort, Bernie, and I used to fish on Opening Day when we were kids. We fished at a spot we called the Big Bend, with worms and spinning lures, and we took great numbers of trout. I resisted telling Justin how many.

It was still there: the rock ledge against the far side, the heavy current down the center, the deep eddies on the near side, the sand bar on which the three of us would line up at midnight, year after year, like mannequins.

I put on a Hare's Ear Nymph, added a couple of split shot, and started to work my way up to the head of the run. Justin heard a woodpecker, saw a kingfisher skirt the alley of the river, and went back to the car to get his camera; he seemed casual enough. I intently fished the nymph upstream, lost a few flies on rocks, and finally hooked a rainbow of about fourteen inches. Then, fishing hard above the bend, I got two more, about the same size. They were stocked fish, I reckoned: triplets and too washed out. But I was happy to catch fish on flies in this old place, nearly noxious with nostalgia. And then, fishing under the bridge in water that seemed safe as pie, I felt my boots slip on a rock and I went rump over elbow into the drink, got up, and keeled over again, dousing myself up to my eyeballs, spitting East Branch, watching a fly box glide to oblivion.

Justin insisted I change—only a maniac would keep fishing in wet clothes, with the temperature dropping—but I said there was another hour of good fishing possible, there might still be a hatch, and I sure wasn't going to miss it.

An hour later we saw a few spurt rises, guessed the fish were coming to a small dark caddis, and each took a small one on a dry fly, the way I prefer to take my trout, when I can take them at all. They were our first trout of the season on dry flies and we were as giddy as if we'd been in Montana, though I was colder.

My desk is a patchwork quilt of all the cards, licenses, money, and papers from my wallet. A few hundred flies are drying sensibly on the mantelpiece. I have a couple of scars from my baptismal fall and a sore throat and a bit of a spring cold. No matter. We got a few fish and saw a few birds. We felt the wet banks underfoot again and saw the first lush growth of skunk cabbage and a few yellow trillium and trout lilies. And

I have the image in my head of that lovely little spurt rise
when the bright native rainbow came to my fly. Justin called
to see if I was all right and I said sure, did he think I was an
antique? "Well, you get a little overexcited, Nick. I mean, you
really fish hard." And we made a date to get out again soon.
So I've traveled back and will travel forward again; the skein
thickens; another season begins.

PART TWO

SOME FISH I'VE CHASED

5

THE GENEROUS
BLUEGILL

They were the first fish I—and most of us—caught: bright flopping jewels of blue, crimson, green, and coral. I caught them on bent pins first, then snelled hooks and eyed hooks, on breadballs, crickets, grubs, caterpillars, bits of pork rind, corn kernels, and worms. Mostly I caught them on garden worms.

I spit on the breadballs and the pork rind for luck, and I used bobbers made of quills, balsa wood, and wine corks threaded right onto the line with a large needle.

I started to catch bluegills before memory began, so as far as I know I've always been catching them.

After a while I caught them on flies. Bluegills were the first fish I caught on flies and with the first flies I used—deliciously gaudy wet flies, the brighter the better: McGinty, Parmachene Belle, and Silver Doctor. Drab flies, like those I later used with such success for trout, never worked as well. Anything with rubber legs, though, was a killer.

I first fished flies for bluegills on a Berkshire foothills lake called Ellis, wading the shorelines in sneakers on July and August evenings after I'd finished waiting on tables. I used one of those clumsy white-glass fly rods and a level line, and first put the line through the keeper ring. I could barely slap the line down twenty feet out when I started; until I rethreaded the line, outside of the keeper ring, the casts were considerably briefer. But the bluegills didn't much care. If they were there, you could see them trail after the fly as I retrieved it with short slow pulls, a few inches below the surface; you could see them come after it, their little mouths pursed and ready, and then they'd snap at it and pretty much hook themselves.

Since all the action was visible in the shallow water, from the moment the fly hit the water until the fish was hooked, bluegills gave me a short course in how fish strike and why. The regular, steady retrieve, for instance, rarely brought the number of strikes that irregular twitches brought—slow, then fast, quick and erratic. I could see how deep the fly rode in the thin water and the fish's response at various depths, to kinds of retrieve, particular colors, and so much else— knowledge of fish behavior that, over time, became instinct and helped me catch a thousand fish with bigger reputations but no more heart.

No, they were not what trout fishermen call "selective"; but they had their preferences. They did not mind when a beginner's bad casts fell like balls of hail on the flat evening lake. They did not ask for seventy-foot casts. They were the most generous of instructors and I couldn't catch enough of them—and I seemed to learn more with each fish that trailed my fly.

Bluegills are of course the ideal fish on which to start fly fishing. Since they take the fly so readily, you can have the pleasure of catching *something* immediately, and they always fight with circling pluck and ardor. They are tolerant of our mistakes and are willing to give us a day's sport as soon as we get the line out of the keeper ring.

Though colorful wet flies and chenille-bodied flies with rubber legs were how I started, I soon found that small cork popping bugs were much more fun; I still prefer them, whenever they've got the slimmest chance to work. That first summer, as I taught myself to cast thirty, then forty feet, to reach some parallel stretch of the shoreline I could not wade, I found that I had a distinct preference for the floating bug. I'd choose the very smallest I could find in a local hardware store—about twenty cents apiece, from a card that held a few dozen of them—and choose, too, the ones with little cupped heads, which would make a bit of disturbance when I tugged them. I'd fish them near the lily pads, let them sit for a moment or two, pop and ploop them gently, and if there were bluegill around they'd crash up for the bug, with a happy pinching and clefting of the surface. Oddly, they always stopped at dusk—which was when I caught my first few bass on flies; and all I had learned fishing for bluegills immediately stood me in good stead with their larger cousins.

How I wish I had started my three sons on bluegills instead of trout! We took long trips in their early teens to great rivers to which I'd lost my heart, and usually they caught nothing but a huge dose of boredom. There has got to be *some* encouragement for a beginning teenager with little other fishing experience; a day of listening to a lunatic father talk about bugs with Latin names, and about fish that *might* start rising in another hour or two or four, and slapping down casts a couple of dozen feet for those trout when they do finally rise, will not get a youngster interested. We did best on Great Pond, near Amherst, Maine, where we bunked in an old cabin for a week many years ago. Here there was excitement: the water near the island was lousy with bluegills and we all got a good dose of them, several of which, on the way in, found their way into a pickerel's mouth—which added to the fun.

After I lost my heart to trout and became involved in the minute and exacting business of learning to extract a few now and then, sometimes under very challenging circumstances, I forgot about bluegills for some years. They were fine, I thought, when there was nothing else to do, but I wouldn't travel very far for them.

I guess it was Thom Green, an oil geologist from Tulsa, who got me to travel for them—and when he did I traveled a full two thousand miles. That was fifteen years ago. We were fishing Henry's Lake in Idaho for very large rainbow and hybrid rainbow-cutthroat trout and Thom was one of the most tenacious—and skillful—fly casters on the lake, up at 4:30, in at 10:30 A.M., out again in the evening and on the lake until dark. And he got some of the largest trout, on a special leech he tied and could cast spectacularly. With a shooting-head line he regularly cast a full hundred feet; here was a big-fish fisherman if I'd ever seen one. One night, seeing his pleasure, I asked him if he enjoyed this lake more than any other fishing he did and he replied without hesitation: "No, I like bluegill most. I really like those bluegill when they're up on the beds and you can take them on little popping bugs. Gosh, that's a barrel of fun."

I said I'd always liked them too and a few days later we'd arranged to meet in Utah the next spring to explore a lake that, allegedly, had two- and even three-pound bluegills.

Utah is two thousand miles from where I live . . . but those are *very* big bluegills.

We were a few weeks early but the fish were every bit as large as the reports Thom had been given. This was a rich alkaline lake and a delicate combination of abundant food supply and severe winter kills had created—at least for a while—a large number of gargantuan bluegills. Thom saw at once that they were not yet on the beds, so he tied up some of those chenille-bodied flies on long-shank hooks, with drooping rubber legs, and we took a slew of fish up to two and a half pounds in the deepest water, and had a marvelous time, worth every mile of the trip.

Most bluegills are much smaller, of course, and the best sport is usually close to home. That's one of their greatest virtues: they remind us that the heart of fishing, the great fun we have at it, is not high-tech, far-flung, expensive sport. It's as close as the nearest farm pond. It's the meeting of an angler or two, with the least possible gear, and a game fish in another element. There's always a bit of mystery and with bluegills there's always a whole measure of fun—and there's a certain unpressured, noncompetitive, happy, Huck Finn–like, earthy quality to it all that I've longed for more than once when I've done "Big Time" fishing.

Give me small-time bluegills half a dozen times every year, to keep the human measure to my angling; give me a long light fly rod and a single plastic box of bugs and wet flies, and I'll have as much fun as I can have anywhere on the water.

I like a stiff #4 rod these days—light but strong enough to throw a bug into the wind. I like a variety of small bugs, usually with dyed feathers for the tail and a couple of strands of rubber coming from the sides. I use a simple double-taper line and a seven- or eight-foot leader, tapered to no lighter than 4X; I think that lighter tippets flop in the wind, won't straighten out a bug, and break off too quickly on obstructions. You tire a fish less using the heaviest possible leader, which of course enables you to bring fish in quicker, and bluegills are not leader shy.

Along with bluegills, you often catch perch, pickerel, rock bass, crappie, and other panfish. All can be lots of fun, too, on a fly rod, and all can be caught with pretty much the same techniques that work for bluegills, though I always retrieve flies with the greatest possible speed when I'm specifically after pickerel.

I like to wade wet for bluegills in the late spring, fishing to the beds with a little popper. I generally do so alone, so I can travel at my own pace, though this is genial, friendly fishing, not nearly so intense as fishing—say—a tough spring creek, and it's often pleasant to talk over the water to a good friend, sharing a fish that may be a full inch or two larger than the average you've both been catching, comparing notes on which bugs work best. But I often fish for them from an old wooden rowboat or a canoe, tooling down the shoreline slowly and casting in to those targets of lighter sand that are the bluegill beds, each, often, with an auburn shape in it that is the fish.

After that trip to Utah I've never traveled very far for bluegills, though they've several times saved a slow day of bass fishing that I'd come a great distance to try. I know five, six little ponds, some that you can cast across, some a mile or so around, some with larger bluegills, some with bluegills that must go seven or eight to the pound. I'll fish any one of them any chance I get—often in the late afternoon, when the heat of a late spring day just begins to break and the sun is beginning to angle off the water. My casting is much better now than it was when I first fished for them, and often I'll practice a double-haul or see if I can reach a log some seventy feet away, and then turn the cast into some good fishing by working the bug back with little twitches and pops. But mostly, bluegill fishing requires no more than thirty feet or so, and I simply make my casts as gentle as possible and work each fly in with care.

I'll amble down to a certain half-acre pond I know about six o'clock on an August evening, and feel the same sense of expectation I feel when I fish one of those great named rivers for big trout. The water is flat and there's just a bit of swirling mist on it, as the temperature changes. A couple of mallards climb off the water as I approach, shattering the stillness; a few robins exchange one branch for another. I'm wearing sneakers and khaki pants, a long-sleeved khaki shirt to keep the bugs off my arms (and the chill that will come up in a couple of hours); I've got a single box of flies and bugs, an old rod, dark glasses that I'll shed when the sun goes down, and a baseball cap. If I want to keep a few fish—and they're of course sweet and delicious when fried, though bony—I may take the old wicker creel I no longer wear near trout streams; I always liked the weight of it on my shoulders and lining it with wet grasses for the fish I caught. Mostly I travel very light.

The pond is shaped like a watermelon, with a swimming dock that floats on barrels at one end. I can just about cast fully across it at its narrowest point. The cattails and marsh grasses are high this time of the year so I'll only have two or three spots I can cast from, but from those I can reach every corner of this pond. It is an intimate place and I love it, and as I work out a couple of dozen feet of line for my first short casts I remember dozens of fish I've taken over the years from this very spot.

I've chosen to make my stand with a tiny cork bug painted yellow, with soft red feathers for a tail and a couple of pairs of rubber legs—like cat's whiskers—near the head. It casts well and its concave head lets me pop it loudly when I'm of a mind to see such a pleasant disturbance on the flat surface of the pond, or think it will attract some attention; I like to watch the little thing chug and swirl on the surface of this little pond, its rubber legs vibrating back and forth, and I've seen fish come from even the deepest parts to the top for it.

This is a good night. I get a fat old pumpkinseed with a bright orange belly, big enough to take two hands to hold, on my fourth cast. It may be the largest fish I've ever taken in this pond, except for a three-pound bass I once got at dusk. Then there are four or five bright bluegills, considerably smaller, but quite satisfying. The fish are coming to the popper readily tonight.

A frog jumps in near the dock. I see a deer up the hill, near a stand of aspen. I shift to another side of the pond and then, when I catch nothing, to the dock. On top of the dock, a couple of feet into the pond and above the water, I can fish most of the far bank and I start to do so, systematically, as if I were fishing a salmon pool. About eight o'clock there's a sudden pocking of the water near the reeds and I hook the biggest bluegill of the evening—not nearly the size of the ones I caught in Utah, nor even as large as the pumpkinseed, but twice the size of those I've been catching, a trophy.

I smooth back its dorsal with my hand so I can grasp it without the points sticking me and look at it as the light begins to fail—the fish of my youth and of my late middle years: an eager emblem—small but of stout and generous heart—of all the simple good sport we all too often forget when we fish these days.

Then I head home. Or was I there already?

6

SMALL FISH

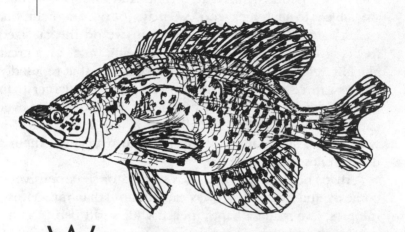

"Wal, son," the Florida bass guide Bill Miller consoled a friend who had not taken a bass big enough to match his dreams, "just about everybody comes down here wanting to catch Bubba . . . but hardly nobody ever does."

We all want the big fish. We've traveled great distances to get to Lake Big Buster, and we don't want to settle for a couple of shrimpy bass, thank you. Little pickerel are just fine in the nearby farm pond, but you don't travel two thousand miles for them. When you pack your bags carefully and ready your equipment, you think big. A fifteen-pound bonefish this year. A hundred-pound tarpon. A trout over two feet. A thirty-pound salmon. Rainbows to knock your eye out. My friend Mort caught a fifty-pound Atlantic salmon in Norway last year, which is about as big as anyone, ever, would want a salmon—but what now can he possibly do for an encore?

Some people only like big fish. No travel fee is too large for the largest fish, no distance too far. They want to better their personal best and beat everyone else's biggest and best. They fish for records and for the "thrill of a lifetime."

No one would deliberately pursue small fish, though I have friends who consistently catch runts and minnows—and I am subject to such luck, too. We may not pursue them, but we all catch a lot more of them than we do the outsized freaks. Even when I traveled two thousand miles on a great bluegill trek, I was after alligator bluegill, fish that reputedly grew to three pounds or more. We caught fish larger than two pounds—which is a lot of bluegill, the largest I've ever caught—but they were bluegill and it just seemed as if it would have been more appropriate had we caught them a dozen miles from home.

Perhaps because the big fish is so rare, or so expensive to come by, and since I've always caught more than my share of midgets, I've made a happy peace with small fish. When I was seven and eight years old and a confirmed—and exclusive—bait fisherman, I several times had outlandishly large pickerel, bass, and trout take a small shiner, chub, or bluegill while I drew it back to the boat. Once a four-pound pickerel ambushed my five-inch shiner, and before it would let go I hoisted both fish into the boat.

But I love small fish not merely because they sometimes draw the dramatic strike from their bigger betters and because they're the best of baits, but because they remind us of other reasons to be on the water, reasons bigger than big fish.

Once Craig Mathews walked me far back into some swampy flats to beaver ponds that reputedly held huge brook trout. It was a long trek in but I had made such treks before with Craig, during which we usually found battalions of mosquitos, lots of muck, and sometimes three- and four-pound brown trout; so all the while I thought of three-pound brookies—which qualify as "tortugas"—with dark backs and bright rose marks and that softer, seemingly scaleless skin that felt like something from a dark wild place. The fish had dark backs and bright markings, but they topped out at five inches in length. Still, we laughed a lot and we couldn't catch enough of them; and we called them "tortugas" anyway . . . and maybe they were. Vince Marinaro once told me he liked bright little wild brookies best.

Several years ago I had spent a long and interesting day in the backcountry section of the lower Keys—fussing around, looking for bonefish, permit, perhaps a small tarpon or two. I was with John Graves, and it was a perfectly pleasant day, talking with a new friend, exploring a new kind of fishing for me, even practicing casts for a day with Jeffrey Cardenas, for big tarpon. We looked hard at some sand flats for bones and found only a small sand shark, which ignored us. We fished a section that reminded me of a river, where a falling tide swept off mangrove flats and out into the Gulf; and that might have been a barracuda that cut my line so neatly—or only a piece of coral. But we caught no fish, and the day wore on until we'd walked the boat through a long shallow stretch that sometimes held permit but today didn't—though, never having seen a permit, I wasn't at all sure I knew what I was looking for, or if I'd recognize anything whatsoever beneath the mottled glaze of sun on broken water.

At the end of the shallow passage, the water ran flush up against the corner of a mangrove island. "Now that's where I'd fish," I told John with a smile. Fish *had* to lie in the eddies where the ocean swept in under the mangroves, curling under them, buffeting exposed roots. Fish would be protected under the overhanging twisted branches, food would come to them on the conveyor belt of the tides, and we'd surely catch some now.

"They'll be small," John said, "probably mangrove snappers."

At the end of any long fishless day, any fish sounds all right, so I put on a Crazy Charlie meant for grander sport and chucked it a couple of feet out from the mangroves, letting the rush of water take the fly down and deep into the mysterious, dark, swirling heart of the overhanging trees. It felt like the wet-fly fishing I'd done after I'd shifted from worms. The line leaned away from me, grew taut; I released a few inches of line, gave the line a few short tugs so the fly would ride high and then drop back; and then I felt the pecking tugs of something alive. I repeated the cast a dozen times, and each time the fly would suck down into the maze of roots. Every cast would bring that pecking strike and a bright little mangrove snapper—the size of perch or bluegill, wriggling madly.

Small fish are not always so generous. A decade ago, a happy circumstance got me to Europe on business matters the same time as my twenty-fifth wedding anniversary. It was a happy trip, by sleeper from Paris to Aix, where we saw Cezanne's studio and his Mont St. Victoire and some of his earliest work (which was so awkward it would give any young artist supreme courage to go on). And then we found a cheap *pension,* within sight of the blue Mediterranean. I had fished hard on my honeymoon, and fishing had not played well; and I only had one of those five-piece fly-rod outfits with me because a business colleague had given it to me; so I wasn't thinking of fishing. I had no intention to fish. And what would I fish for?

But by the third day, I'd had my fill of the topless beach and began to look more seriously at the water. It took me only a few minutes to spot some fishermen on the rocks. "I just might take a walk over in that direction," I told Mari.

"Have you found some fishing?" she asked without opening her eyes.

On the rocks I found three men fishing with long bamboo sticks, wispy line, tiny quill bobbers, and a bait so small I could not see it. They were fishing for tiny mullet, but the mullet were having none of whatever they offered. I watched for an hour, maybe longer. The three fishermen were as patient and committed as the fishermen on the Seine, who also catch no fish. My French was too rotten to extract precise advice about this refined fishery, but careful observation suggested that the mullet were taking a hatch of green weed.

In my new kit I found a few #18 flies, but they looked nothing like mullet food. So I clipped most of the grizzly hackle from a Griffith's Gnat, tore a piece of bright green yarn from the bottom of Mari's new twenty-fifth-anniversary sport jacket, wound the thread over the peacock herl, tied it off with itself, and left a quarter-inch strand for the tail of the new Lyons Mullet Weed Fly.

In the next two days I fished for nine hours, diligently. In that time, I saw one of my three brothers of the angle catch one silver fish, at least five inches long—which led to immense shouts of elation, louder than any I'd heard for hundred-pound tarpon. My score was exactly: eleven follows, two nips, one sore casting arm, several sun welts on my casting hand, no fish caught. It was the toughest fishing I'd ever done.

"You mean a big boy like you couldn't catch a tiny fish like that?" Mari said when she walked over and I showed her my fellow angler's catch.

I had no reply.

LITTLE WOLVES OF
THE WEEDS

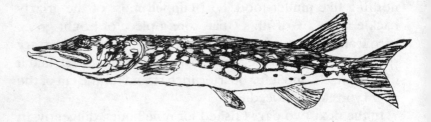

At the far end of the lake, at the edges of the stands
of pondweed and lily pad, we stopped catching bass. This
looked like fishy water, and Larry said he often caught bass
here in the very early morning or late at night, but it was now
10:30 A.M. and another largemouth would be a freak. "Why
don't you put on a streamer with a bright Mylar body," Larry
said. "Retrieve it as fast as you can."

I found one, cast it flush against the lily pads, as I'd been
doing all morning for bass, and got nothing.

"Strip in faster," said Larry.

We were in an old gray rowboat, repainted a dozen times,
on a small Connecticut lake, about half a mile around, and
we'd had a wonderful morning of bass fishing. One of us
rowed and the other cast in against the shoreline, into the

varying maze of deadfalls, jutting rocks, coves, and patches of weeds and lily pads. I'd gotten a few and Larry had taken a few; all were chunky fish and their rises to our surface bugs were thunderous. I'd pitch the bug in close to a stump or fallen tree, let it sit for twenty seconds, twitch it, chug it a few feet, let it sit, twiddle it a few times, chug it again, make it gurgle and dip, throw a little arc of water or a splash, then rush it and skip it a foot or two, then let it sit again.

I don't really know whether I'd enjoyed doing it my-self, watching my bug on the water, or watching Larry's bug—full of more surprises—perform on the surface sixty-five feet away.

Bass, with a rise half a foot across, would take the bug early or late in the retrieve; we never knew when. It was great fun, and I couldn't think of any fly fishing I had enjoyed more, though I've yet to find any fly fishing I don't like.

Now the fishing was slow. I caught a fat bluegill that circled and put its weight against the tug of the line, then two more bright orange panfish. This wasn't so bad. I could take an hour or two of it before lunch.

"Retrieve even faster," said Larry, and I did, stripping the line in with short, emphatic jerks. Just before I lifted the streamer out of the water, no more than three feet from the boat, a long, thin fish bolted for it, touched it but wasn't hooked, and set my heart aflutter.

Pickerel. I hadn't fished for them in years, not since I was ten, not since long before I owned my first fly rod. I took my first pickerel when I was six or seven. I had been fishing for pumpkinseeds in a weedy Catskill pond and had hooked a fat shiner of perhaps half a pound. I didn't especially like shiners and was in no hurry to get it in; anyway, it was just heavy enough to let alone for a minute, until it tired, and I remember distinctly, nearly fifty years later, peering down into that twenty-foot pocket within the weeds and seeing it there, three feet below the surface, flashing its silver sides, pausing, flashing again. And then, with electric speed, a great fish shot from the dark water beneath the lily pads, grasped the shiner sideways, and lurched away. I knew nothing better than to lurch back, and the fish, not hooked but holding dearly onto its dinner, flew out of the water and into my rowboat—about four pounds of pickerel.

Later I caught small shiners especially to fish for pickerel and must have taken thirty from that pond over the next few summers. I also caught them in the pool below the dam, on a piano-wire noose I had fashioned. I'd lie stretched out on the top of the wooden dam and watch them for a half hour or more, they as motionless as I, long, thin forms, still and facing the little fall of water over the top of the dam, watching for food. In all the time I watched I never saw them take actual food and never saw them on the prowl. They were always motionless, as alert as wolves, as still as hunting herons.

After I had watched a while, waiting for something to happen, I'd lower the sapling to which I'd attached three feet of fine piano wire, with a slip noose at the end. I'd lower it into the water well behind one of the fish, move it by millimeters toward the tail, pause, let it wait motionless while I watched for any sign of concern in the fish, then with one terrible swift movement bring the noose sideways to the pickerel's gills and up, snaring the hapless fish and hauling it high.

From such low origins do even fanatic fly fishermen start. I don't feel I have to justify my early pleasures by claiming they taught me patience!

The pickerel in Larry's lake averaged about 18 inches long, with some as small as eight inches and a few that would weigh from 2 to 2½ pounds. Once I got the hang of it, I caught a slew of them, more than I could count. I stripped in line as fast as I could, until my left hand ached and I could hardly tug faster. I don't believe that you can retrieve *too* fast, either for a pickerel or a bluefish.

The fish were up in the weeds and under the lily pads, in relatively shallow water, facing the pockets among the weeds and the deeper parts of the lake. At first I cast from the deep water in against the edges, as I'd always done for bass. This caught fish, but then it occurred to me that lining up with the edge of the lily pads and casting parallel to them would let the fly tempt more fish. The idea worked. I tried to keep the fly within a foot or so of the pads, and the fish tore out after it and ripped apart the Mylar and bucktail. After a half-dozen fish I had to put on another fly.

The fish came in twos and threes, vying for the kill, snapping and slashing at the fly. Whenever I retrieved slowly, though, they'd follow the fly steadily at a respectable distance and then only streak toward it, mouth open, at the last instant, just as I lifted the fly out of the water. No doubt about it: they craved the chase.

But I found that they also liked a hair frog or mouse fished quite as slowly as you might fish a bass bug. I'd put the fly onto the pads, as I did for bass, then twitch it off and let it lie quietly. The pickerel would come at it with their characteristic mad rush even when it was quite still. They also took a surface lure retrieved as fast as I could bring it in, ruffling the surface like one of those new bass lures that twirl.

Fishing that morning, I was carried back to my childhood, to days less fussy than those I'd spent in recent years on difficult trout streams. It was pleasant not to have such critical inspection of my flies, to see that readiness I remembered from my early days with bluegill, to remember that first huge pickerel taking my shiner. The fish were extremely active (though I have since found them almost so docile that I did not think they were present) and eager. Their requirements seemed simple: something bright and something moving fast. Like a wolf, they did not particularly bother to worry whether the rabbit was gray or brown; so long as it moved and wouldn't bite back, it was dinner.

Spinning, with its faster retrieve and brighter metal lures, would have been more effective; but the pickerel is a lovely fly-rod fish, and a couple of hours passed by with sparks of excitement, lots of action, and not too much worry about why I wasn't fishing to trout on a spring creek. It was fun to see the long, thin fish with the big mouth streak like lightning at our flies.

We kept a mess of them, which Larry assured me was good for the lake; there were simply too many and they would grow larger if we harvested some. Anyway, he said, pickerel were delicious.

I told him I thought they were too bony.

"Just wait," he said.

When we got back to his house, Larry laid four of the largest fish on a cutting board. They were handsome fish, their opalescent green fading now to gray but the black oval markings on their flanks, like links on a chain, still clear.

Larry skinned and filleted the fish and laid the white strips in a row neatly. I touched one of them and felt bones. Larry cut the strips into three-inch portions, then sliced the remaining bones, halving them but leaving them in place. He soaked all the flesh in milk for ten minutes, then fried them in sizzling oil. The bones must have dissolved, because the little chunks of pickerel were sweet and choice with only the faintest heaviness of bones, like fried smelt, which was quite pleasant.

I always carry some streamers especially for pickerel when I get within one hundred yards of a bass lake these days. Though pickerel will eat insects as well as other fish, frogs, and mice, the streamer is the ideal fly-rod lure for them. If they can be tempted—and some days they can't—that's what they'll take. I like streamers with a hard head and painted eyes, a bright red tag below the head, a firmly tied-in Mylar or other silver body, and white or dyed yellow buckskin. I much prefer kip to marabou, perhaps because I like every part of a pickerel fly to be as durable as it can be made. Two and a half to three inches seems a good size— large enough to interest them, not so large that they'll only snap at it.

I've begun to give some serious thought to eight-inch streamers for their larger cousins, the pike and muskie— but that seems like a major commitment, and for now I'm quite content to have found again the quick little wolves of the weeds.

LARGEMOUTH MAGIC

Green-gray, chunky, with a gourmand's palate and beastly eating habits, the largemouth bass has probably given more pleasure to more people than any species other than its little cousin, the bluegill. I am addicted to the brute. I caught my first largemouth in my early teens, on a live sunfish, and they've never been far from my mind, even during some lengthy love affairs with trout.

They're not finicky or fussy or easily scared. They'll eat anything they can catch and get their big jaws around. They mean business when they strike but grow bored—as I do— with the ensuing fight. There is just no freshwater sight as heart-stopping as a truly big largemouth busting up for a hairbug on a muggy night, blasting the surface with the sheer weight and ferocity of its strike, sending a lathed fan of silver in every direction, hustling away like a spooked muskrat when the bass realizes it's been hooked.

I first caught largemouth at a summer camp in the Berk-shires—first by mistake, while slowly hoisting out a three-inch bluegill, then on nightcrawlers and crayfish, then on minnows caught in a bread-baited jug, then on spinners, spinner-and-worm combinations, Jitterbugs, Pikie Minnows, and finally on big deer-hair or molded-body bugs. The bugs were merely a plump turtle-shaped body with crisscrossed clumps of hair for the four legs. That's still the bug I use most, nearly half a century later.

When I found the fly rod, I never let it go. Even in those early days when I half-tossed, half-slammed a bug out on a level line—sticky from too much grease—I was hooked by the rise of a largemouth to a surface bug. You saw everything. The expectation—as the fly lit, twitched, wiggled, waited, stuttered, and rushed headlong toward you, almost independent of any movement you made—was thrilling. I could barely cast the big thing thirty feet, but when I got it out (and perhaps cheated by nudging the rowboat away from it a few more feet) its presence on the calm surface of the lake mesmerized me. Several times fish struck (and came off) while I looked away, dreamily, and I learned then, for all time, to rivet my eye to that little object on the surface and keep it there for dear life. And once I learned never to look away, I was hooked to the bug, felt its every movement, waited, every moment, for that explosion on the surface, that sudden eruption of calm, that stirring, heart-stopping moment when a great largemouth attacks a bug.

Besides, I liked the way the fishing was done. I didn't have to fish all day, to find fish in deep water, to use hardware of such weight (and number of hooks) that the fight was diminished. I liked an old rowboat that went at exactly the speed I propelled it; I liked the oars making their rhythmic sound against water and oarlock; I liked the constant sight of the shoreline with its myriad shapes and forms: eelgrass, lily pads, old rotted stumps, fallen trees or branches, jutting rocks, drop-offs, points, rocky flats, coves, islands, channels, overhanging brush or branches, and so much more. Here, you did not fish to a fish, as you did on the flats or for trout; you fished to a spot where a fish might be. Slowly you learned the spots, all of them, not from a book but in the most pragmatic way: you got strikes in certain places, none in others. You did not pitch a fly and let the current take it to a trout but cast to a stump or a patch of weed and then, by wiggle and pop, tried to induce a fish to come and play. It was great fun. It was leisurely—and dramatic.

My friend Mort and I went to the Thousand Islands section of the St. Lawrence River for smallmouths a number of times. We fished for them with live minnows in thirty-five feet of water, below ledge drop-offs. The largemouths were in certain defined channels, not far from the shallows where we caught northern pike, and when they took a plug or live shiner their bulldog fight was distinctive, powerful, memorable. They did not go in for the acrobatics the smallmouths did—angling away from the boat as they came up from the depths and then leaping once, twice, high and wriggling. We'd catch them—largemouth and smallmouth—an hour apart and then talk endlessly about their differences, about which we liked most. The largemouths were heavyweights, even the smallest of them—one-punch knockout artists—smashing the lure or bait, making their play hard, with bad intentions.

Technology came to bass fishing as it did to everything else, from typewriting to kitchen appliances, and it brought finer reels that didn't backlash, subtler and stronger and lighter rods in a wide variety of patterns, and a cornucopia of whiz-bang lures from spinnerbaits to plastic worms. I listened to their advocates sing their virtues, read about them, watched them work on video, and—at one time or another—tried them all. They caught fish. Often one of them caught largemouth when another worked not at all. Some caught them on the top, others in midwater, still others along the bottom. They were versatile, keyed to dozens of different fishing occasions, often highly effective, always capable of expanding our fishing options. But in the end they did not catch me. As we get older we make choices. We narrow our sporting options because we've found that one route simply gives us more pleasure than another. Isn't that why we're out there? For the quality of the pursuit, the discrete joys the hunt gives us?

I had lost my heart to the long rod, the fly rod. I liked its rhythms; I liked the fact that *I* had to work a bit harder, was more involved; I liked the lighter, more responsive flies and bugs it could cast; I liked the sight of a fly line floating out behind me and then reaching forward. I even liked casting less and being a bit more involved with each cast. And I found, every time I went out for bass, that it filled all my needs. I did not want or need to catch fish all day, every day; I could wait. I had quite enough fishing to try them when they could be caught on the top, at the extremities of the day. And on a long hot summer afternoon on a New England pond, I could take all the pleasure I wanted by easing a rowboat or canoe toward the edges of a weedy cove and casting in against the rim of the lily pads for the odd fish that had squirreled in for a midday rest, with half a hope that an unlucky frog would come its way. I have taken a lot of bass from such spots in the middle of the day, when even bait and deep-water fishermen are having lunch or readying their gear for the evening. If I'm alone I may anchor the boat where I can fan out my casts for perhaps sixty feet of that line that separates open water from the outer edges of a large bed of lily pads. Some bass will be there, even at high noon. I'm in no hurry. It's better than badminton or golf or a gin rickey in the shade on shore. One fish for an afternoon of it will be plenty of reward.

But mostly, the magic of largemouth fishing comes at dawn or dusk, and not only then but the time just before and the hours well after dusk. The pond is mysterious, moody, silent then. In the very early morning, after a night on the prowl, big bass can be anywhere. And they're looking for food. I've seen one blast the gently floating plug a friend had left in the water while he untangled a backlash, an hour before dawn; I've seen their streaks and bulges among the weeds; I've had them storm a bug dozens of times, at any of a dozen different moments during a retrieve.

I like to get down to the dock by four o'clock, before there's any light other than the moon's on the water. A loon calls; faintly, a dog barks. The water, what I can see of it, is flat-calm and, in summer, light mist circles above it. I whisper to my friend. Neither of us wants to make the slightest unnecessary sound, even when we leave the car, a couple of hundred feet from the dock. We slip gear into the wooden rowboat, ease oars into their locks, untie the joining rope, and push off. I barely allow the oars to touch the water, just dip their tips gently against the surface. It does not require much more to propel the boat. Only a couple of dozen feet outside of the dock area, I bring the oars in and we both scan the dark waters for the best place to cast first. My friend is using a plug, I the long rod. He casts far out into the deep water, toward the center of the pond, claiming the bass will as well be there as anywhere, and I, from the bow, pull line off my inexpensive fly reel, false cast twice, and cast toward the faint outline of the shore. I can see the shoreline brush, a few rocks, but not much more. On my third cast the water breaks and bursts, as if someone has thrown in a cherry bomb, and I feel the hard satisfying weight of a good bass. It does not make a long run, like a bonefish or a salmon; it jumps twice—hard, loudly, with a rude power, and then, against my stubby leader, comes toward me. It's about four pounds. I grasp its lower lip, extract the big hook of the bug, and slip it back into the water. Then my friend has one, a bit larger, on his four-inch jointed plug, and then another. And then we see the first lightening of the sky in the east and head for the other side of the lake, where we take another four fish before the sky brightens and everyone else's day begins.

Largemouth bass are on the prowl in the very early morning hours—and the more you can manage to avoid gentleman's or banker's hours, the better the fishing will be. If everyone gets to the lake "early," at, say, 6:00, I'd get there at 5:00 or even 4:00; there is no hour too early to fish for largemouth bass in the summer—and you will find it a different lake, to the eye and for the fishing.

Best, though, is dusk, those great hours when the heat begins to leave the day inchmeal and the lake and the fish gradually become more and more alive. I like to have an early dinner and be on the water about 7:30 in high summer. There will still be some activity on the lake but not that much that you can't find a quiet section where no one will go in for a late swim, where the faster-casting spinners and baitcasters have been and gone. I like to row or paddle quietly, ten or fifteen feet farther out from the shoreline than I can comfortably cast. If I'm alone and the lake is calm, I'll often ship the oars and allow a slight breeze to take me along a shoreline, regulating direction by a brief pull on one oar or the other now and then. This is the time I love best. The sun is off the water, a sunset may still linger in the west, the evening calm has struck the water, and the cool air brings a strange mist to the surface. I can *feel* largemouths beginning to stir, beginning to look for their first meal of the evening.

I have with me the same order of tackle I used thirty-five years ago—as large and powerful a rod (in glass, graphite, or bamboo) as I have at hand, even a #11 or #12, even a tarpon rod. The fight is not my game; casting a heavy air-resistant bug *is*—and it requires a big tool. I use a simple reel with not much backing, for I've rarely had a largemouth run far; I use a weight-forward line (with perhaps two feet of the end cut off, which seems to help casting the heavy bug), a six-foot leader tapered to ten or twelve pounds; and I like a hairbug or a molded-body bug with a big cup, which will pop and throw a lathed wake when I tug the line to manipulate it.

I like progress. But I have found no reason to change—except perhaps the rod, since graphite is so much lighter and has exceptional power. And I'm still blithely content to fish a bug, on the top, where I make everything happen, where I can see it all happen.

I am astonished that more people don't fish for largemouth this way, that they rush around in high-powered boats with huge boxes of lures, that they plunk the lure out and draw it back with a grinding motion, that they need a lot to make them a little happy.

Lengthening my line, I double-haul and send a long cast out toward the fallen branches near the edge of the cove. The bug—that big four-legged one I love so much—lands a foot from the tangle of branches. With a lure I'd have to get it moving quickly or risk it sinking into the possible tangles of branches beneath the surface. But I can let the fly sit. And it does: settling itself from the long toss, rocking less and less, finally motionless. Now the game is all mine. First I twitch it twice, trying to keep it very close to where it fell—thinking that that must be the best spot of all, as near the branches as possible. I am all expectation. My eye is riveted to the bug. I leave the bug there for ten seconds, twenty seconds. Nothing happens. I give it a few abrupt tugs, which make the bug lean underwater a bit and then pop up. Then I leave it alone again, for forty seconds. I barely trust myself to blink. Then I rush it back toward me a foot or so in a steady tug, then pop it once or twice, then twitch it, then strip it back quickly.

I've had fish strike at every moment of such a retrieve: when the fly hit the water, when I was ready to yank the fly out to begin my next cast.

On my next cast I let the stationary bug sit, inches from a stump, for a full two or three minutes. I'm in absolutely no hurry. Then I twitch it slightly and let it sit some more. Then I twitch it again. There *has* to be a bass near that stump. That stump was made to harbor a big largemouth.

And so it does.

With a sucking in and out-rushing of water, a bruiser of a bass takes and bores deep, and then lifts up on sky hooks and rattles its sabres and falls back hard, with a heavy crash. Twice more it is up, into air, and several times it scurries off, with determined force. And then it comes in—five pounds' worth, green-bronze, thick as a loaf of bread.

There is no better freshwater fishing. There is no more delicious expectation than working a hairbug on the surface of a calm lake at dusk. There is no more excitement than the eruption, as if someone had thrown a pig or a garbage can into the water, when a largemouth takes. There is no day when I would pass up a chance at such largemouth magic.

9

RIVERBASS

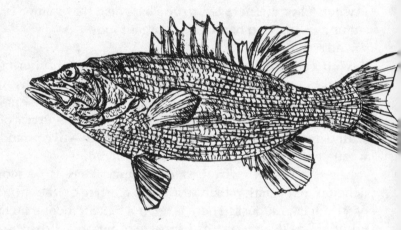

Sometimes we judged the Ten Mile River wrong. We came for trout, but the season was too far advanced and we caught only bass. They were in the pockets and eddies behind the rocks that were now half out of the water. They came short to a bushy dry fly but slammed our streamers. They leapt higher and fought harder than trout, but they were not as pretty and we were always disappointed then to catch them.

Though we knew they were smallmouths, we called them riverbass. We had caught chunky largemouths in Lake Ellis, on plugs and live bait—big ones, up to eight pounds; these were sleeker fish, never as large, more durable fighters than their dogged kin in lakes, but they had neither the coloration nor the size to hook us then.

Still, they sure saved some long, slow days.

On warm afternoons in late spring, after six hours of hard and fruitless fly fishing for trout, we began to drop down-river to the slower, warmer water and spend the last two hours of our fishing day after smallmouths. In fact, after three or four whacks at it, we began to carry some primitive bass flies—bigger streamers, cork poppers, small hair frogs.

It was pleasant work: we'd cast a bug up into an eddy, into pocketwater, twitch and chug it a few times, let it drift briefly downriver, and then there would be a heavy pocking of the water and a bright green twisting fish would bust up out of the water and splatter liquid silver into the slants of sun. We might catch eight or ten or twenty of them; I don't remember. I was always an indifferent counter of the fish I caught, and I have still not developed much of a flair for it. We might raise one or two a bit larger than the others—say, a pound and a half. This was not delicate work; we used eight- or ten-pound tippets and rarely lost fish except when they threw the fly on a jump or the hook simply pulled out. A fish better than a pound was always a prize.

Later my roommate Mort and I fished the huge St. Lawrence River for smallmouth, though not with flies, and I had my first true sense of how powerful the larger members of the species could be. Fishing in water thirty-five feet deep, with live minnows, we caught smallmouths up to five pounds. They'd take with a dull, steady peck. We'd wait. We'd wait a little longer. Then we'd strike hard to counter the sway in the line, and then the line would angle up toward the surface. We'd watch them run away from the boat and higher in the water and then, suddenly, they'd leap—high, powerfully, rocketing out, big enough to send a chill through us.

Recently I've taken a second hard look at riverbass—in the lower Schoharie, the Ten Mile, the Housatonic. They're simply lots of fun, and people like Dave Whitlock, Harry Murray, and Bob Clouser are bringing smallmouth more and more into the mainstream—if there is one—of serious fly fishing. Clouser's Crayfish are brilliant concoctions—good enough to put into a Creole gumbo or the mouth of a three-pound riverbass.

I make special trips for smallmouth now, and as they did thirty years ago, they still save the day when I've gone for other species that just don't want to come out and play.

I like to start late and wade wet on a lazy late-June or early-July morning. I work my way upstream, looking for some of the deeper runs. There are no rises to search for. Every cast is prospecting: behind the big rock; in the dark run, like a seam, in the dead middle of the river; in the shadows under those low oak branches; in the tail, where the run widens, flattens, grows deeper. My arm is in continual motion. I cast, watch the yellow cork popper come toward me in the foam and chop of the river, twitch it, and flick it up, back, and down again. *There's* a likely spot, where a tree quarters the river and serves as a kind of wing dam. I swivel slightly and cast three times, each time a little farther along the heavy tree, always as close as I can manage.

I'm never really sure where the fish will be at midday. They always surprise me. I've found them in midwater, behind boulders where the water is most roiled, and along the shady shoreline. They seem to like water cooled by riffles and shade. But they'll move six feet for a popping bug, so I'm never sure where they've actually been lying.

Fly fishing for smallmouth bass in rivers is a rougher game than fly fishing for trout in rivers. You generally fish in larger, rougher water (though not always), with larger and rougher flies or bugs. You rarely see the fish. You rarely see the food they're taking. I'm sure there are many times when some reasonable brand of imitation is possible, especially for larger moths or mayflies. I've heard of such times, but I've never been on the river when smallmouth are rising steadily to a specific insect. Mostly there are four or five kinds of food that riverbass eat, and they eat such foods anytime they can find them. A frog struggling in the currents is always a choice morsel, and so is a crayfish. Any popping bug, of cork or hair, will imitate the former; and there are some excellent crayfish imitations: Bob Clouser's, which I like best, and several that are less subtle—chiefly the defined shape of the crayfish, and drawn backward in the water, like Clouser's—but often quite effective. Smallmouth will take other large insects on the surface, like grasshoppers and crickets; and like their big-mouth cousins, the larger ones will take voles and small field mice. Underwater they're always partial to any of a dozen smaller fish, including minnows, dace, sculpin, sucker fry, and the young of just about any other species in the river, and they'll take nymphs and always worms. So a whole variety of streamers works well—fluttered, darting, ambled, or even dead-drift. I prefer patterns with marabou and the Matuka-style streamers, including those with a strip of rabbit fur on top. Any of the Woolly Bugger patterns, which can be bait-fish, leeches, or worms, are effective, too.

I've found riverbass slow at times but rarely uncatchable. Their clocks, I think, are less finely tuned to some hatching food than those of trout; they're greater opportunists—and I've found them to be so at the deadest hours of a summer day.

As these things go, with a large family of varying needs, you sometimes have to fish when you can, not when you'd prefer. A few years ago, for instance, I found myself at midday in Middlebury, Vermont, on a high-summer afternoon, with the sun bright and hot. My daughter was scheduled to graduate from a summer program that afternoon, and the entourage—

some five or six of us—was wandering through this pretty New England town. My daughter and wife found a clothing store to entertain them; from a bridge in the center of the town, far above the water, I naturally found the Otter River.

From the height at which I saw it, it seemed a pretty river, so naturally I decided to take a closer look. Since I had a rod, reel, and some flies in the car—though no boots, no vest, and no net—I naturally decided I ought to take those, too. And naturally I needed a license.

The proprietor of the local shop, whose vested interest was surely in optimism, just shook his head and said there was no fishing this time of year in the Otter.

"No fish at all?"

"Too warm," he said.

Still, I bought the license and a couple of cork bugs and walked down to the edge of the water in my only pair of shoes and slacks. To make a decent backcast, I had to manipulate myself into the right position—and in doing so I noted that I had muddied my pants and that my shoes had taken some water.

The water was sixty or so feet across. I managed that just fine, putting the popper a foot from the opposite shore and about fifteen feet upstream. This was pleasant fishing. The bug came down a bit; I chugged it and let it hug the shoreline; then I began to bring it across the river, with fits and starts, always letting it drop downstream a bit, like a frog (I thought) struggling mightily to get across the stream.

It was a pretty scenario, and I was enjoying myself hugely, undisturbed by thoughts of catching a fish. Local genius is rarely wrong. But I was much happier casting than shopping.

And then, of course, I was rudely disturbed by a wake and a short strike—my heartbeat quickened—and then, on the next cast, by the fish itself—a plump 14-incher. After that, while townspeople, some half-dozen of them, on the bridge looked at the strange creature up to his thighs in their river, I took four fat bronzebacks in less than an hour—one a bit smaller, several a couple of inches larger, which is a lot of smallmouth for a dog-day afternoon, or anytime.

I went to the graduation, with squooshy shoes and muddy, stained trousers, and a smile for the graduate. I just smiled and smiled, and several people said they could see how proud I was of her, and I was, but they were only half right.

10

FIRST BLUES ON A FLY

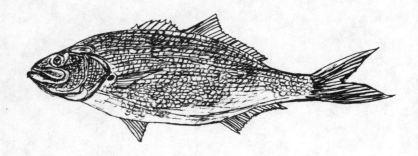

The winds were savage our first four days on the island. You could hear them even under the covers, at five in the morning, and they rattled the summer house all day, and rushed in the trees. One morning they were ferocious and later we heard reports that, far inland, they had dropped twenty inches of October snow. We got no snow but after six hours of surf casting that morning, of casting for twenty minutes then rushing back to the car for warmth, then venturing out again, I thought I'd never rid myself of the jittery chill in my bones.

Of course, fly fishing was out. I'd hauled a #9 outfit up to the island with great expectations and for the first few days I dutifully took it from the car when I went to the surf; but it was hopeless. No one could cast into a harsh wind like that— not Steve Rajeff, not Lefty, not Joan Wulff, not me. Most especially not me.

Worse, after that truly blustery and cold morning, some local experts I knew said the fish would surely be scattered; they could be miles offshore; they might not come back for two or three days; and the water would be littered with seaweed, eelgrass, and debris. Fly fishing, they said, was improbable.

I'd been trying for years to get a bluefish on a fly, a thing of no particular difficulty to most of the rest of the world— those who cared about such matters. I had especially come to this island in early October, with greater expectations than ever, only to be thwarted again by the fickle finger of fate. I'd practiced my double-haul; I had counseled with Tom Rosenbauer and Lefty and Lou Tabory; I even had flies from Lou, the best you could get; and as I'd feared, I was going to miss them again. There was too much wind. The fish were scattered. They were here last week but now they were who knew where.

After the fourth day I thought I'd had enough of this madness and did not set the alarm clock for the next morning. Why punish myself more? The trout season would open in another six months; let better and wiser men do this saltwater thing; I'd sleep late and dream.

But I was up at four and, miraculously, I heard no wind; that jolted me awake. In twenty minutes I was on the bay side of the island. It was warmer and calmer than I'd expected but I reasoned that the fish would be scattered and that I needn't bother with my fly rod or my chest waders here. There wouldn't be any fly fishing, I felt quite sure; I'd take the big surf rod and could cast a mile with that. I liked the long hard casts and the sight of a big popping plug chugging back, throwing a roll and spurts of water as it came toward me. It wasn't precisely "dry plug" fishing but it could be exciting to see a good fish come to the surface for it.

The bay was barely rippled, black except for the glint of the moon in a long streak on the water from the west. A couple of guys had a little camp going—with a gas light, a freezer box, a pail of live eels, and four or five rods set out in sand spikes. They had been fishing all night and had caught two bluefish of about four pounds each, one of which they'd cut up for bait. I walked down the beach three or four hundred yards from them, and began to cast far out into the bay, working my way slowly farther from the bait fishermen with each cast.

About an hour later the first light began to break in the east. The light started just at the skyline of the harbor and the hills and then spread upward, minute by minute, slowly. It was pale pink and salmon and very beautiful, and I stopped casting to watch.

A moment later, to my left, I thought I heard a splash and turned instinctively. A fish had broken water. And wasn't that a swirl straight out? And another off to the right?

I poised my big surf rod, then, at the next swirl, cast quickly beyond it and chugged my lure into that area within seconds. A good fish struck at once and I had him on.

I'd thought these were striped bass taking sand eels—and in fact I'd seen a lot of sand eels washed up on the shore. The swirls were more measured than I'd have expected of anything but a bass. But my fish was a blue. It jumped twice, then made a strong run, then jumped again and somehow shook the single large hook.

When I looked again out into the bay there were a dozen swirls and boils in every direction—not the slashing, churning of water I'd always seen during a bluefish blitz but swirls just beneath the surface, like huge trout taking nymphs. And now and again a fish would porpoise completely out of the water, in a lithe arc. All the fish were blues, acting a gentler part.

I was about to cast again, then stopped and began to run across the sand, back to the car, now a considerable distance away. I got there breathless, grabbed my fly rod and box of flies, looked at my waders but decided they'd slow me down, and raced back, my feet paining sharply as I high-stepped through the deep sand.

When I came to the first swirls I stopped, tied on a green Lefty's Deceiver that Lou Tabory had given me, and cast quickly. I was breathing hard and my cast was clumsy and short; also, the big fly jerked around badly at the end of my nine-foot leader. I cast again—again short and clumsily.

So I reeled in, caught my breath, watched the water, cut the leader back to three and a half feet, tied the fly on again, and waded out into the bay in my trousers and the only pair of shoes I'd brought with me.

The water was cold but I went in up to my thighs, remembered my wallet, took it out and put it in my upper jacket pocket, and waded deeper.

Now I'd be able to reach them comfortably.

I stripped off as much line as I thought I could cast, watched the water, saw a boil off to the right, cast just beyond it, stripped the fly in briskly, and felt a tremendous jolt.

I had caught hundreds of bluefish in the surf on heavy surf-casting tackle and large lures. They are savage fighters. But I was unprepared for the feel of one on even a heavy fly rod.

The strike was a sudden, wrenching lurch at the end of the line; it was followed by a heavy surge of power as the fish fled, trying to save its skin. I raised my rod, put a broad bend into it, and held on stupidly as the fish took me well into the backing, the rod tucked into my pelvis, the reel spinning madly.

Lou had told me he did not use wire leaders because both bass and bonito were shy of them. He felt that the long-shank hooks he used would keep the line away from the razor teeth of the blues. I had tied the fly directly to the monofilament but didn't trust it. The more line the fish took—it had two hundred feet by now—the more I was sure I'd lose it.

The force of the fish was tremendous—and I was quite sure I'd never bring it in.

But in five minutes of pumping and reeling I had the fish back on the fly line, and a couple of minutes later—my wrist aching—I saw the flash of blue-silver and knew it had begun to tire. Another two runs, a few hard splashes at the surface, a lot more steady pressure, and the fish was near the shoreline; and then I slid it up the beach.

I was astounded at how small it was: six pounds, no more. I'd thought it twice that size.

In the next two days I got another couple of dozen fish on the fly—often when men tossing metal or plugs got nothing. Perhaps it was the undulating movement of the large fly, the way it fluttered and paused and sped in the water; the fly was clearly a magnificent lure for blues and I could scarcely believe I'd thought for so long that I'd never get one this way.

I was up at 4:00 A.M. the last day, wildly excited about this new sport I'd found, after years of frustration. But there was a sharp wind coming head on into me and I could barely cast into it. I tried. For three hours I fought the wind, wished

I had on an intermediate line that would cut into it better, switched casting angles to beat it, somehow. I walked a half mile to a bend to beat the wind but never did, not that last morning.

It was a tough way to end the trip—but I didn't care; I'd found a new addiction and I knew I'd be back.

11

SELECTIVE BLUES—
AND STRIPED BASS

Bluefish (*Pomatomus saltatrix*), affectionately
known as "choppers," are notorious slobs. They maketh the
sea to stink of oily bunker when they've been feeding;
friends pride themselves on being able to smell blues a mile
away. Give them just about any sort of steak and they'll turn it
to tartare in an instant. Over the years I've taken them on
swimming and popping plugs, spoons, bucktail jigs, diamond jigs, drails, a dozen live and dead creatures, something
called an "umbrella rig," can openers with hooks affixed,
surgical tubing, and three or four sturdy styles of the feathered thing.

When they get a little blood on the brain, they'll generally
make a sorry mess of anything you chuck at them. Still, I've
had my odd times when they were what would pass for

selective: evenings when they were thick in the surf yet would take only surface lures; nights when you had to retrieve a lure or fly just as fast as you could; mornings when—patrolling the shore in ones and twos—they showed an exclusive preference for a very thin, very chartreuse-green sand-eel imitation, wiggled ever so slowly. I'm not an expert on blues. I have gone to them these past ten years, now and then, to escape the tyranny of trout, to change pace drastically, to explore a part of the watery world I know too slenderly—the sea. It's bigger than any trout stream I've fished and has more places in it where the fish aren't; it also has bigger and more savage denizens than a trout stream, fish I understand not at all.

More often than not blues beat me quite as badly as most other gamefish do me in, though I've fished four or five times during blitzes from which I've walked away with fish still active, quite sated by the sheer volume of their eager strikes, their raw violence. They must be one of the strongest of all gamefish and among the most generous.

Last fall my friend Steve Fisher and his son David had me out a couple of times in Greenwich Bay, chiefly for stripers. They'd pick me up in front of my city apartment on warm fall mornings before the first light, weeks after I thought my season had ended for the year, and we'd head less than an hour out of the city. I had rather grown comfortable with midmorning starts for trout, when the western flies came, but these early-morning forays reminded me of my youth, of adventure, of how we often love fishing best when it breaks the bonds of the ordinary for us, the routine, the usual hours, the regularized life, when it puts us in touch with something a little more elemental, even for a brief while.

The Fishers' boat, a twenty-two-foot Winner called "Piscator," isn't elemental; it's a sophisticated modern fishing machine with sonar and CB radio and twin motors and a john and a houseful of the best flies, rods, and reels for assaulting blues and stripers.

We assaulted the stripers with impunity, but they played hard to get. What those big fellows with stripes were doing, and when, was not clear to me. I had once taken them on the bottom, on diamond jigs, one after the other, but that wasn't our game today. I was sorely anxious to get a truly big one on a fly. Steve said he had gotten all of his stripers on a pale-blue popping bug so I tried one of those and did what he did, after my fashion, casting in against the breakwater and the exposed rocks, and generally doing what I would do with a slightly smaller bass bug. Steve did it all well. I enjoyed watching his popper drop near the breakwater and work its way back to the boat, sending out a "V" wave and a series of curls, plops, fits, and starts. I had taken my big tarpon rod, on some theory or other, and I liked the feel of the big stick and heavy line pulling against my arm and shoulders; I liked the deliberate and heavy rhythm of it, the long powerful cast and then the bug unfolding and dropping a bit better every half hour or so.

We got nothing.

"What am I doing wrong?" I asked.

"No one's doing anything wrong," said Steve.

"How do you know if the fish are there?"

"You don't," said Steve, "unless they roll or break the surface."

"Have you seen them here, right here?" I asked.

"Many times."

We fished quite hard on the strength of that history for several hours and neither of us had a follow or a touch. It was just like that sometimes. Yesterday—or was it last week?—there had been fish all around the breakwater; it was as good a place as any other to make a stand. Today, the deliberate, sturdy rhythm of my #11 tarpon rod began to saw into my back. I thought a chunk of me might just break off.

I switched to a Deceiver, let it sink a couple of feet, and then stripped it back. Sometimes I could see the fly a foot or so under the surface, sometimes not. I switched to a sand eel, on the theory that once, several years earlier, they had taken fish for me on Martha's Vineyard. The theory was poor medicine. I switched back to the Deceiver. David thought that as the light got brighter the stripers kept getting shyer. I'd heard that theory and it made sense; so I fished the Deceiver much deeper, where it would be darker. I was being very shrewd. And my shrewdness was rewarded. In a cove near some high grasses, on a White Deceiver, I finally caught one.

"How big is it?" asked David.

"Five or six pounds, I think," I said.

I was less than half right; it might have gone a fraction over two; I always like to be wrong the other way. But a little striper goes a long way. It has to.

So we turned our attention to blues, which were now doing terrible things to bunker in the harbor. What a sight! Acres of mossbunker skittering, leaping, charging at the surface, bringing the water to a wild boil. Some flew a foot or two into the air, in terror, to save their skins. Everywhere, in a great elemental massacre, there were desperate bunker, forced up against the surface by the blues. Half a dozen boats had blues on. This was a school of gorilla blues; they were in the fifteen- to seventeen-pound class. I'd have liked to be connected to one of those for a while. All those caught had been hooked on cut bunker.

There was now some serious and pointed talk about what was going on. Everyone had a theory about how these fish could and could not be taken. Steve said that blues never took flies when they had this much bunker available. This sounded sensible to me. I had read that they didn't even take whole live bunker when they were on this brand of orgy; I reported this theory, which nudged the discussion toward a concept of selective blues, but there were no takers. I also reported having read that they never took heads— which fell to the bottom and were later picked up and prized by stripers. I heard a faint chuckle or two. Steve thought they were selective to a good bloody midsection or tail section of bunker and that's what I saw my fellow anglers pitching out, overhand, and taking the big ones on. When the discussion finally drifted back to fly fishing, and I felt on firmer ground, someone wondered if there was a good Chunk of Bunker imitation or a Piece of Flesh fly that might turn the trick. Was this "fly" fishing or (as Conrad Voss Bark says) "artificial bait" fishing? Did it matter? Was it fun anyway? Was fun enough?

These were weighty questions for an autumn bluefish trip and I pondered them soberly as the sun came up, forgot them, and cast my biggest Deceiver almost fruitlessly into the churning water, catching two plump bunker on the fly, one even in the mouth.

For a moment, as I watched one of my bunker cut into three bloody portions—the fate of *Brevoortia tyrannus,* the Atlantic menhadden, familiarly called mossbunker, affectionately just bunker—a bunker's lot did not seem an especially easy one. If the blues or the bluefishermen didn't get you, the makers of cat food, chicken feed, fertilizer, fish paste, paint, or canned chum would.

In the end we caught no blues by any means, fair or foul, and by 12:00, from a good deal too much of the elemental, I could barely stand and looked around eagerly for something with sugar to which I might rise, and found three chocolate donuts.

An hour later I wondered if I could walk up the stairs to my apartment or would have to get to my door on all fours.

Two afternoons later, Steve called and said they'd taken some people out that morning. The people had never fished for stripers or blues with a fly before and had even brought trout equipment. You know what happened but I'll tell you anyway: a striper on the first cast; blues all morning long—on cast after cast, a boatload of them; broken rods; chewed-up flies; shouting, excitement, no theories, busted reels.

All that elemental jazz.

12

CIVILIZATION AND THE BLUES AT EAST HAMPTON

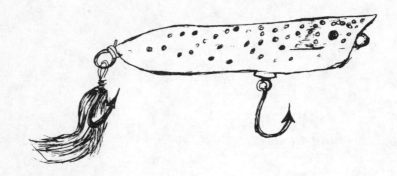

She hauled me quite as far from rivers as you can get: to the shore, for a few restful days in East Hampton, "looking in the galleries, shopping in the pretty little shops, lying on the beach." I went quietly. After all, I'd been hauling her in the opposite direction all summer, to trout streams, with a flyrod. But behind my luggage, far back in the trunk of the car, neatly hidden, I hauled along my surf-casting rod.

The local newspapers flashed pretty pictures of Mrs. D. Evelyn Metroland's party, at which were present faces one could not help but see—hard as one might try—on the big screen and the little screen and in society columns. They all smiled from the pages and seemed to be having a perfectly splendid time in East Hampton, civilized East Hampton, and I lay on the beach for an hour and practically went bats.

After beach and before dinner on the second day, I found an hour and a half that went begging. But not for long.

At six-thirty, I said: "Take a shower. I'm going to make a few casts—nothing serious—and I'll be back at eight sharp."

"Oh, no!" she said.

"Eight. I promise."

"Another midnight supper," she said. "Damned! I thought we were going to spend a civilized weekend."

On the beach I saw an elderly chap in chest waders, casting a metal Hopkins lure deftly. I looked for birds circling the surface but saw none. I looked up and down the shore but there were none of the telltale signs of feeding fish: birds or some surface disturbance or some other fishermen with fish on the line.

The bright umbrellas were gone. The bronzed bodies in beach chairs were gone. The breakers curled like lathed glass, and no one swam in them. The beach, where I had stretched restlessly all afternoon and the previous afternoon, squinting at the sea and the horizon and the bodies so much better tended and browned than mine, was now almost deserted. A man and a woman, fully clothed, walked arm in arm. A couple of kids tossed a Frisbee. A spaniel chased a ball thrown by a boy. The elderly man kept casting his heavy Hopkins lure far out into the ocean and retrieving it without interruption.

So I rigged up the huge surf pole with the outsized spinning reel slowly; it was a gigantic, unwieldy tool for someone who loved delicate bamboo rods and flies the size of gnats. To the end of the line I attached a two-foot wire leader that my little brown trout would have thought a water snake, and to the snap-clip at the end of the leader I attached a six-inch Atom Striper Swiper lure. It was not as pretty or civilized a name, I thought, as a #20 Blue-Winged Olive.

I had not fished the surf for five years and the first cast I made with my blue and white Striper Swiper was modest, tentative. You like to lean into a cast when you fish the surf; you like the ache of your whole body bending back and coiling forward and the sheer power and distance of the cast. My first cast had none of that. But it was far enough. A second after the lure splashed down, there was a gigantic swirl, a spurt of water, and a moment later a huge bluefish rocketed out of the swells, shaking silver and blue and, spectacularly, attached to me.

When I'd beached my fourth blue, all about ten pounds, the man fishing the Hopkins lure said he'd never seen anything like it in all his years of surf casting: a school of blues, obviously feeding underwater, refusing a Hopkins and smashing a surface plug. We saw dozens of baitfish wash up on the wet shore now, and there was clearly a feeding frenzy under way. I reasoned that there was so much real food under the surface that only a splashy lure on top would attract their attention. The man cast five more times with his Hopkins, then, when I caught three more bluefish, grudgingly switched to a surface plug and his rod arced at once.

Now there were eight, ten casters on the beach. A young man next to me, flinging a piece of metal, was the only person who caught nothing and I gave him a surface plug and he was promptly into a fish, which he lost because he didn't use a wire leader. He became quite frantic and raced back to his car; I hoped he wasn't going to strip wires from his transmission or lighter. I remember a crazy friend doing that.

These were big, powerful blues and I could not reel in fast enough to keep the lures out of their mouths. The fish were everywhere beneath the calm surface of sea and it was a savage business down there, I thought, as well as on the shore, where six, eight rods arced every time I looked up, a couple of hundred yards in either direction.

It was hard to disengage the treble hooks from the toothy fish and return them to the sea but I didn't need them, could not use them, and did so time after time, after each fierce bout. They fought so hard they almost came in dead. But all revived. Eighteen, twenty—had I caught that many? I had not cast five times without taking a fish.

And then, suddenly, I'd had enough of it. They were big, they were strong, and I'd had fun catching the first eight or ten of them—but they had exhausted my interest. The drama was over. I could leave them alone. Without looking at my watch, with the blitz still going full blast, I dismantled my gear and headed back to the car.

Mari thought I'd gone berserk, leaving such a spree, returning a full half hour early. "I'd have waited," she assured me.

"Sure," I said, making the most of it.

The next morning I drove to the beach for a last look, not to fish. An old car was lugging a huge dory out of the beach and onto the roadway. Behind it, a couple-of-ton truck was lumbering with a vast load of bluefish bodies, breaded with sand. Netters. They had circled the vast school and decimated it. It seemed a less-than-civilized thing to have done, especially in East Hampton.

13

WORLD OF THE
SILVER KINGS

"How's your heart, Nick?" Jeffrey Cardenas wrote, and sent me a photograph of what a 16-foot hammerhead shark did with one bite to a 150-pound tarpon: there was a head and half of a torso, and a lot of blood on the deck of the *Waterlight*.

My heart felt pretty good, and not so lost to those pretty little speckled things that I couldn't dream of at least one trip south for the great silver kings. So when an opening broke for two days in prime tarpon time with Jeffrey, I said, "Why not?"

I ordered a 12-weight 9'3" graphite rod that was very fast and very powerful. Then I traded half a dozen reels I never used for a huge Fin-Nor with an intermediate line and six million yards of backing. I bought the strongest sunscreen I could find—to prevent more basal cell carcinomas, which had recently begun to pop out on my forehead like freckles—and scrounged sixty or seventy tarpon flies from friends and bought twice as many, and read Lefty and Dimock and all the articles on tarpon I could find in magazines going back ten years. And in the end I wasn't sure I really wanted this kind of fishing at all.

I'd never had a 12-weight rod in my hand; I'd never caught a fish larger than twelve pounds on a fly; and I'd rather gotten to like tiny flies and tough trout lately. Four pounds of such tough trout would be more to my liking, I thought, than these silver monsters I understood not at all.

Still, I'd made the commitment and kept planning hard. I worked out everything with the greatest care. I even took a left-hand Fin-Nor, though I always reel with my right hand, thinking my right hand could hold the rod better. And day by day the letters came from friends who had tried tarpon fishing: "It's addictive." "You'll give up trout forever." "They're awesome, prehistoric fish!" "I envy you like mad."

Several weeks later I was back home, safe—my rod broken, middle finger of my left hand scarred, bruises on my chest, my left arm, and rump, my nose and left arm scaling rudely from the sun, my head awash with dreams of big water and big tarpon.

And even now, many weeks later, scores of images keep porpoising in my brain, like great silver backs rhythmically rising from the sea and falling back.

I see the flats from Miami to Key West as the Jetstream J31 cruises low: so clear and calm I thought they were land, except for the sailboats and skiffs, like skittering caddis, on the flat surface of the thin water.

What a different game it is: standing on the prow of the *Waterlight,* which dips and rolls in the high winds, line coiled below me; Jeffrey high on the poling platform, eyes peeled to the horizon line, looking for dark purple shapes beneath the surface or silver backs porpoising or nervous water. "One o'clock—about two hundred yards," he calls. "A big school. Large fish. And they're very happy."

I look and see nothing but the thousand refractions of light on the choppy green surface.

"Point your rod to where you think it is."

I point the rod.

"Farther right," he calls—a voice out of the wind, in my ear.

I point the rod to 2:30.

"Farther. Yes. See them?"

I do.

"They're closing quickly. Make sure your line is ready. Keep them in sight. Here they come . . ."

Thinking back on those two days, I see the giant rays like magic carpets beneath the boat; the sudden appearance of a turtle's head, the size of a grapefruit; a happy tarpon's head out of the water, Cuban anchovies sprouting from its mouth; cormorants working down near the abandoned barge; pelicans diving thunderously; huge nurse sharks mating. Jeffrey says the nurse sharks gather near these islands and sometimes mate as long as twelve hours, twisting and turning together, white belly high, tails thrashing, milt awash in the green seas.

I see Mari making watercolors on the brief sand beach of an island, us rushing from the permit flats as the rain clouds angle toward her.

I see the sheets of rain as we turn tail and race back to Key West, water blasting me from the boat's spray in choppy seas and from above, my eyes stinging from the salt, Mari smiling through it all like a kid on a roller coaster.

I see Jeffrey madly untangling the knot in my fly line, the second day, after the bright forty-pound tarpon took and began to leap with abandon, and Jeffrey untying it and the fish soon coming close under the pressure of the 12-weight and Jeffrey shouting, "If he goes under the boat, take it around the front end," and the fish diving under, me following stupidly with the rod, the new 12-weight busting cleanly with a bang, Jeffrey leaping in to get the tip section that came free when the fish was off, me seeing that photograph he'd sent me of half a tarpon, and then Jeffrey hoisting himself back on board and all of us laughing.

It was very different for me out on the flats. I saw and understood too little. I felt untutored for it. In that one moment when tarpon and poled boat began to intersect, I had moments to get my line in the air, double-haul, and place it quickly in the line of the huge fish. I got one cast, perhaps two. I got buck fever and crashed key casts, after Jeffrey had spent twenty minutes poling into position. I nearly put a fly into his neck when I cast at twelve o'clock. I cast too fast. I cast late. I forgot everything I'd read, everything I'd been told, everything I'd practiced the day before in a skiff in the backcountry with a friend. It was after we'd fished the backcountry that afternoon and practiced with the big 12-weight that I tripped getting out of the boat— nervous before I was within thirty miles of a tarpon—and smashed my chest, my left arm, and my rump. Out on the flats I forgot the sunscreen I'd brought and only used the one fly that Jeffrey gave me.

I took a tarpon on my first cast the second day, jumped another, cast poorly much of the time, decently on occasion, and half began to think I understood something (though I didn't), and wondered if I could ever master this exhilarating sport.

The two days had started with a minute of high drama, and I may even have thought then that I understood a bit more than I could possibly understand.

We had no sooner arrived on the flats the first day than Jeffrey tied on a fly with a bright red head that had been hot the past week. He said to keep alert. I remember a sailfish captain telling me that a dozen years earlier, and my sitting in the big fighting chair for five hours—highly alert, dragging a rigged bait fruitlessly.

Not this time. Two minutes after we arrived, Jeffrey spotted silver backs, not eighty feet away. You couldn't miss them. My legs turned to jelly. But I stripped out line, stepped onto the casting area, saw the ruffled water angling toward us, and seconds later they were at eleven o'clock, forty-five feet off to the left, and closing.

For three weeks I have been trying to get a truly clear picture of what happened next. All is awash in silver and confusion.

Seconds after I made my first cast ever to a tarpon, a huge fish—over 100 pounds—took the fly. I struck three or four times hard (as I'd been instructed); the fish careened dead away from the boat and leapt once, thunderously, rising like some great silver missile, shaking, vibrating in the air, and then crashing back into the sea.

It was off the hook.

There were voices behind me, but my first thought was that I might get in another cast before this large school passed. The line was too far out to put it in the air, so I began to strip it—fishing it, as I always do when fish are near.

Another tarpon picked up the fly. I felt the sudden surge of power, reared back three or four times, and this time the fish was on. Up it went—bright silver and electric, quivering with life—and I bowed (or at least leaned enough) and the fish stayed hooked.

There is an old 1920s cartoon about a Mississippi fisherman hooked up to a truly gigantic catfish, with the legend: "Fish, do I have you or do you have me?" With my tarpon I could not tell. The fish took line when it suited him; it leapt magnificently; at times it felt unbudgeable. It proved to be modest-sized—about seventy-five pounds—but it was more than enough fish for the likes of me, and while I fought it, Jeffrey taught me how to gain line, keep the fish from rolling, apply maximum pressure, and haul opposite the tug of the fish. Reeling hard with my unused left hand, I put a huge welt on my middle finger; I could barely lift my right arm. An hour later the fish turned sideways and the fight neared its end.

Those two days—my first on the flats—haunt me. My heart held—but I lost a piece of it to the world of the silver kings.

14

FRENCH PIKE

The fly fishing in Paris was extremely poor. I could find no trout in the Louvre; there were none in the Orangerie; only the Musée d'Orsay had one—in a Courbet. Nor were there any fishermen with their long rods along the Seine. I walked the quais and looked but saw only one fish in four or five miles: amid the floating debris, among the heavy shore weeds, a carp, belly-up.

I did find two shops, one of which was surely my kind of place. It was called La Maison de la Mouche, on the Ile de St. Louis, and it was crammed with flies, rods, reels, and all the delicious paraphernalia that drives us nuts. The proprietor spoke little English, and I speak less French. Our conversation amounted to a muttered "Ritz" and a "grand mouche" and a "cad-ese" and a couple of "cul de canards." I bought several of the latter, blond, in #18, which reminded me of some Pale Morning Duns I'd once seen, in another country. And later I packed them up carefully and sent them to my friend Herb, well west in that other country. I told him to run them by some large speckled friends we knew in a certain pool called Paranoid. I told Mari: "We've come to the wrong place. The fishing's lousy here."

Matters picked up considerably, though, when Pierre returned from Portugal.

He had been at the beach with his family, far from rods and flies and any chance to fish, and his frustration had swelled to a fine frenzy. He wanted to go out right away. At once. The next morning. We could fish the upper Seine; we could fish for carp below the Pont Neuf—at 4:00 in the morning; there was a small pike pond an hour from Paris; there was the chance of a helicopter ride to a chalkstream only fifteen minutes as a fast crow flies; there was a pond with big pike on the border of Normandy and Perche.

I looked at the big pike on the wall of Pierre's Left Bank apartment. It was a considerable fish, better than thirty pounds, and it had come out of the big-pike pond about which Pierre had spoken.

My friend pushed the chalkstream option; he said it had a good head of wild browns and had been fishing very well—the big mayfly was on. I'd never fished a French chalkstream and the idea appealed to me. But the pike on the wall, with the mouth of an alligator, had put the hex on me. I asked Pierre lightly if that was the largest fish to come from that pond. No, there had been forty-pounders, and one day the previous October he had seen something that suggested some were much larger. He had been on the lake alone, during bird-shooting season. Now and then he heard shots. After one cluster of blasts, a pheasant came rocketing out of the woods, fluttered, and fell to the surface.

"Don't tell me the rest," I said.

"It lay there on the surface, Neek . . ."

"I don't want to hear about it."

"It lay there for a few moments, and I watched its wings struggle, and then I had to turn the boat a bit and for a moment I couldn't see it."

"I don't believe this, Pierre. It didn't happen. Not a whole pheasant."

"I turned away and then there was a tremendous splash . . ."

"No!"

". . . and when I turned back, there were just . . ."

"No, Pierre!"

"On the surface, Neek . . ."

"Stop it!"

". . . there were only three feathers. Fifty pounds. Fifty pounds that pike was, min-e-mum."

The pond, leased by Pierre's friend Alex from a duke, is two hours from Paris, if you drive over one hundred miles per hour most of the way. We stopped for coffee and then for the makings of a sumptuous lunch, and made it in 121 minutes.

Wobbling slightly, bundling myself against the rain and chill, I allowed myself to be ghillied by rowboat to an embankment where the water dropped abruptly to fifteen or twenty feet. At least seven twenty-pounders—if I kept the various pike distinct in my mind—had come from that very spot. Even one of Alex's girlfriends, out for the first time, had caught one that size. Twenty pounds seemed the size at which serious counting began.

I could see this was a remote, modest-size pond, perhaps twenty acres, surrounded by forest, with weedbeds in the coves, some deep channels, and the embankment dropoffs. Alex leased it very cheaply, with a house and some incidental buildings, and since I'm restless and always looking for a "home," I considered that option and concluded that I could live in this place forever and write shaggy fish stories, especially if I could get a twenty-pounder every couple of days.

The three fish Alex and Pierre caught were one-quarter that size. I caught nothing but a running nose and a rather large, full branch, well beneath the twenty-pound class but of a much more complicated species. That and the rain did their best to discourage me. I thought briefly of the warm museums in Paris. Then Pierre hooked one a bit larger and handed me the rod. I told him I didn't need his pike— in the fullness of time I'd get one of my own, thank you. Alex caught another, and I had one flash at my lure and struck much too fast and hard. Then Pierre jumped one on a big popping plug, and I got out a fly rod and began to flail away. The rod was light—only a 6-weight—and the bass bug, with wire tippet, was unwieldy. In the wind the rig jerked around spasmodically, and I could not help noting that my companions had stopped fishing; they were now low in the boat, head tucked into chest, arms in protective embrace, strong French words emerging rapidly from each pile of person.

In the candlelit camp building we built a fire, had charcoal-roasted steaks, country pâté, warm local bread, and a pleasant beaujolais—and my spirits picked up considerably. Then we walked back to the lake, and in a steady rain, rowed to the opposite side.

The water there was dotted with tiny rock islands, each fitted with one of the duke's duck-nesting structures. Each structure had a neat little metal ramp leading to the water. We saw one week-old duckling totter out to its ramp and then, wisely, have second thoughts and scurry back, for the pond looked very nervous where the ramp entered the water.

Though we did not have duckling or pheasant imitations, we fished near the ramps a couple of times, and Pierre had one good pike leap right over his big popping plug. He is one of the great fishermen—a former champion caster with several kinds of rods, a demon-pursuer of all the great gamefish. He once told me, "All I want to do, Neek, is fish. I want to fish for every species in every part of the world. I want to fish all the time, everywhere."

This is a sort of large commitment, and my little passions pale before it. Pierre also finds fish and eventually, late in the afternoon, when hope had almost metamorphosed into despair, he found one for me. "There, between the two weedbeds," he told me, and I cast the big frog bug in, chugged it, rushed it, let it wait, chugged it some more, and began to lift it out when my first pike struck—and missed.

"Back, back!" shouted Alex.

"Quick!" shouted Pierre.

I was quick and sure-handed, the bug bounced once, there was a heavy splash, I struck, I felt a heavy rush, and four minutes later I grasped my first pike behind the gills and lifted it into the boat. It may have been French but it sure looked like a Northern to me.

The fish was shy of twenty pounds by about fifteen and could not have fit more than a couple of furry ducklings into its maw. But I felt very happy about the outcome, got my picture taken a dozen times with the grizzly thing, then chucked it back.

* * *

The fishing in Paris is generally poor. Go for the museums, the food, the history, the culture, the ambience, the picturesque winding streets. Go if you want to try to regain your youth, even though you won't. The fishing isn't much, but if you know Pierre, you can do all right.

15

BROOKIE

They were the first trout I caught. So small they seemed merely a brighter and quicker brand of minnow, they'd dart and dance in the clear pools of that little feeder creek where I began all my fishing. They were wild, dark, furtive things, as evanescent as flashes of sunlight between the branches of dancing poplars, and when I hooked one, it came leaping toward me, wriggling like mad, as brilliant as a live jewel.

Those fish might be char, not trout, but such diminutive versions of *Salvelinus fontinalis* became great totems in my heart, and I forget them at my peril.

I thought of those wild little brookies a few weeks ago, when Roger Menard showed me a hundred or so slides he had taken of some wild brook-trout fishing in some backwater unnamed creeks. Sitting in the dark room, with the bright screen like a great window into this world of fern, rivulet, tiny falls, overhung caverns of poplar, birch, and willow, I kept seeing through Roger's shrewd camera a world I'd neglected for larger game. Small silver pocketwater. Quick short casts, the line reflecting the bright slants of sun. A fish on. A dark brookie in the water, a Hairwing Royal Coachman in its lip. A wicker creel. Three perfectly gorgeous brookies laid side by side on a rock. And as the scenes clicked onto the screen, I looked, too, through that other eye that peers back into the past.

Those first brookies I knew rarely reached five inches. They were in the creek near Haines Falls on which I prowled for frogs and newts and crayfish and had the great hook set firmly in me for a lifetime of fishing. Barefoot, with a ten-foot piece of raw bamboo I bought in town, and to which I tied a six-foot length of green wrapping cord, gut leader, and the smallest hook I could find in the mixed box I bought for ten cents, I searched for pockets deep enough to hide the largest fish, six- and seven-inchers. I'd seen and even trapped fingerlings, no more than two inches, in the shallower runs; unlike the dull dace, the coloration of these strange fish was brilliantly varied and bright, their parr marks so much lighter and varied than the coloration of their larger kin that at first I took them to be another species. And to the touch they were like wet velvet.

In the deeper pockets, under mossy rocks, in the darker recesses of this tiny mountain stream, there were the prizes I sought: dark, soft, eager fish. After weeks of stalking I began to catch them regularly on a half-inch of tiny worm placed just over the point of the smallest hooks, with a bit of cork for a bobber and two BB split-shot to take the bait where I could not see it.

Since then I have caught brook trout in dozens of different waters, in a score of shapes and sizes. The largest, caught on brown leech patterns tied for me by my friend Thom Green, came from Henry's Lake in Idaho, and they seemed no more like the little brookies I caught in that unnamed Catskill creek than a great maned lion is like a kitten. These were big outsized footballs of brooks—with the thumping power of a striper and the shape of a black bass or a ham shank. I would tool the boat up to eighty or so feet from the shoreline, where a little creek entered the lake, anchor, and then cast in as far as I could.

When my leech had sunk slowly toward the bottom for fifteen seconds, I'd retrieve it with a series of three short tugs and a pause—a rhythmic pattern lethal in that remarkable fishery—until, heavily, the line would grow taut and begin to throb. It was lots of fun. I could, in those days, cast out and retrieve for hours on end, lulled by the repetitive motions, blasted into wide-eyed astonishment by the size of those huge fish. My son Paul caught a five-pounder in Henry's, and I got a batch not much smaller. They were the largest brook trout I've ever caught.

These were not "brookies," though they had been born in the feeder brook, but huge, plump, lake-dwelling brook trout, like those caught in Labrador or South America. They were brilliantly colored and strong, and their flesh was as pink as that of salmon.

Not so the hatchery brooks—those domesticated quarter-brothers of the brookie—that I caught on Opening Day in local rivers I fished year after year through my youth: those were dull, silvery, liver-fed creatures with little of that haunting dark vermiculation common to natives, pale fish that came dumbly to a nightcrawler or a C. P. Swing or a Mickey Finn, fish that epitomized how misguided so much of our fish-stocking philosophy can be, how deluded. Mort and I, fishing twenty feet apart on a cold Opening Day morning in Westchester County, would call out in delight when we got even a hatchery brown instead of one of those herring; at least the brown had fetching spots. Later, when we fished waters in which the Hornberg, graced with a few slices of lead, was the killing fly for newly stocked brooks, we theorized that they took the fly so readily because they thought it a fine imitation of upstream-swimming bread.

I once saw two of those freshly put-in brook trout acting in the strangest manner. They were making a terrible commotion behind a log that blocked out an area for them between it and the shore of some three feet by eight feet, and at first I thought ants were dropping en masse or some other cache of food had suddenly come their way. But they did not look as if they were feeding. And they were moving too fast, too harshly, for this to be any sort of premarital hanky-panky. They weren't competing for food; this was not a feeding spree; they could be doing nothing connected to spawning. Their behavior was agonistic—but its cause baffled me.

Then they crossed over the log into open water, and I thought they'd surely stop. Trout rarely fuss with each other for more than a moment in such spaces. But they didn't stop. Now, though, it became clear what they were doing. They were chasing each other's tails, turning round and round, forming a complete circle, in an odd game of gymnastics, too unusual for a streambred trout and too mechanical to be beautiful. And then the logic of it stunned me: they were trying to nip each other's tails, as they'd done in the hatchery—or did they have what I later learned was another hatchery gift, whirling disease?

Little native brookies are worlds away from such fish. They may be eager, happy feeders, a bit too easy to catch, but there is a wildness about everything they do. They charge a fly with a bold gleefulness and wiggle madly as they are merely hoisted—not fought—from the clear headwaters they inhabit. I fished one of the headwater creeks to the Madison River watershed some years ago, and it was crammed with small native brookies, right up into the springs, and a six-

incher in such miniwater was cause for shouts of glee. A
feeder to the Firehole has such fish in its upper regions,
too; and I once fished a charming Eastern club whose most
interesting fishing was the small upper water, close to the
springs and seepages and swamps, overhung with birch,
willow, pine, and poplar, in which small natives were all
we caught.

This is *small*-game fishing, and we all need to be reminded
of its beatitudes now and then. There is no hour-long tug
of war with a tarpon after it strikes, nor the savage lunge of
a pike on a yellow streamer nearly the size of a native
brookie. Your cast is generally under thirty feet—a short
toss upstream of some bright little fly like the Coachman.
The fly floats a foot, or less, and there are a couple of
pockings of the water around it as, perhaps, several of these
little brookies vie for the honor of taking it first. Near
that seepage coming from the area of the cattails there's a
pod of fish, and under the pine branches (requiring an under-
hand or sidearm cast), and just where the broken water
flattens in the shallow pool. The fish love these cold headwaters, often where the sun cannot shine full-blast on the
water. Often you can see them in clear water over sand
bottoms when they're active: skittery, nervous, untamable,
quick little shadows.

And when you see the fish take, you make a quick strike
and as often as not they fly free of the water at once, wiggling
in the air toward you, far too small to tug against the line, the
fishing pleasure being narrowed and concentrated on two
moments: the sight of the quick take and the sight of the little
fish dancing on the end of your line, with its wormlike back,
bright black, white and red fins, and strawberry spots, the
color of the Ray Bergman brook-trout flies that caught it so
readily fifty or sixty years ago.

Up in these headwaters, the sport cut loose from exact
imitation and high technology and exotic place, we come

closest to the things that led us here in the first place:
simplicity, untrampled bogs and banks, sweet silences, and
perfectly exquisite beauty. At the heart of such a small, happy
world is the brookie: gorgeous beyond measure, too generous a fish, dooming itself, delighting us always.

THE SNOBBISH
BROWN TROUT

Salmon are larger and leap higher. Bass strike more savagely. Bluegill have the more generous heart. The fierce bluefish fights harder. And in various ways, at various times, the good case can be made for pike, bonefish, tarpon, striped bass, bonito, muskie, snook, barracuda, and a dozen other gamefish. On a given day, one might even be persuaded to vote for the fluke.

But I prefer trout. I like dark, mottled, and brilliantly rose-pocked native brookies from the headwaters of clear mountain streams; I like bright silver rainbows, with their honor stripe of crimson, in the brisk rapids below; and I like wild cutthroats, with their colors of mountain mosses and wild raspberries. But mostly I like the beautiful brown—sleek, dappled with crimson moles, its yellows the color of fresh butter. I love the wild brown trout beyond all other fish. But I love it not for its fighting ability nor even for its beauty.

I love the brown trout because it is shy to the point of being a wall (or shore) flower, but mostly because of its eating habits—habits so fastidious, so snobbish, that I'd probably abhor them in humans.

With infuriating finality, the thoroughgoing snob turns up its nose at what it refuses to eat, saying, "I would if I could, but, really, I simply cannot—not now." Nothing in the behavior of any fish, when coupled with its pleasure in taking food from the surface of the water, makes it more appealing to me.

Myself, I'm more like a bluefish. When I'm hungry I simply hunt out the oiliest fish, the nearest chum line. Even my wife, who is picky, will eat broccoli anytime, asparagus day or night—which, ironically, I won't eat, even when it is served in a gourmet restaurant. The brown trout eats what's served, but he's picky, temperamental; when he's living up to his best potential, he is a dainty picker of tiny morsels from the stream surface. The brown may have a brain the size of a pea but he knows what he wants for lunch and when he wants it, and when he wants it on the surface, the top of his world, I want to be there. Trying to figure out what he wants and when he wants it, though, I—who presumably have a much bigger brain—often fail miserably. Without the failure, I'd love the brown less.

When a brown trout wants a *Paraleptophlebia*—which is not a foot fungus but a mayfly—he wants a *Paraleptophlebia* and no substitute. He's got backbone and values. He'll only eat a *Paraleptophlebia* sandwich when *Paraleptophlebia* sandwiches are being served, and he'll come to the table only when summoned by the official dinner bell, not before, not after. Sometimes, being a very particular fellow, he'll prefer an immature *Paraleptophlebia;* sometimes one that's just hatching; sometimes one that has fulfilled all of its sexual obligations in this world and, wings spread-eagled on the surface, is quite spent and done in.

I have tasted *Paraleptophlebia* and have no sweet tooth for them, not anytime, though a big *Ephemera guttulata* tastes a little like butter. A braver friend tried a giant stonefly (*Pteronarcys californica*) once, then drank a glass of white wine, and said, "The wine's not quite right." Each to his own, I suppose, though I've worried that if I can't taste food like a brown trout, how can I learn to think like one?

What's the appeal of all this fussiness?

Simple. It makes a savage old bluefish like me think a bit more when I pursue the fish, that's what. I haven't the slightest idea of why a salmon takes a fly that looks like the British flag, and no one has given me a convincing reason; the fish is up the river to spawn and probably gets irritated or remembers some lunch it had a couple of years earlier, but doesn't remember very exactly. It can't put a hand out to touch it, so it takes it in its mouth. Big deal. A pike would as well dine anytime on frog or perch or duckling or lizard as shiner. When a fish takes my fly, more and more I want to know why—and, frankly, though some people may think *me* a snob, more and more I want to see him do so.

Part of the fun I have, of course, when I pursue wild brown trout, especially in tap-clear water, is that I've got to figure out which of the hundreds of possible mayflies or caddis or stoneflies a particular fish is lunching on, and then offer him a reasonable facsimile thereof. To find the right fake bug, I must think about the natural insect's color, its size and shape, its attitude on the water, and how the bits and pieces of fur, feather, and space age plastics can best be concocted to represent them. The brown trout's brain may be the size of a pea, but he's no dope. More than any fish that swims, he's determined to save his skin. He'll rarely take a piece of food on the roof of his world if it looks like a piece of grandma's old sweater—and he can spot an *inermis* in the midst of his

Paraleptophlebia adoptivas any day of the week. The honorable brown trout in his middle years—before he has become a toothy old cannibal that will eat any old living thing that it can get its hooked jaws around—wants his plate of fake *Paraleptophlebia* to look and act pretty much like a plate of real *Paraleptophlebia*.

I'm less fussy myself. I'm partial to smorgasbords and stews. Like the pike, I'll take liver instead of beef, chicken in lieu of duck, if that's what's available. I didn't choose my wife for her fussiness—nor my friends for their eating habits. It seems a curious criterion. But I like those of the brown trout. He's a thoroughgoing culinary snob, all right—and that makes all the difference.

PART THREE

How we do it — and with what and whom and when...

17

HOW WE DO IT

In fly fishing, as in fashion or knitting or love or painting or eating a grapefruit or war, there are styles of behavior, ways we do it. It cannot be otherwise. Try as we will, we cannot escape who we are; style, say the French, *is* the man—or woman.

I've fished with some people whose fishing style was to work so hard at it that I grew tired watching them, and others for whom it was such a delicate aesthetic exercise that their fastidiousness made me think that fishing, for them, had descended into an art form. Some dress *up* for their fishing, some down. Some wear skin-tight waders, some wade wet. Some consider fly fishing a chance for "lifestyle" dressing, others wear only the drabbest, oldest clothes they can find. From dress to equipment to the doing itself, the ways we do it are wildly diverse.

And if for a moment we extend our range from fly fishing to any fishing, the divergent styles grow greater still.

Once, on Martha's Vineyard, I saw a fellow heave his bottom rig into a high surf positively wild with white-caps; it was in fact one of the worst October storms in the history of the eastern seaboard and I could manage only ten minutes at a time out in the wind and cold. This fellow was quite mad. He'd rush up to the edge of the surf at a gallop, lean hard into his clumsy cast, and heave the thing no more than fifty feet. Then he'd scamper back to avoid the waves and a few moments later he'd furiously reel in, always with a full three feet of heavy weed at the end. It must have been as much torture to do as it was for me to watch. The guy simply believed: if you're in a warm car, you ain't fishing! His was a sad case of too much matter, no art—or common sense. He was related by temperament to that guy Charlie Brooks once told me about who fished an entire day with a Sofa Pillow pinning both his lips shut.

There is a saner commitment to hard fishing. Art Flick had his fly on the water more than anyone I've ever seen. Art was a vigorous, restless fisherman who liked nothing better than to fish a Grey Fox Variant in pocket water—pitching his fly here, then there, then up against a rock and into a broken-water run. He always caught fish.

Often the kind of water one fishes most regularly, or prefers to fish, determines the kind of fisherman one becomes. Art's Schoharie has a great deal of broken water and those runs and riffles and pockets were the sections he liked best; on other rivers, that's what he looked for. It matched his temperament. After a long slow morning on the Battenkill, fishing flat water, Art found a brisk patch of shallow riffles and, at midday—when no one catches fish on the Battenkill—tattooed the trout.

Vincent Marinaro, with whom I never fished, liked the limestone rivers of Pennsylvania—chiefly the Letort—and fished only to rising trout, which is the English way and the way of many people who fish the spring creeks of the West. Perhaps because it is so often associated with "refined" fishing on the English chalkstreams, where some anglers still do "dress up" for their fishing, in tweeds and ties, fishing only the dry fly and only to rising trout is often considered elitist. It isn't. There's no populist law that says we have to fish all ways any more than there's a law that says we have to fish one way. We fly fish—I hope—because it's fun; and we do it in ways that give us, individually, the most fun. Some people simply consider the rise of a trout to a surface fly an especially exciting experience, and casting to a specific target, requiring a specific fly, more challenging and fun.

Some of the best of these flat-water fishermen I've seen are John Goddard in England and H. G. Wellington in the United States. Both are superb casters, both fish only to rising fish, upstream, and with flies that imitate the insects on which the fish are feeding. Goddard has spectacular eyes, which are necessary to spot the form of a fish "on the fin" as well as actual rises—and I am intrigued that the kind of fishing one does prompts the development of certain skills: if you *have* to see fish first, you *must* develop the faculties with which to see them. Herb, who fishes the large open areas of the West, is a powerful caster; with the western wind, he must be so. Both can wait long periods of time, still as herons. Not for them a line constantly in motion, spooking every fish in the clearest of waters (where most of the fish's predators come from above, just like a fly line). Goddard once told me that the most valuable piece of equipment he owned was a portable chair; it folded into a kind of walking stick, then could be opened when he wanted to sit and watch. Herb finds even that height wrong. He'll sit on a bank for as long as necessary, and then make one spectacular cast, eighty feet or more, low to the water, angling upriver away from the fish, hooking the leader so that the fly comes over the fish before the monofilament.

It stops my breath to watch them both. And at least some of the better fish they catch could not be caught without those finely honed and athletic skills, without a style keyed to their precise fishing needs.

Doug Swisher, the one day I fished with him, had his fly constantly on the water. We floated the Big Hole and he'd cast with left or right hand, switch hands as the line came down river, juggle and jiggle the line on the water to get a better drag-free float, and invariably catch twice the number of fish that anyone else in our party was taking. He was like a boxer, attacking the river, and that aggressive, restless, hunting quality was the sure source of his success.

One fly fisherman casts fast and has his line constantly in motion, another waits. Ed Van Put, the Catskill master, casts so slow a line that I've sometimes wondered what keeps it in the air. But that catlike quality about everything he does on the river makes him a great predator.

A memorable display of grace came from the late Al McClane. He'd just flown to Montana but his luggage had wandered off to left field. He came to the river in his traveling clothes, which included a light tropical shirt, designer shoes and slacks, and a straw hat. He borrowed a rod, walked downriver with me, and scoffed at my insistence that he had to crawl through the mud along this stretch if he wanted to catch fish. He stood straight upright, cast with a happy stylish care into some broken water, presented the fly where he wanted it to go, controlled it on the water, and took a number of fine fish on not very many casts.

Some fly fishers like to fish all the time; some (like me) must make a little go a long way.

Some wear pins, patches, and Stetson hats, designer vests and Austrian brogues; others settle for a baseball cap, a hip carryall, blue jeans, and torn sneakers.

Some talk a lot, some fish mum.

Some spout Latin, some know only size and color, some take the whole subject of bugs (wrongly) to be affectation.

Some fish a mile of water in a morning, some a hundred feet.

Some like a dozen friends spread out around them, some none.

It's a varied game.

As for me, who fishes too little and in a few too many places, I doubt that I'll ever develop one style. In fact, I sometimes think I have *no* style, indifferent as I am to what I wear, how I comport myself. I once sat at the same table as Diana Vreeland, then the doyen of high fashion. It was a corporate party, we were the last in, and there were only the two of us at the table. I tried several times to speak with her but she refused. She never once acknowledged my presence.

Invisible me likes to try to let the water dictate how I'll behave; I try to grow a bit more versatile and diverse; I learn a new trick or two; I generally dress drab, with what's at hand, with what can't be too easily ruined; generally I try not to make too great a fool of myself in front of trout or priestess of high fashion or friend. Unlike that surf caster, I lean toward that which is pleasure, not pain when I fish. I try to learn a bit more entomology because that deepens my understanding of what happens when I fish but—as my friend Gil Eisner said, on his fiftieth birthday—I try not to say *Paraleptophlebia* when strangers are around or when it would sound pretentious.

If I catch a few fish now and then, that helps.

18

FLY FISHING FOR
ANYTHING, ANY WAY

The letter from Dermot Wilson began with this injunction: "When you're tired of catching snakes on the dry fly in Montana, it appears that you should come to England to perform similar miracles with eels."

There are those who think I have always been a closet eeler —and since there's some truth in this, I was all ears. I have practiced the fine art of Hudson River fence fishing and mastered some of its subtler minor tactics; and when my friend Joe Pisarro lived nearby we studied old maps of New York City to determine which manholes might sit innocently over choice glory holes for the eel. We wanted to write a book called *Masters on the Eel,* but Joe defected to Vermont, where they have more common pursuits, like trout and bass.

Then Dermot quoted this passage from *River Trout Fly Fishing,* a recent book by Peter Lapsley: "there are carriers and sidestreams on the River Test on which falls of spinners can be so heavy at certain times of year that the resident eels have been seen there, lying just beneath the surface and rising to the spent flies just as trout do."

One snake satisfied whatever curiosity I might have had in that regard—but eels! My head swarmed with possibilities.

I hastened to call my old friend Clyde, who has a natural interest in such matters. Twenty-five years ago he set out to catch every possible species of fish—game and not so game—on a fly, but I knew that he had taken only one eel, and that surely not on a dry fly. He had once drenched a battered Marabou Muddler in chicken blood for five days, added a couple of shakes of garlic salt and some Worcestershire sauce, and fished this behind four wraps of soft lead. He was fishing for channel cats and since he finally did not count the eel as fairly caught—it was a two-pounder, 31 inches—I don't count it either. There are limits—and Clyde had exceeded them.

"Eel on the dry fly?" he shouted.

"That's the story."

"On spinners?"

I confirmed that this was the report.

"On a chalkstream?"

"The Test itself."

"Astonishing!"

Clyde has done well for other species over the years and I had always listened with awe and envy to his litany of accomplishments:

Carp on his Mulberry Fly of crimson chenille;

Dace on a #32 Bread Crumb Special;

Sturgeon on a Duck-Gut Roller;

Piranha on a triple long-shank Finger Fly;

A small paddlefish on an Eelgrass Wiggler;

Mullet, on the Riviera, during his Twenty-fifth Wedding Anniversary trip, on his #28 Plankton Popper.

And the list goes on, including hacklehead and skate on his Cut Squid Fly from the pier at Sheepshead Bay in December and blowfish on a Clam Glob Red Tag anytime. He had so mastered the fine art of chub fishing with a fly that he could pluck one out of a pod of rainbows almost as quick, intentionally, as I always do not on purpose. No one could bring a flounder to a Blue Bloodworm Fly quicker than Clyde, and I'd put him against anyone for fluke with his Fake Stillborn Spearing.

There are people who still send their guppies to a local guppy-sitter when Clyde comes to dinner—and with good cause.

When one associates with such loonies, one is forced to think about what is and is not appropriate for fly rods. Since there is neither a pope of fly fishing nor a pontificating council of elders—well, there *are* a lot of plain pontificators, I guess—one is quite within one's rights to fish however one chooses. As they say: it's a free country. Still, I've stopped using lead because, first, I once put a really lousy set in a lovely bamboo rod using the stuff and once got a tough knock in the head from a heavily leaded fly, poorly cast, which nearly caused a concussion.

As I think of it, that may be why Clyde is so weird. He used to use a lot of lead. He once told me that he'd socked himself silly one windy day with a Doughball Fly he'd made out of melted lead, mashed dough, honey, and peanut butter, permanently affixed with Krazy Glue but hollow near the head so that he could fill it with Alka-Seltzer, which trailed a little line of bubbles that must have simulated an emerging caddis better than Antron, for it was frequently taken by trout as it was raised to the surface. I guess I'd have reservations about that—about all smelly flies, all flies that are that heavy, all flies that require Alka-Seltzer fillings to work properly.

It may be sheer snobbishness on my part.

Still, I wouldn't want to say that something is *not* fly fishing just because it's not what I find myself doing any more.

I guess it's all worth thinking about now and then, though I wish I didn't nod off during some of the better heated discussions. One guy insists that only dry flies are "moral"; a British friend called a Thom Green leech I was pitching—with great success—into his reservoir, a "hairbrush"; the British generally call all flies that don't imitate an actual insect—even when they're nifty fish-catchers—"lures." I once met a fellow who insisted that only flies #16 and smaller could bring him "grace"; many fly fishermen won't use lead; some use only flies that imitate a natural food—natural foods other than mice, leeches, grasshoppers, baby ducklings, salmon eggs, and the like; some use only floating lines or twenty-foot leaders. Someday it may be that you're not really *fly* fishing unless you use lighter-than-air flies that hover above the surface.

There are a lot of ways I *don't* fish anymore and I suppose I ought to have some profound theory about all this but what it all seems to come down to is this: I fish in a certain way because it satisfies my sense of what's fair play—for fish and fisherman; because it's a little more fulfilling to know why a fish takes a certain fly—especially when that's what he's feeding on; because I don't anymore have to catch every fish in the river but am reasonably content to get a couple of fish in a way I prefer to fish, when they can be caught that way—though this sometimes means fishless days; and chiefly because it's a lot of fun for me to fish in ways I've chosen to fish—more fun, in this hedonistic pastime, than other ways.

Frankly, Clyde seemed a little extreme to me and I worried that what might have been read as innovation was really some form of perversion.

The prospect of taking an eel on a dry fly made him positively delirious. He could not get it out of his head. I thought he'd gone nuts. He made ten phone calls to Dermot, at all hours, asking for absolute verification, hatch dates, the body color of these spinners, their size, whether poly or hackle points or fibers will make the better wing, how they will react to drag, the size tippet required. Dermot's letter to me was a masterful bit of understatement. "I didn't think anyone in the States," he began, "was a bigger nut than you."

I reminded Dermot that some respectable bulwarks of the American fly-fishing establishment fished dry flies for catfish when the white fly was on the Susquehanna, and that many serious fly fishers over here considered the catfish-eel controversy six of one, half a dozen of the other.

In the end, Dermot has been persuaded—for Clyde is the most contagious of fly fishers. Dermot has forsaken France, New Zealand, Montana, Argentina, and all other chalkstreams and spate rivers in England for the prospect of some decent dry-fly fishing for eels on the Test come July; he's counting the days until Clyde arrives. Clyde is so excited I fear for his health.

Joe Pisarro is another story. He seems, safe in the lush hills of New England, to have forgotten the eel entirely and cannot be induced to travel anywhere for them.

I'd go but, frankly, my case is worse: I've discovered that in my advancing years I've become a species snob. I'm afraid this is just one more intriguing fly-fishing opportunity that I can comfortably pass up.

Which doesn't mean I haven't asked Dermot and Clyde to call me on July 9th, the day they anticipate the spinner fall will start and the eels—like them—will go nuts.

19

GADGETS AND GIZMOS

Fishermen love to invent. We are forever tinkering with our flies, lures, boats, and boxes to make them more perfect. Thus the enduring popularity of "Tap's Tips," with its monthly stream of practical ways to manage our play more wisely. Thus the restless stream of new tools and materials, flies and fly boxes, gadgets and gizmos that turn up year after year, ever since someone discovered that you didn't have to fish merely for food, but could do so for fun.

Look at any recent fishing-tackle catalog, and the current extent of invention will startle you with its variety. The array for fly tying alone is amazing: a little metal frame that hooks onto your tying table, complete with a plastic bag for cuttings and scraps; wingburners for carefully cut mayfly wings; half-hitch tools, stackers, midge bobbins, dubbing teasers, new body and wing materials such as Antron and Sparkle Yarn, and enough clever devices to fill half a house.

From there we move on to lights for night fishing that attach to your shoulder or head or hang from your neck, new rod materials such as graphite or boron, rod-wrapping stands. Velcro tabs so line won't slip back onto your reel, miracle glues to attach anything to anything else, braided leaders, new lures made of new plastics, new fly coatings, upside-down hooks, pin-ons of all kinds, new vest designs, lighter wader materials, wader spats, and mittens without fingers. We have wading staffs that fold, stream cleats that hold, wading jackets that shed, rods that won't break, attachments to glasses that magnify, tubes that will float you anywhere, and videocassettes that will teach you anything. And of course, year after year, we get a perfectly bewildering array of new fly patterns that imitate everything from the stillborn hatch to the lowly leech.

It's a brave new world, indeed, that features such objects—and it's all bound to make your fishing life more comfortable and interesting, if you're not driven batty by the choices.

Of course, not all innovations survive. What was new yesterday—hailed as the ultimate breakthrough—may be extinct today. Look at a tackle catalog sixty or eighty years old and you'll find lancewood and hickory rods, silkworm gut, Senate "steel vine" rods, and pocket dry-fly vaporizers with rubber bulbs. There was once a "Walking Stick Rod" that, for some reason, was billed as having "not the least appearance of a Fishing-Rod." "Vaseline jelly" was once hailed as "a great advance on paraffin oil" for floating flies, and we don't see much "imported English Deer Fat" around anymore.

I don't know if the "Live Minnow Cage" caught fish. "The minnow is not harnessed, hooked nor mutilated—remains alive and active," its sponsors claimed, as they did also for their "Magnifying Glass Minnow Tube." We prefer plastic worms or crankbaits today. Nor have we much use for the "Patent Lever Fish Hook," which was "constructed on the principle of a lever, and the harder a fish pulls the stronger it holds him." That device as well as "The Celebrated Yankee Doodle or Sockdolager Fish Hook" have vanished, blown away by the winds of good sense. We have our own gadgets for lighting our way on the waters at night, and I'm pleased as punch (since I like to fish at night) that we no longer have to trifle with the "Ferguson Head Lamp," which burned "signal oil, or lard, or sperm oil mixed with kerosene."

Some of the wonderful old inventions were modified slowly over the years, and we couldn't do without them today. The Orvis perforated fly reel, which enabled the line to dry, is one such old standby; and dozens of flies, lures, boxes, and garments have endured a hundred years with only slight changes. They may well last another century, since they work.

Lots of people tinker with items for their own or their friends' use. The late Sparse Grey Hackle, an inveterate tinkerer, may have been the first to attach a jeweler's eyepiece to his glasses, the better to tie on small flies. He also tried to invent waders with a zipper fly—a splendid idea whose time has not yet come. He even rigged his pipe on a string so it wouldn't fall into the water (though he dropped the idea when he found it *did* drop hot ashes down his waders). A friend of Art Flick's makes a brass dry-fly oil container; I used one for years, until I discovered that my left shoulder drooped from the weight. Dave Whitlock snugs a piece of chartreuse fly line onto his leader—it makes a superb strike indicator. Charlie Brooks glues a needle into a simple felt-tip pen, which makes the pen a terrific tool for poking cement out of the eyes of flies—though it causes a bit of mischief when you use it to sign an expensive nonresident fishing license. My friend Justin Askins concocted a finely tooled device for me that was designed to help my bad eyes thread a #16 fly. But the aperture of the device is so small I can find the eye of the #16 fly more easily.

For myself, though I have nine thumbs, I make a nice little fly box from metal cough-drop boxes by gluing felt to the inside base and attaching some lamb's wool against the inside of the lid. It's simple, practical, and I consider myself quite brilliant to have come up with it. For years I've wanted to have my name on a fly, so I once invented a pigeon-quill dry fly, called the Lyons Quill. Unfortunately, it sank like a rock.

But that doesn't stop me from trying.

20

A FINE MADNESS

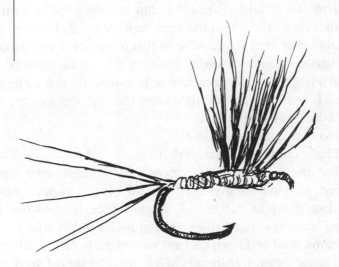

Another season won't begin for too long, and as an alleged balm for cabin fever I have been laying out on the dining-room table my tens of thousands of trout flies. They are in half a hundred plastic boxes and metal cases of varying sizes and conformations; there's even a half-full shoebox. I surely don't need this number of flies. I could not use them if I fished every day for the rest of my life, which I can't. But I never have enough flies. I am mad for them.

With some delicacy, I pick bad ones out of the shoebox with my surgical tweezers and drop them into the wastebasket. Some that I bought twenty years ago—full of great expectations—I now do not think could catch a chub; some hooks are rusted; and a couple of dozen flies were mangled last summer. I set a Catskill Cahill next to a Western Pale

Morning Dun, tied parachute style, and check the proportions of each. I wonder where I fished that Adams with the sloppy tag of nylon still through its eye, or the mushed Hendrickson, or the Paradrake. These little bits of fur and feather are filled with stories—but they are first themselves.

Looking at all the flies, I begin to contemplate both my addiction to them and the odd meld of aesthetics and practicality that are the measure of this minor art form. In order to succeed, each of these thousands of steak tartares must gull a trout into thinking that it is worth the risk of its skin. This is not mere art for art's sake; the aesthetics of the trout fly concern life and death.

Do I need all these flies?

I have convinced myself that I do.

For these artifacts—made of fur, feathers, and various yarns, tied cunningly with thread onto a proper hook— imitate many of the several stages of the four or five hundred mayflies, caddisflies, and stoneflies that live in trout streams. And you need half a dozen of each. So I need several thousand or so, minimum. What would I do if I were three miles up the creek and didn't have a proper *infrequens* emerger? That isn't all. The trout's palate is of course more ecumenical, and I have at one time or another bought or made or borrowed imitations of sowbugs, scuds, inchworms, grasshoppers, leafrollers, crickets, dragonflies, voles, damselflies, riffle beetle larvae, moths, caterpillars, leeches, frogs, worms, sculpins, slugs, blacknose dace, crawfish, salmon eggs, beetles, gnats, newts, jassids, ants (black and cinnamon), other trout (including their own and their neighbors' young), and dozens of other little creatures that, to their ultimate misfortune, satisfy the trout's sweet tooth.

Looking at all my flies on the dining-room table—where I have now dumped them randomly in preparation for the massive reorganization—it is pleasant to think that because the trout's appetite is "selective," or at least keyed to a particular food served at a particular time (a sensible trout would question the propriety of grasshoppers, say, in early April), adds hugely to the fly fisherman's, and tier's challenge—and to my fine madness. Many of these flies I'll never use again because my prejudices mount and my preferences grow pickier each year. Imitations of bait—like salmon eggs and worms—just aren't my cup of tea anymore. Yet the selectivity of the trout requires a lot of options. We have to be prepared for the fact that if it is afternoon of a late-April day in the Catskills, a trout will probably want, almost exclusively, the mayfly *Ephemerella subvaria,* the Hendrickson. Trout would grow suspicious, as we would, if served a dish that did not look correct in color and form, whether Hendrickson or frog; I should be wary myself if my steak came to the table green.

To meet all the options, we need more and more flies.

We need to solve the great questions about what the trout sees from its unique position in the universe—so the tier, or buyer, of trout flies always tries to think like a trout. I try to do so now. I look at ten flies sideways and from beneath. I pop one into a glass of water and, holding it against the light, look slantways and up at it from below. In my youth, I once brought goggles to a bathtub, submerged myself, and viewed flies from the trout's angle. I learned nothing.

Since I am not a trout and haven't the foggiest idea of how they think—if in fact they do anything remotely resembling thinking—I know these issues will never be resolved except in the most abrupt and pragmatic terms: a trout will either accept the imitation as the real McCoy and try to eat it or offer the most ungracious of snubs. The trout is your ultimate arbiter and snob concerning the acceptability of the trout fly.

To help us whip this snob, we exploit all available resources trying to imitate some natural food on which the fish is snacking. The whole world of fur and feather offers itself to the fly tier's palette, in a cornucopia of colors and forms: turkey wing feathers, elk hair, coastal deer hair, specially bred blue-dun hackle, mink, sable, fox, woodchuck, rabbit, peccary, nutria, peacock, mallard, teal, grouse, and a couple of thousand others. Lately, a wide array of new synthetics have enriched the palette even more. This kind of stuff can be bought from special purveyors of fly-tying materials, or found in barnyards, fields, or along roadsides, in drug stores, or on ladies' counters. I have even found some of the finest bits of sable and fox in the gutters near New York City's garment district, my best luck coming on Twenty-seventh and Twenty-eighth Streets, between Sixth and Seventh Avenues, in the late afternoon.

As I look at my flies, one after the other, I see clearly that structure, design, pattern, shape, color, and a certain fishiness are all elements of the art of the trout fly. Like art, the genre has its schools—realism, impressionism, expressionism—as well as types that defy category. Over the years, I've found that realism has its limitations, for reality is not frozen in life, in art, or in trout streams. The best fly is often the one whose feathers—bruited by wind and moving water—look most alive. The best fly for a tumbling Catskill freestone river may be hopeless on a Western spring creek. A fly that looks brilliant to the human eye—a Tiepolo of bright inventiveness—may to a trout look like moldy stew, or, worse, a bright concoction of alien furs and feathers.

Since anyone with the proper number of thumbs can tie a fly that will catch a trout, this is an egalitarian art. One of the finest modern fly tiers I know, Del Mazza, earns his living driving heavy earth-moving equipment; but the fly of his I'm holding to the light of the window suggests otherwise. Fly tying is also an ephemeral art, since most flies (if they aren't lost in trees or ear lobes) will collapse after catching half a dozen trout. But flies do survive and the art has its masters. I've owned at various times flies by the hermetical turn-of-the-century genius Theodore Gordon (whose flies now sell for $1,000 each); Preston Jennings, whose flies advanced the clean, classic, Catskill style; Harry Darbee and Walt Dette, two Catskill aces; René Harrop, the master of spring creek flies; Jay Buchner, whose grasshopper imitations are good enough to eat; and Al Caucci and Bob Nastasi, whose durable and deadly comparaduns have saved a lot of tough days on spring creeks. I've also owned flies by Art Flick, Al Troth, Dick Talleur, Larry Duckwall, Dave Whitlock, Poul Jorgensen, Ted Niemeyer, Del Bedinotti, Vince Marinaro, Frank Wentink, and scores of others.

Hold a Red Quill by Art Flick to the bright light of your dining-room window, as I am doing now, next to one tied by a ruffian like me, and you will quickly see the difference. In the Flick fly, the tail comes straight off the shank of the hook to exactly the right length. The body is luminously tawny red, the duplicate of the natural. The lemon duck wings come briskly off the head, canted to provide just the right silhouette—not, like mine, the shape of some prehistoric insect. The hackle is of the finest blue dun. It glistens and glimmers in the light and seems to change color as I turn it; it seems brilliantly alive, like a great gem, tangy, like fine wine. It is able to ride high on the pocket water that Flick loved best to fish. I'd eat it myself if I could, though, sadly, I can't.

As I fuss and fiddle with my thousands of flies this afternoon—placing them in new boxes, in new arrangements, and culling the bad ones—I see clearly that the art of tying a trout fly begins with the gathering of the proper ingredients. It is the art of minute architectonics, the art of illusion, a meld of craft, vision, and imagination, whose chief goal is the simple one of gulling a trout whose brain is tiny.

That a trout with such a small brain often *won't* risk its skin for some of these brilliant flies is why I keep brooding about them this gray winter afternoon—scrutinizing them and quietly going mad.

21

SPACE AGE STUFF

Art Flick, who reduced the hundreds of fly patterns then available to a manageable handful, loved to tell the story about a fellow he met on the Schoharie, sitting on a rock with dozens of fly boxes laid out, bewildered as to which fly he should choose. He told Art he was searching for exactly the right fly—and really needed a computer. Art would tell the story, shake his head, laugh minimally, and then fix a true frown on his face; he said it was stupid to make a simple sport so complex. He caught plenty of fish on his few flies—in fact, mostly on his Grey Fox Variant, tied with light and dark ginger hackles, one good grizzly, the quill from a cream cock for the body, and a couple of ginger barbs for the tail.

Art still used a Dickerson bamboo fly rod when I first fished with him. He'd been a Dickerson dealer for years. But then he changed to a good glass rod—and he did so for the best of reasons: it was lighter and brisker, and he thought it cast better; it was, somehow, a simpler tool. I don't think Art had a special predilection for natural fly-tying materials; they were what he knew and he knew they would work. He said it was his Scots ancestry: he loved most what was economical, durable, and effective.

I'm just old enough to remember greasing HCH fly lines, stretching gut leader material, fishing with flies that had lovely names like Parmachene Belle and looked like Kandinskys, fussing with cheap bamboo heavy enough to wear out a quarterback's arm in half a day.

I still use an Underwood Standard, Model "S," vintage 1945 typewriter. My four children and just about everyone else I know think me a dinosaur. But it's neither a point of honor nor an act of stupid fidelity to the antique. I just like the feel of the thing, the sound of it, the exact pressure needed to make it work, the faint ache in my shoulders when I've been pecking at it for most of a day. I've learned to *think* into the old machine, to fit the speeds of my brain and its mechanism together. And I haven't found a good reason to give it up yet, though each year the number of shops that can fix it or supply it with ribbons diminishes.

I'm probably terrified of computers, but for my needs my old Underwood serves just peachy. I've bought seven of them, with a couple of Remington Royals thrown in, and ribbons enough to last until I'm ninety-three.

I love bamboo deeply and often swore I'd never give it up. I like the look and feel of it, the craftsmanship of it, the special pleasure I take in holding something special in my hand, something made with skill, even art. I even like the purple poetry it draws from its fans. But when I tried some good glass—the kind Flick used—I liked it enough to prefer it on trips into tough terrain, like the boulders on New York's Ausable, chiefly because I'd have to worry less about it than about bamboo. I tried some early graphite and found it lumpy; worse, I saw a friend break a rod when coming forward with his cast. Bamboo was a pleasure and the best waters almost cried out for it—until, one summer, I fished a spring creek in the West and switched horses forever.

Here I had to cast quickly and hard. I had to use a minimal number of backcasts. I often had to punch a line into the wind. I fished doggedly for a week with a wonderful old bamboo noodle, with intermediate windings. It was fine when I had a fish on but less than fine as a casting tool. This could well be my problem. In fact, it *was* my problem. But that's what we ship for when we fish: the arbitrary, the personal, the idiosyncratic. We want simply to do what will work best for us; we want always to make the fishing experience more pleasurable.

I don't think we go fishing to hold up the honor of the past—though the past is honorably part of the pleasure for many; but to me, suddenly, bamboo was not quite as useful or pleasant as a graphite rod I tried. Bamboo was heavier; it did not cast with as much authority as I wanted; I worried about it; apostasy be damned—I could cast better with graphite, and so I switched. I would have switched back to bamboo without hesitation—but I kept finding more and more reasons why I, at least, preferred this space age material that dinosaurs were supposed to loathe.

Then everywhere I looked there was more of the same. The new fly lines were more amiable to live with: they did not require greasing; they came in a variety of special tapers and coatings for special use; and each year they improved. Leaders, too. Even eyeglasses. Even waders. There were a dozen new variations on the vest, but the old one—like my Underwood Standard—served me so well that I didn't change. I felt no urgency to change, to be thoroughly modern. If anything, I'd always wanted to put a bit of sand in the mechanisms that hurtled us forward at such dizzying speeds before we had a chance to get used to one change or another.

In the realm of flies something quite subtle was taking place—something that offended a lot of old purists. A few tiers, like John Betts, began to work in synthetics alone; others, like Craig Mathews, began to blend them with natural fly-tying materials, using a bit of Z-lon for a tail while keeping elk hair for the wing.

The proof was in the fishing. I caught more fish with the new flies—well, with some of them; some, perhaps because I lacked trust in them, fished as poorly as they looked.

Some folks I know still use bamboo, and some will always use only natural fly-tying materials for their flies. Some even only use one fly—a Hairwing Royal Coachman, perhaps, an Adams, a Woolly Bugger, a bead-head nymph—and are not only as happy as clams but terrific catchers of fish. Fly fishing will always be lots of different stuff to different folk: a genial pastime about which the less said the better; a respite from other lives; a sojourn in pretty country; an adventure, pure and simple; a chance to be on the water with a few old friends; a place to work out what the poet John Engels calls "a coherent discipline"; a chance to play Huck Finn; a place to solve dilemmas; an opportunity for maniacal frustration; and much, much more. And why not? It's one of those areas where we can hang out the flag of our independence, our chance to carry one fly or 4,728. Fly fishing is neither "getting too technical" nor too complex. We can ignore high tech or embrace it—and we can pick and choose.

I guess it's more important to remember that intelligence, humanity, courtesy, skill, and heart exist whether one carries bamboo or cutting-edge graphite, and that the spirit with which we practice fly fishing means as much—even more— than the tools we use. And that reminds me somehow of what Sir Walter Raleigh said as he was prepared for the axman. Asked if he'd like the block to face the east, whence his soul would shortly travel, he replied, in his last words: "What matter how the head sit, if the heart be right."

22

IN A BARREL

This is the saddest fish story.

Sylvester, my friend Clyde's brother-in-law, went to Casablanca for a year to create his "Moroccan Vapors," a series of minimalist sculptures that he could put into a small Orvis satchel and bring back to the States, where his dealer could promptly convert them—by some weird modern alchemy—into a couple of million bucks, minimum, hard cash. Sylvester's previous two shows at the Dice Gallery had made him an extremely wealthy man, and he now—as he once told me—never picked up a chisel for "less than a couple hundred Gs." Such a person needs a house sitter. Stupidly, he chose Clyde. Also, he wanted his sister Brooke, Clyde's long-suffering wife, to have a glimpse of something beyond the poverty into which Clyde's mania for fly fishing and his interminable piscatorial scholarship had thrown them.

The house was in a luxurious suburb of Chicago. It had nine rooms, a solarium, a studio, a Jacuzzi, a study in which Clyde could write Volume 7 of his classic *Fly Fishing and Neurosis: An Inquiry* (University of South Leftfield, 1973–1990, 2,923 pages), and an outside swimming pool. The pool was twice Olympic size.

The day they moved in, Brooke was ecstatic: it sure beat their four-room apartment in Brooklyn, filled with 47 boxes of flies, 13 fly rods, nets, 4 pair of waders, 2 float tubes (inflated), 19 reels, photographs of Clyde on 27 different rivers, and 17 crates of notebooks for his opus. On the door of their apartment there was a plaque that read SOCIETY FOR THE INVESTIGATION OF PISCATORIAL NEUROSIS. Brooke found that awkward when friends came. But she saw something special that afternoon in early May. The something was in Clyde's eyes, and it gave her great alarm. She had seen varieties of the expression before—too many times to count. This time, Clyde was looking at the swimming pool, not yet filled.

On May 11 I received the first of thirteen letters from Brooke, and thus began the saddest fish tale I've ever heard.

"Help!" that first letter began.

I had heard that word from her before, and I suspected the worst.

She said that from the eat-in kitchen overlooking the pool, Clyde had several times positioned himself so that he could watch the great concrete cavity fill with water.

"What are you looking for?" she had asked him.

Clyde did not answer. He had a glazed, faraway look, just like the one he'd had when he received a letter from Dermot Wilson telling him that eels were rising to white flies on a tributary of the Test.

In a day the pool was filled. In a week the men would come back and add the chlorine. "What are you watching that pool for all the time?" she asked Clyde several more times over the next few days. "Clyde," she finally said with a pout, "what do you expect to see in that pool, seven miles from Chicago—rising trout?"

Now Clyde looked away from the window toward his wife. He smiled and nodded. "You lunatic!" she shouted. "All you think about, night and day, is fly fishing, fly fishing, fly fishing. There are other things in the world, you know. There really are."

"Perhaps," he said, turning back, "we can just keep the chlorine out, until, say, June tenth."

She shook her head vigorously. "I know you too well, Clyde Fish. I know exactly what you're thinking." But the temperature was in the mid-fifties, and there would really be no chance to swim before June, and Sylvester would never know, so, after a two-hour discussion, she relented and said, "Well, all right, but they have to be out by the tenth."

On Thursday Clyde came home with three large milk cans that contained ten two- to four-pound brown trout, and that's when she wrote me. "Nick," she said, "it's just that I like things in their place. I'm perfectly happy to see trout in a stream or a lake. That's where they ought to be. It's appropriate for them to be there. But—I can't explain it—I just don't like this situation. It's unnatural. It's unhealthy."

Of course it was—for the trout; and for Clyde, too, whom she meant. But I had to admit to myself that in weak moments I had myself pondered alternative uses to swimming pools. Still, I assured her that she was correct: it was one of the dumbest things my old lunatic friend had ever done, and it offended me to think of any trout—even hatchery cousins, twice removed from the breed I loved most—in such a situation. Might it all be justified by Clyde's researches? His book, though it would never make a smash musical, might someday put my beleaguered friend in the pantheon of angling greats.

Anyway, there was little I could do, a thousand miles—and, as always, several universes—away from Clyde, but

I called him after I got Brooke's third letter. "They're beautiful," he said at once. "But they'll just be too easy. In a
barrel." He described the pool, with its beds of tulips along
the far side, the crystalline water, the sight of those big
trout swimming slowly in the clear depths. "Of course I'll
have them out long before the tenth," he said. "I've got
my strategies."

"I don't doubt that," I told him, and felt that the dread-
ful situation might well be over in at most a week. Clyde and
I might be fish of a feather in many respects, but we have
these differences: he'll fish for anything, anywhere, any way,
and he has always caught what he fished for. He was a demon
fish catcher, a man monomaniacally driven to succeed in
finny matters.

Two days later he called my office and said, smugly, "Got
two this morning on Mickey Finns. Tried drys first, but they
wouldn't rise." He asked me whether I thought if he heated
the pool the fish might come to the surface more easily.

"If you don't boil them," I said.

"Seriously. Seriously."

"Well," I said, entering into the sad problems as best I
could, despite all my qualms, thinking that now the game
was afoot it would be best to end it as soon as possible,
"you might turn the lights on after dark. That will attract
moths and then you might get some dry-fly fishing in the
swimming pool."

"Brilliant!" he said. "I knew you'd get into the spirit of the
thing"—and I immediately wished I hadn't.

A week later he told me he'd tried my scheme, the moths
had come and even fallen on the surface, but the trout
had stayed close to the bottom. Smart trout. "Try a bead-
head nymph," I said, anxious to have this sad business
over.

"I can't stand this madness anymore," Brooke wrote.
"The neighbors are furious."

"Got two more on the bead-heads," Clyde faxed me, having discovered this machine in Sylvester's study. "But they won't take it anymore."

The story then disintegrated badly, and I can barely give the sad, sad details of it. When I refused to take some vacation time, fly out, and help Clyde extract the poor fish, when the days remaining before Chlorine Time dwindled to less than a week, I received a barrage of embarrassing faxes relating to a broken pool pump, cats, worms, live goldfish, a falcon, doughballs, corn, a fermenting pool, grubs, chicken gizzards, bits of strawberry, ground-up mackerel, live sculpin, Asian cockroaches imported by Express Mail from Florida, neighbors' screams, and the use of a new Sonic lure "with a tiny battery-powered oscillating fan embedded in an airtight chamber surrounded by a tight fluid seal."

I can barely write the words without cringing.

The number of remaining trout reduced to four, then three, then two. And then, on June ninth, there were none.

Clyde caught the ninth trout, happily, on a fly he found written up in an obscure footnote in John Randolph's brilliant monograph *Architectonics and Hermeneutics in Wet Flies*. The last trout vanished.

A year later Sylvester returned from Morocco with thirteen small North African sticks, occasionally joined, worth $1.8 million, minimum. In April he found the skeleton of a four-pound brown trout in the flower bed. No one knew what the fish was looking for, tripping through the tulips, if it had tried to walk on land or just escape, or if a cat or falcon had taken it, or Brooke.

Poor Clyde.

Poor trout!

23

THE JOURNALS OF
CLYDE FISH

Three weeks ago my old friend Clyde Fish left a small package in my office with this note: "I don't want this to come between us. If you don't like them and can't publish them, simply pack my notebooks carefully and send them to me without a note. I'll understand."

By the fall of the dice, I spend a lot of my life digging into piles of manuscripts and trying to pluck forth those I can't resist, which is never precisely what someone else can't resist. Some of the manuscripts don't even come in piles; I get some in the oddest places. I once turned a corner at one of those terrific shows that have proliferated in that anxious time between the new year and the new season and bumped into a fellow who might well have been lying in ambush for me, because he promptly handed me a huge shopping bag full of pamphlets, index cards, typed and untyped manuscript pages, and a piece of a bear's flank, and said, "I think you'll like these." Then he fled into the crowd. After three hours of hauling that bag around, I couldn't have liked the contents if they had been strawberry shortcake.

Once while fishing the Yellowstone at Buffalo Ford, I watched curiously as a sturdy fellow rocketed through the shallows with an odd object in his hands—neither rod nor net, nor any other necessity for the middle of a trout river. It was a large manila envelope—and he was headed toward *me*. In minutes he offered me the thing, reverently, like a precious gift. At that time and place my best response would have been to hold it up to the sun for a benediction, say, "Oh, isn't this nice?"—and then drop it directly into the drink, right where I saw a pretty cutthroat rising.

You never know what a new manuscript will be like, and I love to consider every one of them—but, come on, not while I'm fishing, a passion I practice too infrequently.

What Clyde submitted to me were his journals, filled with maxims and anecdotes and perhaps observations that might eventually appear in his opus *Fly Fishing and Neurosis: An Inquiry.* They ran to eight journals, all done by hand in a small tight scrawl that begged for an Egyptologist to decipher. I immediately groaned. They would take months to read—and the season was already well under way. I soon realized that much of the stuff was too narrowly focused on fly fishing to be made into a family movie, and some of it was libelous, venomous. Still, the journals had their moments.

Some of them were parodies of famous clichés or lines of poetry or prose piscatorially slanted:

"A fly in the water is worth ten in the bush."

"Fools step in when the water is near 36 degrees."

"Nothing can bring you peace but a six-pound brown on a #20 *Baetis.*"

"If money is the root of all evil, a new Bogdan reel is its antithetical flower."

That sort of stuff, though some of them were a bit more extended:

"A fight in the street is a terrible thing, says John Keats, but the passions displayed in it are wonderful—and under any circumstances, it's more interesting than a fight with a chub."

There were scurrilous portraits of world-famous authors whom he had caught in disreputable acts (a thoroughgoing scoundrel himself, Clyde never failed to point out the moral flaws in others)—and to one such profile he appended: "But why do these stars enjoy holding up fish for the camera that they didn't catch? Don't they understand the virtue of modesty, even its P.R. value, or the truth that their adoring public does not even expect them to catch fish of that size *all the time?*"

The best, I thought, were actual anecdotes, taken from his own experience, which might have some point to make or perhaps not. Here are a couple of these:

"I once came to a pool in which I'd never been able to take a fish. Either the water was too clear or too thin or my movements just rattled the trout. They were big—and indifferent—browns. I'd fished the pool a dozen times, with the most exacting imitations developed over the long winter of scheming and designing, and with the smallest leader points, and a fish had never once moved toward my fly. I came to the pool one afternoon in the bright sun, saw no flies or rises, cast poorly, used an Adams, and promptly caught three good fish, one after the other, even before the roiled water calmed. Was it the Adams? The fact that it had rained the night before? Had someone given these shy trout a pill? Was it their Mardi Gras? Or was it just dumb luck? Sadly, after all my researches, I am inclined to think the latter.''

And then there was this harrowing passage:

'' 'I wouldn't mind exposing myself to the sun,' I told a friend who asked about the ridiculous full-brimmed hat I've started to wear, 'but the last time I got a couple of basal cell carcinomas on my forehead, I let them advance too far before I went to a doctor. The dermatologist told me that he'd just be a few moments and that it wouldn't hurt; I didn't even need a painkiller—though I asked for one anyway. He shot my forehead full of something and started to cut—but the painkiller didn't work, the carcinomas wouldn't break free, and he pumped in enough anaesthesia to knock out an elephant. Now he began in earnest—digging and cutting. While he was digging and cutting he began to hum a passage from Wagner, and he got so warmed up to the music that he shot from the table and put a tape into the player on the nearby table. I recognized the piece as the "Ride of the Valkyries" from *Der Ring*. The nurse, who had a robust behind, must have bumped into the volume knob on the tape machine, because the sound suddenly tripled in magnitude. The nurse shifted her position to switch it down, but the doctor barked, she turned again to my forehead, and saw that he'd cut some manner of blood vessel, which she tried to cover with a gauze pad before the spurting blood and splattering on my face sent me into shock. I saw it all—though my head was a stone. I saw the doctor reach for something we used to call an electric pencil. A moment later he touched it with a wet finger, and I heard a sizzle. The nurse took the pad away, and my head began to spurt again. Wagner, with heroic distemper, got louder. Then I smelled burning flesh, which complemented the "Ride of the Valkyries" nicely. A moment later I was ushered off the table and down the passageway to cough up eight hundred bucks. The doctor said, "Now that wasn't too bad, was it?" '

" 'That's not a fly-fishing story,' my friend said.

" 'I don't go outside to play golf!' I said.

" 'Where can I buy one of those silly hats?' he asked."

I was happy to see rudiments of the modesty Clyde had begun to admire in Clyde himself, after years of bald boasting.

"I now realize that I can't catch every fish in the river."

"Gingrich suggested that fly fishing is a thousand occasions for hope. I now see that it is also a thousand occasions for disaster."

He even showed social awareness.

"There are still too many clubs," he said, clearly from hard experience, "where the members are adept fly fishers but more adept in the dozens of razor-sharp techniques of the put-down—some as brilliantly honed as the flick of an eye, the most minute inflection of tone, the smallest— unprovable—curl of lip, turn of phrase."

And then, at the end of the fourth volume, there was this sobering observation:

"Two pals quit fly fishing this past year: one because he 'didn't like the idea of that thing struggling at the end of the line,' the other because the rivers he fished were just too crowded. The wriggling of Brother Trout doesn't trouble me, but I'm no longer interested in converting friends who will make my Big Bend Pool into a rush-hour subway. And there's too much refinement lately—of which I've been guilty—until refinement borders on nothingness. This afternoon I'll try for some fat bluegills in that muddy pond out past left field."

24

HONEY HOLES

It was a bare patch of water, about fifty feet around, surrounded by water lilies. Its floor was pickerel grass, and I always caught the biggest perch, bluegills, and shiners there. I was six and this was my first honey hole—a contained area richer than any other in the lake, often filled with astonishing surprises.

I used to fish it with a long bamboo pole I'd bought for a buck, to which I'd tied a dozen feet of stout green cord, a snelled #10 Eagle Claw hook, and a red-and-white bobber. I fished only with worms until the day a pickerel—with the speed of a sprung mousetrap—swiped at a small shiner I was hoisting in, and missed. My heart picked up a few extra beats, and after that I used small live shiners caught near the shore. I impaled them through the back with a larger hook and let them swim freely beneath a larger bobber. I rarely waited long. The lilies were lousy with pickerel, and I could catch four or five on most afternoons—fish 14 to 18 inches long mostly, though I once got a four-pounder that was nearly twice that long. The fish broke the bamboo pole as I derricked it out, but fell in the boat where, near my bare feet, it looked like a prehistoric monster. I dispatched it with an oar, nearly tipping the boat in the process.

Strange, exciting adventures always took place near the honey holes I found. On a small creek that ran through the grounds of a college I attended, the water shot up against a stone embankment, swirled and eddied, and then made an abrupt right-angle turn before scooting downstream. The hole, perhaps ten feet deep, was at the farthest corner of the property, and its dark depth was protected by brambles and tangled locust trees. Few people fished it. I did—every chance I got. I fished it before classes in the early morning and at dusk. It *smelled* of big fish; I *knew* they were there. On a late-April morning I found them.

The first was about 18 inches long; the second was nearly twice that size.

I had rushed out early, armed only with a can of worms, my spinning rod and reel, and a small canvas shoulder bag of tackle. I caught the first fish about 6 A.M. by casting a worm upstream and following the line down with my rod, striking when the line stopped. For the second fish, I had waded into the pool until I was in over my waist; I wore no waders and, in the chill dawn, I began to shake from the cold. I could have fished the far run from the bank, for the spinning rod could easily cast that far, but I'd waded in so that I could fish the worm with more care, upstream and then down into some eddies and slack water near the stone embankment.

The fish took lightly, fought sluggishly, and I thought I might have had a carp or sucker on the line. But as I brought the fish into the slack shallows, backing out of the pool as I did, I saw at once that it was a huge old hook-jawed brown trout. I could not believe its size. The fish was comfortably over 30 inches long. I played it lightly and steadily, easing it up over the mud in a couple of inches of water. I was sure I could back it out and beach it.

But then the great fish flopped and shook, and the hook slipped out. I fell on the great brown, drenching myself, and grasped for the thing beneath my chest, securing it finally. I told no one where I'd caught it—except my girlfriend, on whom such priceless information was utterly lost.

I've found a dozen other honey holes within a couple hours' drive from my home—each different, each holding remarkable fish. You tend not to be a kiss-and-tell fisherman about such places; they're private, and you want to keep it that way. You may take a trusted friend or two there, like a grouse hunter who will share a covert or two. There's some danger here; I've known long friendships to break when such trust was violated. But friendships are often richer for having shared a private, fecund place.

There was a huge bend pool on the East Branch of the Delaware River that I first fished with Art Flick and Mike Migel more than a dozen years ago. They'd fished it for years by themselves, and it was clear that day as we drove from Flick's home in West Kill, around the Pepacton Reservoir, that I was being let into a sacred circle—and that I ought never to tell anyone else the path in. And what a holy place it was! Flick had half a dozen good trout before lunch; then, as we finished the last bites of our sandwiches, almost as if on cue, a hatch of Hendricksons started.

My friends insisted that I take up a position just below the bend, where the current began to flatten, and I was too excited to argue. The fish were high in the water, taking the duns as they rode the current on that chill April afternoon; you could see the trout in fixed feeding lanes, within easy casting distance.

Even *I* couldn't botch this chance.

I took three on my first dozen casts. Then Migel got a couple, and Flick, fishing the lesser spots, took five. We were off the water by four, with all the fishing anyone could want, and we talked of nothing except that honey hole on the long drive back to West Kill.

I dreamed of that glorious afternoon a thousand times and told no one about it, even after Art Flick had died. It was a private place, and we always saved it for special days and special moods. Even on those days when it didn't produce, it remained special, and I always could call up the memory of that first day.

We remained loyal to the pool, fishing it at least once a season, and later, after Migel had died, I went back religiously, once a year, alone. One year, on the last day of the season, I was on the pool and caught a fat chub of perhaps 11 inches. I had to pinch its head to get my fly out of its soft mouth, and when the fish slipped out of my hand I watched as it turned slowly in the low, clear water a few feet from my waders.

I turned my head to pick a new fly, and when I turned back I saw an astonishing sight: slowly, with the measured movement of film in slow motion, a three-foot brown trout came out of the depths of the pool, angled toward the chub, and without hesitation, took it sideways—like a dog taking a bone. After making a leisurely turn, the trout headed back for its safe, dark depths.

My heart smashed against my chest, my fingers shook, and I cast the biggest flies in my box into every corner of the pool for a full half hour—fruitlessly, of course. That old leviathan had gotten himself enough food to last a month.

Such scenes keep me going back to that bend pool every year—though often enough I'm skunked.

On rivers, many of the best spots are these big bend pools, where the water rushes in from a heavy riffle, takes a sharp ninety-degree turn, and cuts a deep excavation in the floor of the river. Twisting currents and eddies intermingle with slack areas, and food sloshes down to big old fish that don't like to move as far as they did when they were young; these fish also like the security such places provide.

I love these honey holes wherever they occur—rivers, lakes, even beaches. I've often seen men on a long stretch of beach fishing an area that looks for all the world exactly like the rest of the shoreline—but it isn't. There's a dropoff or underwater rocks, or some other feature that gathers the baitfish or sand eels; the blues or stripers know this, as do these men. I have half a dozen honey holes on several Northeastern lakes that I fish for bass, where coves, patches of pickerel weed, or a couple of fallen trees create structures the largemouths can't resist. And I have a dozen holes on Western rivers that I always fish when I'm in the area. I dream about such places, and I find myself approaching them with great expectations.

Sometimes too many people learn of these special places—there are never that many to begin with—and they're skinned for years to come. Sometimes you just hit them at the wrong time. But enough honey holes are always good for a decent fish or two. And even when they've declined, they rise in my imagination, and I find myself going back, seeking old moments of glory or the memories of old friends.

25

SIZING UP NEW RIVERS

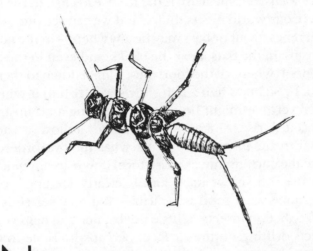

No two rivers are alike, but they all overlap. What you learn from one, with variations, you learn about them all; and the experience of fishing many different kinds of rivers, if rightly used, can provide the wisdom you need to fish almost any new river.

For years I used to gallop madly around a new river, flailing away with fly or bait or lure, trying to see it all and fish it all, taking a shotgun approach. With spinning lures, which enable you to cover so much water, that sometimes worked; it rarely worked with bait or flies. But lately I've been looking more carefully before I even begin to fish, and I am astounded by how much I already know about a river I've never seen before, and how well I can fish it if I'll only think before I cast.

All knowledge of rivers for a fisherman's purpose begins with the fish, and with the question, What do the fish in this river need? All fish, everywhere, need food and protection, so beginning with this premise, you should look for those features in a river that will provide one or both.

If there is the sudden availability of food, the questions are more focused, especially if the food leads fish to the surface, where our world meets theirs, and we can see our quarry. At such times, trout or bass may be anywhere—in the eddies, in the runs, in the flats, near the banks, and even in the thin tail of a pool (where all the food must funnel down to them). You work by sight. When a fish shows, you fish to it where it is, wherever that might be—perhaps casting a bit upstream of the actual rise, since fish sometimes follow a sandwich downstream to make sure it's what they've ordered, and since the current moves a rise form downstream quickly.

If the fish shows itself and is clearly feeding, you must determine what food is available. You may see rises on the surface but no insects. A little pocket net will help you catch insects drifting on the surface, perhaps invisible to the eye against the green or slate lid of the fish's world. Perhaps you can see insects in the air or in the bankside foliage. Sometimes the way a fish has taken its food will disclose the kind of food it is taking. In late summer, for instance, a great splashy rise could well mean a grasshopper—always as irresistible to a fish as a bonbon to a boy—has landed on the water and was wolfed down by a ravenous fish. Then, it would be helpful to see what size hoppers are in the fields and what color they are (especially their underbelly, which is primarily what the fish see). And it would be good to know that grasshoppers are less active in the mornings before the sun has warmed them into activity, and thus are more likely to be taken by fish in midafternoon, when it's bright and there's a breeze to blow them onto the water. This gets the fish thinking about them, anticipating them, and looking up for them and coaxes the fish to move near the shoreline, where a larger number of these terrestrial insects might logically be found. Trout that at other times might be in the slicks taking dying spinners—insects that conveniently float to them with no means of locomotion for escape—might well be tucked under a bank during optimum hopper times, protected from their enemies above (like mergansers and herons) by the overhanging bank, watching, waiting, and listening for the characteristic *splat* of a hopper. Even the sound of the insect hitting the surface is important—which helps the indelicate caster, like me, immensely.

A caddisfly rise is generally splashy as well, since the fly is active, sometimes bouncing up or dipping to the surface. A big stonefly, such as the giant *Pteronarcys californica* in the West, will draw mammoth rises like those to a hopper. Tricos, in size 20, and *Baetis,* the same size or smaller, might draw sipping rises. I've frequently identified a Green Drake hatch by the spurting rise of a good fish unwilling to let such a choice morsel escape, or by the dipping flight of sparrows. It's always worth watching for the movement of birds; on a river, the swoop of swallows for mayflies in flight on the surface, the aerial acrobatics as they look for their share of a sudden bonanza, even their presence along the streamside grasses as they wait for an expected hatch, herald good sport.

Sometimes fish feed beneath the surface, and only careful observation can pick up the wink of a white mouth opening under water, or the movement or even the position of fish. Trout may be taking nymphs right at the bottom of the stream, heads down, rooting among the rocks; or they might be in the mid-depths, as I've often seen them, poised, moving to the left or right or up or down, their mouths opening; or they might be taking an insect just below the surface, just before it hatches or as the nymph drifts. Fish feeding in such a manner might not take anything other than what they're feeding on, where they're feeding. Fish take up a specific feeding position and key to a specific food just as we might sink into a comfortable leather chair and munch potato chips or peanuts. Some British friends say such fish looking for food or taking it below the surface are "on the fin"—and it's worthwhile to learn to spot such fish and to distinguish between them and fish that are just keeping out of harm's way.

Food, then—both seen and hinted at—should be the first thing one looks for on a new stretch of water. Sometimes you can't miss seeing it, but often a trained eye is needed. I've met a dozen superb stream fishermen whose greater success in every case was the product of careful observation before they made a first cast.

If there is no food showing, you must go to the places where food might be concentrated in greater quantity or where fish might have a better chance of finding it while enjoying good protection from their predators.

In all rivers there are great concentrations of food in eddies (places where the water swirls back upon itself, trapping insects and baitfish and also providing some respite for the fish against a more militant current). Runs—areas where the water is quick over a small-rock or rubble bottom—are good, too; here, the rubble is a great source of food—everything from crayfish and hellgrammites to dozens of aquatic insects—and the broken water at the surface provides a good measure of protection, shielding fish from the sight of predatory birds. I suppose if no fish were showing and I had to fish two sections of a river only, I'd choose the eddies and runs every time. Art Flick, with whom I often fished, loved nothing better then to "pound up" fish in a likely run, and I saw him do so several times in the bright middle of a day when everyone else had given it up for lost.

But variations of these two areas are often highly productive, too. In a river with a rather heavy current, like New

York's Esopus or Montana's Madison, fish will often hold in midwater behind a large rock or boulder. The water sweeps around either side of such an obstruction, creating a slack area directly behind it. Trout can hold in the slack water much better than they can in the heavy current, and from their vantage point they can see food swept down to them on either side. Such obstructions also cause eddies, as some of the water hits against the straighter current and doubles back upon itself; this provides "tangled," slower water in which the fish can find a greater density of food for which they need not work so hard.

Often, fish hold well in the slacker water and take food from the continuous belt of current that comes down on one side or the other. The point where the current hits the slack—perhaps eddying—water is called the "seam," and this water is invariably excellent. The concept of a seam is always important in sizing up a new river. Seams can appear where feeder creeks or channels enter the main body of water, or where a current abuts a slack section along the shorelines. There is often a quiet area directly along the bank because of the frequent indentations and irregularities. The line of the current as it circumscribes the shore—perhaps a foot or two out—is a continuous food belt for the fish. I have seen smallmouth bass and trout literally stacked up—one every few yards—in such feeding lanes. In the absence of a hatch or some sudden availability of food, the fish become opportunists and will automatically go where they have the protection they need as well as a constant (and concentrated) conveyor belt of food.

All the above is modified, always, by other significant elements—season, time of day, region, and weather. In the absence of a hatch and in the presence of a bright midday sun, you could scarcely find a self-respecting trout in a shallow slick at the tail of a pool. The fish would be too exposed, and would know it had only a minuscule chance to find a meal in open water. But come to the same spot on an overcast day, perhaps when there is some food on the water, and the fish might well move into such an area, which provides several great benefits: it is generally shallower and narrower, meaning that there is less water in which a live meal can escape, and there is a great concentration of food because the water pinches in, becoming a kind of funnel into which all the food is channeled. This is an excellent spot to fish when there is a heavy hatch of flies, for the fish—which always favor economy and like to expend as little effort as possible to get their meal—will often drop back down out of a large pool to have more food available to them in less space. I used to frequent a very heavily fished river some fifty miles from New York City. Several times I fished it straight through the night, and I was astounded on one occasion to see four or five truly large fish chasing minnows in the thin slick below my favorite pool—at three o'clock one May morning. I'd never once seen a fish there during the day and the water was only a foot deep and so clear I could not have missed them.

Very early morning, when the first faint traces of light are warming the sky, can be an excellent fishing time in the East—especially in summer, when the water may be optimally cool before the sun rises; but I rarely fish in the West before 9:30 or even 10:00 A.M., when the water will have warmed from the cold nights and the fish have become active. There is little night fishing in the West, though dusk (on a hot night) can be remarkable. Each river has its patterns—most of which make good sense once you've learned them. Learning something about optimum temperatures helps—and therefore, so does carrying a thermometer.

In small, cold brook trout rivers, the fish may feed all day along the sandy bottom whenever food is available to them; in warm smallmouth rivers, fish can generally be caught all day long in the runs and in the pocket water behind the boulders, though when the weather is warm I've had my best luck in the evening. In the spring, fish may be deep most of the time—and lethargic. This may necessitate drifting bait slowly, or fishing a spinning lure at less than regular speed, or tumbling a leaded nymph along the bottom. On a bright day in July, with no fish showing, you might want to take a long lunch—unless you're on a Western meadow river, the grasshoppers have infested the fields, and there's a strong breeze.

That's what's so exciting about sizing up a new river: it's so richly layered with variables and there's always so much to learn. But it's also possible to turn a mysterious—even near-impossible—new river into a much more positive fishing experience if you learn some of the basic rules of rivers and if you apply more of the knowledge you already have.

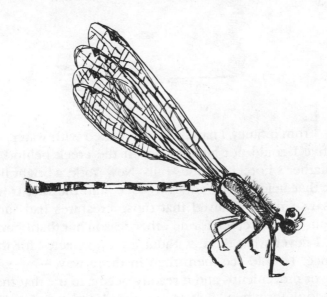

26

WATER WATCHING

From infancy, I have been infatuated with water.

At five I could not be kept out of the creek behind my grandfather's hotel in Haines Falls, New York, a bright little brook that held newts, crayfish, dace, and the first trout I ever saw. Since I believed that those creatures had surely been put into the creek for no other reason but that I pursue them, I never went there without my eyes peeled for their presence. I could see them then in three ways—by color, shape, or movement—and it readily occurs to me that that's what I look for when I go to water to fish today, unless I am looking up, for birds or insects.

Barefoot, I learned to spot the backward-darting crayfish, the shape and color of the newt, the movement of the fish. And later, when I fished the pond from which the creek originated, I leaned far out of the old wooden rowboat, put my face flush up against the water, and peered deep into that other world with its mysterious wavering forms.

There is no science without careful observation and without it there is also only a primitive form of fishing. The best fishermen I have seen were constantly watching the water and I saw barely a tenth of what they saw and reported.

Water, of course, is an element of endless fascination to the child—whether the great force and life of the ocean beach, the movement of a river, the liquid strangeness of a pond, even a splashy bath. Water has its own laws of gravity and biology and hydrology and when a barefoot freckle-faced kid looks at the beautiful suspended forms of perch and pumpkinseed and pickerel, he touches what animates all study and all outdoor sport: *he wants to understand.*

Why is the striped perch at precisely that depth? Why is the pickerel always so motionless? Why do the pumpkinseeds stay in groups, near the lily pads? Why don't the lily pads grow in that big hole in their midst, which is filled with a softer, grasslike plant that rises but a few feet off the bottom? Why? And why? And why again?

Ezra Pound, in *ABC of Reading,* tells the story of a postgraduate student, "equipped with honours and diplomas," who went to the great scientist Louis Agassiz for some "finishing touches." Agassiz showed him a small fish and asked him to describe it. The student observed that it was a sunfish. When Agassiz pressed him, the young man offered a textbook description of the creature, including its proper Latin name. Agassiz again told him to describe the fish and got a four-page essay, and then told the student really *to look* at the fish. Pound ends his anecdote: "At the end of three weeks the fish was in an advanced state of decomposition, but the student knew something about it."

Or, even wiser and more succinct, Agassiz's report: "I spent the summer traveling. I got halfway across my backyard."

Too many of us, I fear, rush to the water, make our play, and rush away.

Going faster, we see less.

Rushing, we miss everything except whether a fish chooses to lunch on something we've pitched in its general direction.

That's not enough—either for the basic skills needed to catch a few fish or for the function of teaching us something about our quarry and its world, something that will lead us to respect it more, protect it more wisely, and pursue our piscatorial pleasures with more understanding.

Some people, of course, start out with better eyes, keener instincts, more opportunities than most to observe a fishery. When I met the great river keeper Frank Sawyer I told him that what I admired most about his books was how much he'd seen and how helpful his observations were to me. He was a gentle, modest, white-haired man and told me quietly, even as Art Flick often told me, that his experience was limited to very little water. But, oh, how well they'd learned and how valuable their lessons have been to thousands of others. Spend the summer like Agassiz, with a hundred yards of your watery world, and tell me that he's wrong. Some narrow, deep, specific knowledge may be worlds better than that which the dilettante carries. Learn something (even almost *every*thing) about the bugs, the pH, the speed of the water, the baitfish, the nearby terrestrials, the cover, the structures, the eddies, the slight bottom indentations, the monthly and diurnal cycles of your quarry, and so much more, and then tell me it is not worthwhile. Flick told me that the three years he did *not* fish but studied the bugs of his Schoharie were perhaps the most valuable of his entire fishing life.

Guides—either saltwater or on rivers and lakes—are on the water every day during the season—and even before and after. They *must* find fish; their livelihood depends upon it. I could no more pick a "happy"—and quite catchable— tarpon from a pod than I could a prize-winning music video from the jumble I used to see my children watching; but Jeffrey Cardenas can—and he can "read" a huge amount more to which I'm blind, too. John Goddard, with whom I fished on the River Kennet four or five times, stunned me with what he could see—from the slight bulge of water to the slightest variation in color that meant a fish to a bubble or two to what Skues called the "wink" of a fish nymphing in midwater. And Goddard stressed, too, how much the English code of *seeing* a fish before you fished for it demanded more careful sight and rewarded the angler by increasing, over the years, what he saw.

This does not happen randomly. It begins, as Lou Tabory is fond of noting for inshore saltwater fly fishing, with "time on the water"; only then can you know anything of importance about your quarry and his world. Being near the water more, watching it with more precise care, knowing what kinds of things to look for—from the flashes and changes in color beneath the water to the rips and breaks and currents on the surface to the birds above it—can be crucial. And you often see the oddest things. I swear I once saw water snakes rising to Pale Morning Duns—though Herb said I merely needed a strong drink.

Perhaps the most remarkable eyes I've seen at work are Al Troth's. I floated the Beaverhead with him some years ago and was astounded at the potency of his water watching. He saw everything, ten minutes before I could pick up the sight, even when he pointed precisely. At one heavy run there were "three rainbows and a brown, four to six pounds, nymphing." Frankly, I didn't believe him. I looked and saw only a rush of pale green water. So he took me halfway up a cliff, pointed more precisely, and there they were—and ten minutes later I raised the brown, which was about four and a half pounds.

Later that day, when the sun came in at a sharp angle, he took me to a side branch of the river and pointed to a spot where "four or five good fish" were rising steadily. I had double-strength Polaroids on but could only see the bright scar of the sun on the water. I'd have passed right over the spot. He told me to cast a certain length in a certain specific direction and I told him I didn't want to cast to what I couldn't see. Anyway, I didn't believe him. So he directed me on a long trek downstream about a quarter of a mile, then upstream through swampy terrain and tangled deadfalls, to the opposite side of the river. It was nearly eight o'clock when I got there and the mosquitoes had made my face a massive red lump.

And he was wrong.

There were not four or five good fish rising but eight or ten, and they were gorging themselves with large slurping rises. Either the sun had dropped or I was on the other side of the scar because I could see everything clearly now. Muttering to myself, "I shall always believe Al Troth's eyes. I shall always believe . . ." I tied on one of his elk-hair caddises and began to tattoo the fish. And then I forgot the disciplined water watching that had gotten me to this spot because, as Mae West once said: "Too much of a good thing can be wonderful."

27

THE MYSTERY HATCH

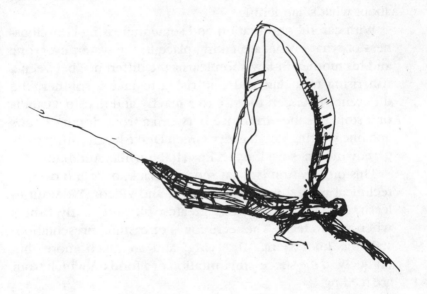

No theme in angling literature repeats itself more often than that of "The Mystery Hatch"—the baffler, the one we can't quite dope out *at first*. For the expert it is the ideal time—in action or in prose—to prove his true worth. "Fish were rising everywhere and not one of the thirty-seven fly fishers on the riffle could catch a thing . . . *until* I figured out that they were sipping only the virgin third cousins of the *Paraleptophlebia* duns—but only those with chartreuse legs. After that it was like shooting fish in a barrel—*for me.*"

I've dreamed of possessing such expertise and—not to be falsely modest—some of my happiest days on the water lately have been those in which I've demonstrated a bit of progress, figured out a bit more, solved a few more of the mysteries of a trout's rise. It's the same for all of us, I think. We take our greatest pleasures onstream not merely when we nail some fish but when we gain glimmers of understanding about what's happening.

With careful observation and some increasing consciousness of what events are taking place in the water, everyone and his mother-in-law soon learns the difference between a fish rising to a dun and one rising to take a spinner; the difference between the rise to a mayfly and that to a caddis or a stonefly; the difference between a trout sipping *Baetis* and one wolfing down every Green Drake it can stuff into its greedy mouth, smacking its lips all the while. Audibly.

This progression is what sends us back, over and over, to technical magazine articles, books, and videos. We want to learn. We take perhaps our greatest pleasure as fly fishers when we do learn: the techniques of casting, presentation, stalking, knot tying, fly tying, and so much more, but uniquely in the successful imitation of a food on which trout are feeding.

People who scoff at entomology, who find it pretentious or blown out of proportion or merely boring, are, of course, entitled to their view. We come to this pursuit, this fly fishing, for our own pleasure, after all. But I can't help but think that they're missing a big part of the show. Unlike, say, upland bird hunting, the pleasure of fly fishing is not so concentrated in stalking and shooting; a lot, especially with trout, is centered on that remarkable moment when the perfect stalk, the perfect cast are not enough—when the fish is intent on its feeding, keyed to a specific food, not interested in peanuts or popcorn or asparagus or Royal Coachmen but mono-maniacally on a #20 olive *Baetis,* with the body exposed, the winging thorax style, a couple of stiff hackle fibers—flanged out—for a tail.

This sounds pretty picky. And it sounds in direct opposi-tion to two great schools of thought: that the fly matters hardly at all but that presentation does, and that most of the technical aspects of fly fishing are a bore and the "why," the "poetry," the "lore," the mist are everything. I have not only belonged to both schools but I have championed their cause. I have seen the brilliant fisherman Ed Van Put use only varying sizes of the Adams, Art Flick his beloved Grey Fox Variant, others a Hairwing Coachman or a Wright's Royal or a Humpy or a Woolly Bugger and take as many or more fish than anyone within shouting distance. Surely, being able to "read" the water well—to locate trout at different times of the day or season, or at different water levels—is a fine skill in itself. And surely my great delights among older angling books don't depend upon a high level of technical expertise: *Golden Days,* by Romilly Fedden, *Where the Bright Waters Meet,* by Harry Plunket-Greene, almost any-thing by Roderick Haig-Brown, Negley Farson's *Going Fish-ing,* stories by Roland Pertwee and Sparse Grey Hackle and John Taintor Foote—these are as much books about the people who fish and their relationship to fishing as they are about the techniques of fishing. In Haig-Brown, perhaps uniquely, you'll also find a high level of quiet instruction, inconspicuously offered.

I guess none of the above has a monopoly on it all. Why should it? In fact, why should we ignore any aspect of any of those schools. But follow for a moment our progression in relation to the world of hatches, a progression generally followed by most of us.

At first we know none of the hatches of trout-stream insects, and scarcely believe that they're important: there are merely some brown or tan bugs hovering around and sometimes an unconnected spreading circle on the water. Then a wise friend named Joe standing nearby dips his fingers into his fly box and presents us with a Red Quill, tied thorax style. "This ought to work," he says with quiet authority, and it does. Miraculously, the fish that lately ignored us take the fly readily, and we think the friend is merely the greatest genius since Leonardo. But that's only one of the hatches—and, to be honest, isn't the success really Joe's?

So on the appropriate days we learn about the Cahill and the Sulphur. Then on a trip West we learn about the lovely Pale Morning Dun. We learn to spot the swarm of caddis we miraculously never spotted before. One day we catch a full-blown March Brown hatch and fall in love with it forever. On a June afternoon we see trout go bats for the big Green Drake—or lose all caution for the giant stonefly, which no one could miss seeing but which we didn't even know to look for. Then one day our Green Drake imitation draws only short rises, and we look more closely and discover that there are two smaller drakes on the water now, one brownish. We figure we have to learn a little of the Latin we've always avoided, to tell a *flavilinea* from a *guttulata,* and we do—though my mother-in-law used to think I'd gone nuts when I first started to spout all that arcane stuff.

And so over the years, gradually, we come to the river better prepared in advance, more knowledgeable about which flies might come, how trout react to the various life stages of the insects on which they feed, which styles of which patterns they prefer on which particular waters. Over a reasonably long period of time we see more phenomena and solve more mysteries. We can't learn it all from books or videos or magazines, though they help—but more than anything else we learn from what Lou Tabory calls "time on the water."

But after thirty-five years of fussing around near trout streams, I still can't go near one without something new, even mysterious, taking place.

On a windy day, blown-over duns are often taken more readily than uprights. I've seen trout move gradually upstream during certain hatches, like the Hendrickson, and during others, like the Trico, slip downstream, just tipping up and sipping and allowing the current to let them drift down. I've now seen hatches with three or four different flies on the water, just like some of the books and articles said (and I didn't believe them), when the fish are keyed to just one of the flies, have a sweet tooth only for the PMD spinners. Sometimes the fly they take is the one easiest for them to get at; sometimes it's the biggest; but sometimes it's merely the one that strikes their fancy. You have to look hard to know. I've seen fish racing around a big pool for no reason I could determine, or lined up in formation on a windy day, waiting for a west wind to blow them grasshoppers. I've heard of trout turning upside down to take snails from the bottom of elodea, mad for mulberries, leaping for dangling leafrollers.

Just a week ago my friend Dick Lower said he'd like me to stop by his ranch on the Big Hole to help him decipher *his* mystery hatch. On mornings in July and early August, on only a particular section of the river where a couple of side channels hit the main current, forming seams across a relatively slow pool, and only between about 6:30 A.M. and 8:00 A.M., this happens: The largest trout in the pool, larger than he ever sees rising at other times, come up with a force that propels them high out of the water. They come all the way out, then flop back. Surely it's caddis, I write him—but immediately thereafter think that 7:00 A.M. is too early for any self-respecting Montana caddis to be on the water, and anyway, didn't he say that he could see no flies in the air? Tricos perhaps. Yes, that must be it. But trout mostly sip

Tricos, don't they? And he had tried several good Trico imitations without success. And he had tried several different caddis. And he had tried a nymph—several nymphs of different sizes—in case the fish were chasing nymphs up to the surface and then clearing the water because of their momentum. The spinners of something that took flight the night before perhaps? On a spring creek I know, there are lots of Green Drakes but no one ever sees the spinners.

Anyway, will I come out and take a look at the situation with him?

Nothing could keep me from it. If I catch nothing, I'm still ahead: I'll have seen it, and it will be in my head, and it will be a thing to decode, by looking, by reading, by writing to more knowledgeable friends.

Nothing used to cheer my mother-in-law like a piece of cake; nothing cheers me like a mystery hatch.

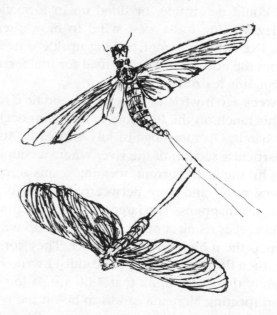

28

LOCAL GENIUS

Lefty Kreh once told me that no one is a deadlier fisherman than a local expert. In its most primitive form, this can be the most dangerous of all trout predators: a local kid with a can of worms or a C. P. Swing. I've seen them at work, and sadly, I had a couple of years in my early teens when I became such a predator myself. No heron, otter, merganser, or kingfisher ever took more fish. Such local people—perhaps otherwise thoughtful and smiling and kind to cats, but mindless of their killer instinct—can skin a river in a season. I once met a terribly nice fellow who fished exclusively on a rather small meadow creek—only several miles long from the pond it drained to the reservoir it washed into. He told me one June that he'd already taken and killed 187 trout that year on a deadly worm rig that exploited in a cunning way a dipsey sinker and two Eagle Claw hooks. He seemed oblivious to the fact that this delicate fishery might have been put in terminal jeopardy by him, who knew and loved it so well.

Fly fishermen often obtain even more astonishing knowledge of the rivers they fish most. Since their success depends upon knowing so many more specific kinds of phenomena about the river than where the fish are and when they might be taken on live bait, they grow closer to its inner life . . . and their skill can be dazzling.

Such a local fly fisherman's universe might consist of no more than several miles of water. He will know it in all seasons, in high water and when it bares its bones in August. He has walked its bank a thousand times—sometimes looking hard, sometimes merely getting from one spot to another and happening upon his knowledge; he has learned and then tested his mettle against the four or five principal hatches; he has fussed with his fly tying until he's got each fly just right for his limited purposes.

I met a fellow on a little New Jersey river who saved a long hot day of frustrating dry-fly fishing by giving me two #18 greenish caddis he'd developed, quite different in shape and color from anything I carried in my three dozen boxes. He lived less than five miles from the river and fished it nearly every day of the season, and he had done so for a dozen years; he had only slender interest in any other water and found this river, which had nearly skunked me, quite enough, thank you. The fly he gave me had a pale-green dubbed body, flared mink hair for its winging, and an odd little collar of peacock herl. The fish came on tracks for it—five or six of them. He said I should come back the next week when the leafrollers would be on, and that I should fish downriver a half mile where there were some old mulberry trees against the shore, and that I should not think of using anything other than these two scraggly chartreuse killers that he had devised and handed me. And he was right.

A brilliant and intense local fisherman like the late Vince Marinaro knew which insects would hatch and when, which patterns were best, the most cunning architectonics for the fly design of patterns for this river, the effect of varying light conditions, what positions were best to cast from, and so much more. He especially liked to locate large and well-protected browns that he would then stalk for weeks on end—watching, waiting, calculating, and then pouncing.

Art Flick—a less fussy but immensely skillful fisherman—was astounding on his Schoharie. "He's simply got them all trained," said my friend Frank Mele whimsically one evening as we watched Art fish briskly up a run of broken water and catch four or five fish, one after the other. His Grey Fox Variant, tied with long or short hackle depending upon his needs, was a perfectly lethal fly, and when I imitated as best I could what Art was doing and used one of his Variants, even I got a few good fish.

Such local knowledge is more various, less formal, less capable of being articulated than we often suppose. It is built of instinct, long exposure, trial and error, and sometimes even gossip. A companion says that he has raised a good brown on a beetle below the Cranberry Rock; a neighbor mentions that the water near his cornfield looks "about right" this morning; a bumbler says the water was boiling with rises in the pool above the bridge, but he couldn't take a thing; ten years ago, in early June, as the water level dropped after a heavy storm had done its worst, the fish near the Elbow Bend went berserk; during the shadfly hatch the fish in the Garage Pool migrated (four years ago) to the *opposite* side of the river; the stomach contents of even the half-dozen trout killed in a dozen years speak volumes—oh, there are a thousand kinds of little bits of special knowledge that help.

In my teens, most knowledge began with finding out where the hatchery truck had dumped its wares. Clyde helped stock the Saw Kill one year, and his "local expertise" induced us to go to those exact spots on Opening Day. Our "streamcraft" progressed from hatchery truck tracks to some intimate knowledge of where any trout might be and a certain fish sense that I still can't define but which held us in pretty good stead. Such knowledge pales beside what the fly fisherman must know, of course—most of whom would surely head in the opposite direction from the hatchery truck.

The kind of knowledge we crave as fly fishermen lies elsewhere and is subject to an infinite number of variables. Yes, we want to understand the water, and where its denizens will be at different times of the year or day. Yes, we want to understand the food forms on which trout feed in this stretch of the river—and when; and we want to learn how best to fish for the most interesting (perhaps also the largest) fish in an area. Local fly fishermen simply have a great volume of information and knowledge about such matters.

I gained such local knowledge of a remarkable river some years ago and—immodestly—learned a particular pool on the river so well that I began to think of myself as its resident genius. This is the only time in my life that I've thought so well of myself, and I felt quite smug indeed.

It was a long bend pool with a brisk head and a broadening body as it turned. The water, quite crystalline when I fished it, flowed over white sand—so I could see every fish that was in a feeding mode with startling clarity. The first time I saw the pool, I had worked my way—rather sloshily—upriver to within a hundred yards of its tail, and I saw immediately the telltale circles of a dozen rising trout, in formation, right up the center, high on the hog. Big trout, too. I shivered all over, licked my lips with pleasure, and soon threw a nice long hard cast right smack down the middle of the pool and put every fish in it down.

Not so the next time I fished it—when I put them all down on my *third* cast.

After I'd fished it a couple of dozen times, I did better. There wasn't a *trick* to the pool but a world with which I had to become intimate. When I learned a bit more about approaching it properly, I discovered that I knew nothing about its entomology; and when I got to know a few of its bugs, I had also to learn about the size line I could put over the fish (no heavier than a 4-weight on calm days, no more than a 5-weight ever) and the tippet point required—and, oh, a couple of thousand other matters as well.

In time I got a chance to share the pool with an excellent fly fisherman. I knew the guy well and told him that this stretch might look easy but was not. I told him he *must* approach it on all fours, get right to the bank, stay as low as possible, and then make the lowest and shortest possible cast to the lowest fish in the run using a #17 parachute version of the *plat du jour*. He chuckled, thought I was putting him on, and let fly an eighty-foot cast across the grass, using a conventionally hackled fly. He tried half a dozen other cute tricks. Nothing. Every fish went down on cue. "You weren't kidding," he said and dropped to all fours, retrieving his line and then holding out his hand for the proper fly.

We love to have such privileged local knowledge, much of which is hard-won; we love to know one thing truly well. How I wish I knew five dozen such pools or stretches of river as well as my passion had led me to know that pool.

But the local geniuses I know who live year-round near the rivers they love often go beyond fish-catching wisdom in what they know. Often they know a river's *needs* as well as its opportunities. They are the first to see a change in its temperature, its composition, its population; they are close at hand as well as heart to heart. And since they are there and have such knowledge, and have such a connection as well, they're often on the front line when there's work to be done, when the local water they love is threatened.

No one did more for the Schoharie than Art Flick; no one has saved the Esopus more times than Ed Ostapczuk. And it's the same with little rivers that look like little more than ditches and great blue-ribbon streams in the West. He who best knows all that *can* be lost has the greatest vested interest in the river. The expert can become the surest guardian.

And we must all praise that.

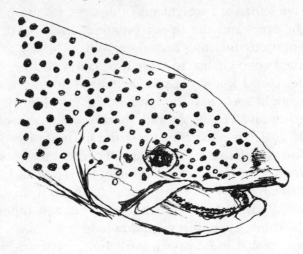

29

COUNTRY HARDWARE STORE

I stop by the window, not intending to buy, needing not a leader tippet on this bright spring day, merely tugged by the old promotional poster. It is a two-foot-long rainbow trout, grinning, brighter red than anything I've ever seen come from a river other than a rusted Prince Albert tobacco can. The old shop is in a town I've never driven through, in a forgotten backwater of the Catskills, and I am curious. That's all.

There's lots of great stuff in the window: a wicker creel, vintage 1940s; a Heddon bamboo fly rod, not quite straight, with a nondescript reel, filled with what is probably a braided level line, or some primitive taper, with a designation that dates back to my teens, HCH, HDH, one of those. There are some small silver spoons on a card, another card filled with panfish popping bugs, still another with crude wet flies, and yet another with dry flies in garish purples and pinks, with soft hackle and forgettable design—except for the McGinty, which still catches bluegill better than any other pattern, and sometimes even trout.

There are a couple of stuffed trout in the window, too— quite weather-worn, looking as if the cat got them, or moths, or just age—laid near a papier-mâché stump, on paper leaves. And there are some signs, announcing that live bait and licenses are available and that I should take a kid fishing. I tried the latter, with all my children, and mostly bored them silly.

This Catskill backwater is far from cities, shunned by tourists, because it is merely itself and has nothing to offer them, far even from rivers with great names; it's near lakes and ponds and creeks you've never heard of, a place where fly fishing still comfortably co-exists with spinning, bait-casting, minnow and worm fishing, even muskrat trapping— fly fishing of a 1940s stripe.

Standing on the rutted and pitted macadam sidewalk, looking down the short main street for my wife, who has found a little clothing shop in which to rummage, I am suddenly mad for this place. I remember its type and hunger for its bounties.

I figure that Mari will surely take half an hour or more to buy a pair of rough-and-ready socks and then will surely know where I am, and I open the door to the tackle and hardware store—which jangles a little bell—just for a quick look.

The inside is dark and shadowy, from bald bulbs under concave reflectors, widely spaced, and from far too many stacks of shoe boxes and shirts and sweaters and jackets, stacked to the ceilings wherever I look. It's better than I dreamed.

It is the place of my earliest youth, a cornucopia of discrete delights that come in little cardboard boxes with handwritten legends on them. I bought my first fishing tackle of any kind in such a shop, in Haines Falls, New York; it was a place that also carried candy, kites, cheap baseball mitts, shovels for sandboxes and snow, notepads, postcards, magazines, suntan lotion, aspirin, combs, toothbrushes, Vaseline, worms by the dozen, and what-not else. I bought a bamboo stick with a little ring on the tip, to which I attached a stout green cord, a red, green, and white bobber, and a snelled Eagle Claw hook. It all cost under three bucks.

Most of the fishing tackle here is old stuff—flies tagged onto willow-leaf spinners, big and little bass bugs on cards, green bait cans that latch onto your belt (for some reason with French words on them), nameless reels, metal and wooden nets in several shapes and sizes on up to gargantuan (which piques my interest), wicker creels, rubber boots, glass rods, a couple of cheap bamboo rods, minnow buckets, and lots of knives. I always like the knives. Everything is somehow mixed in with the hammers and tool kits, cosmetic staples, dry goods, three brands of cheap cigars, machine oil, rakes and shovels, guns, ammunition—an irresistible stew. To the side, as if they are too delicate for the heavier fare, are wooden trays filled with flies with names like Bumble Bee and Parmachene Belle and Silver Doctor. Once they caught plenty of trout. I imagine they probably will still do so when all our parachutes, paradrakes, thoraxes, no-hackles, and comparaduns are gone.

I correct myself immediately. No, our flies are very much here to stay. Those older ones are dinosaurs and won't come back.

These new patterns and designs, beyond fad and fancy, represent some astonishing developments in the past twenty-five years. People keep telling me that nothing changes, that there is very little true innovation, that people fished in the fifteenth century with no-hackles. But they're only slenderly correct. The splitting of tails, the building of the thorax, and the design of a fly without obtrusive hackle— architectonics that allow a fly to sit flat on the surface of a river—were minute but highly significant, not only forgotten but never really perfected. And that tinkering and perfecting, inchmeal, is what's been happening over the past quarter of a century, and it is still happening, and it has been a true revolution, taking us further and further from the wares of this simple and lovely country tackle and hardware store.

I think of a spring creek I know where few trout were caught except in the riffles on the older patterns and how much this shrewd innovation in fly design has made so much more possible. I live in uneasy relationship to technology, I think, standing there in the midst of my past; I still use an Underwood Standard typewriter—and it does what I need it to do, and I cannot imagine retiring it for something called a word processor. I am as wary of progress as the painter Edgar Degas, who, when he saw one of the first telephones, noted that it now meant that when someone rang a bell you had to come running.

"Anything I can help you with?" the proprietor asks. He is perhaps in his late sixties or early seventies, a simple man in a plaid shirt, neither interested in prodding me into what must be an infrequent sale nor able to lose one. He's just being helpful. He just wants to take a chance to talk.

"Lots of nice old things," I say. "But I'm mostly looking, I guess."

"Quite all right. Quite all right. Take your time. Nothing rushes much around here."

My eye fixes on the green worm box with its little circle of holes in its roof, and I remember wearing one very much like it on my belt and fishing for white perch in a reservoir near New York City, the box filled with nightcrawlers I'd plucked from lawns on a moist April night. I fished with a glass fly rod then and lobbed the worms out, ahead of a bobber. I used to grease the line, and it always stuck in the guides.

There really isn't much here that I need, or can use, and none of it really qualifies as "collectible," and I don't "collect" anyway—I just accumulate. But it makes me think of the past, when a dozen items would have attracted me, and it makes me think of a modern tackle shop, twenty miles from here, near a river with a famous name. That one has form-fitting waders and graphite fly rods and trays and trays of cunningly designed and tied flies; and it has racks of books, and on the walls there are handsome paintings; and there are splendid little fly boxes from Sweden, braided leaders from England and France, tippet material from Japan that lets us fish smaller and lighter to bigger and bigger fish, fly lines with clear nomenclature, which float and cast much more smoothly, and enough that is new and truly helpful for me to spend hours looking and touching and testing and buying.

I am mad for all this new stuff—especially if it isn't force-fed to me, if I can pick and choose, if it doesn't pinch those other parts of fly fishing that are full of mystery and surprise and drama and wit.

In the end I buy, for thirty-nine cents apiece, a dozen bass bugs made of cork, with feathered tails and rubber legs; some are quite small and will work well on a bluegill pond, I think; some will work on those alligator bass in that weedy Connecticut pond. They'll all catch fish. I can always use them.

Then I head out of this antique cave and into the bright light of a 1990s' spring day.

Rather than walk toward Mari, I look back into the dark and musty shop. The old man has found himself a chair near the counter and is leaning back, reading a local newspaper. Then I look again at the two-foot-long rainbow trout in the window, still grinning at me.

"I thought I'd find you here," Mari says. "Buy out the whole store?"

"Only a piece of my childhood."

"Don't be maudlin."

The sun is very bright and I am feeling very maudlin, and I know I have no reason to go back into that old shop, but I finally admit that what I really bought was some bass bugs, which will work well in Connecticut.

30

WHEN

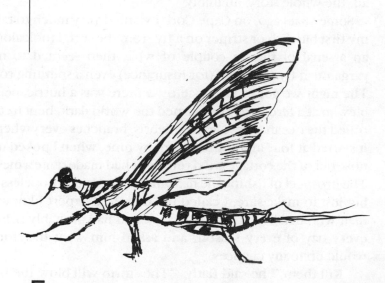

Fishing takes place "in time." We fish at certain times for certain lengths of time. Sometimes we should have been someplace last week or next week or a month from now. We got to Tortuga Pond an hour late, we left the Big Bend twenty minutes early. We cast when the fish were down, weren't ready when they were up, missed the hatch, misread the weather, or, perhaps—a couple of times—got it all exactly right: we were in fact there on time, fished the right length of time, used all those blessed other times we'd spent on the water to tell exactly what we should do—and it worked.

You have to be there to learn, you have to log in your hours to see and to experience more of the odd, remarkable, patterned and unpatterned, unpredictable things that take place in and on the water. Seeing more of what *can* take place, you ought to be able to tell more accurately, more frequently, what will and what won't happen. That's the theory—and it's a good one. Still, there are surprises. And those surprises are why no fly fisherman ever fully knows it all, the whole story, infallibly.

Some years ago, on Cape Cod, I wanted very much to take my first bluefish or striper on a fly from the surf. I took along an arsenal of flies, a couple of what then seemed to me gargantuan fly rods, and (for insurance) even a spinning rod. The night we got to Provincetown there was a hurricane. It blew in at a ferocious clip, turned the world dark, bent trees, roiled the ocean, strew leaves, debris, branches everywhere. It started at four in the afternoon; by nine, when I poked my nose out of the cottage we'd rented, it had made quite a mess. The prospect of fishing the next morning seemed hopeless— but just to make sure, I called the one local expert I knew, a man who had lived there all his life and had probably fished every day of every season, and asked him what the storm would do to my chances.

"Kill them," he said flatly. "The storm will blow the fish miles offshore and you won't get a thing from the beach for three or four days. Minimum."

"Are you sure?"

"They'll be scattered and deep. It will take them nearly a week to regroup and come in again."

"It couldn't possibly be otherwise?"

"Take the kids swimming. Forget fish for a while. It's hopeless, absolutely hopeless. Trust me."

So I slept late and arrived at the public beach about 10:30 with picnic baskets, blankets, and my passel of kids in tow. The beach was crowded but, oddly, no one was swimming.

"Too many big blues around," someone advised me. "See—" and he pointed to a vast flock of gulls and terns diving into a mile-long strip of agitated water.

I abandoned my family and rushed to the water's edge. Of the dozen men I saw with spinning gear, all had half a dozen or more gigantic bluefish, in the fourteen-pound class, which is a lot of bluefish. One said, in answer to my tense query, "They were right in the breakers a couple of hours ago, mixed in with stripers. You could have touched them with your hand—"

"Or a fly rod," I said.

"Don't know about fly rods," the fellow said, "but they sure ate this metal spoon. Wind must have blown them in. Never saw so many. They're heading back out now—so you'd better hurry if you want—"

I raced back to the car, discovered I'd left my carefully prepared fly rods safely at the motel, where they'd avoid the sand on kids' blankets, feverishly set up my spinning rod and cast a dozen times as far as I could to the vanishing school—hopelessly.

There are parts of the world where there is always some fishing—where seasons merge into one another or never end. Friends of mine fish midges in the dead of winter in the Rockies, nymphs before the snow runoff, streamers whenever their hands don't freeze. No-kill sections are in some sections of the country open all year round now, and you can even claim, out of season, that you are really fishing for the glorious chub with that Blue-Winged Olive, not trout. I get calls now from fishing friends who want me out in January, March, December.

It's not something I'm militant about, but I must admit that in this vast world there are a few other activities I like to pursue and, frankly, I enjoy having the season over, flat done, or just about to begin; I like to have the rhythm of my life punctuated with a happy series of stops and starts, expectation and the thing itself.

But in this matter of *when,* once the season is open, to be on the water, I'm on less comfortable turf. I've learned when some of the hatches in my life occur—Hendricksons at 2:00, sulphurs in the evenings, PMDs never before 10:30 A.M., stoneflies a few miles further upstream than they were yesterday . . . this and that. But sometimes—in a scorching spring or cold spring, for instance—the Hendricksons, for their own good reasons, will come later in the day or even at night; sometimes the Green Drakes will come a week early, or a week late, or not at all.

I was fishing a new river in Pennsylvania with Bob Berls some months ago and enjoying the pleasure I always take on new water: watching the way several currents braided in one large pool, the way the water curled against the far bank and under some trees. I contemplated several stretches of pocket water and judged where the fish might be. I watched a long flat pool for some sign of feeding fish, saw one a hundred yards above me, made a decision to fish the water up to it, realized I'd made a stupid mistake in this kind of water not fishing to an actual rise, saw a spurt rise at the base of a riffle, judged the fish to be on caddis or small stoneflies, put on an elk-hair caddis, and caught a decent 13-incher. It was pleasant work—and it was fun to watch Bob, a fine, thoughtful fisherman who knew this water well.

I like to use what I've learned on the water and, as I grow a bit more selective, I fish a bit more when I think something will be happening, in ways that give me the most pleasure. The gods probably don't actually deduct from our allotted span the time spent fishing; and the fish don't rise, as Sparse used to tell me when I fished too little, in Cemetery Pool; but you save a bit of wear on aging bones if you fish less and with more care. I assured myself of this as we began the evening fishing. I looked a lot, cast only now and then. No real hatch had come off but a fish broke water here and there, usually with that now familiar spurt rise.

It was my first time out this season, though, and my rhythms were askew. I could not quite reconcile my old compulsion to fish hard and my new desire to fish more wisely. Around 8:00 I saw a sulphur, then another, and told Bob I was heading upstream to a big pool I'd fished earlier. Sure enough, I saw a sensible rise to a mayfly in the upper right-hand corner of the pool, pitched one of Craig Mathews' Sparkle Duns dressed in sulphur garb, and promptly nailed a nice fifteen-incher. It was cool now and all my best instincts, all my years of time on the water, told me that the fishing was over for the day. Mayflies wouldn't come when there was this chill in the air. The hatch had not officially started. What we'd seen were a few of the advance guard and they were gone now. Anyway, I was shivering. So at 8:15 I left the river, took off my waders, felt I'd done the sensible thing, and headed back to the house.

Wrong again.

Bob did not come back to the house by 9:00 and I began to worry about having left him. When he was not back by 9:30, I thought I might go after him—in case he'd had a problem. He was back, though, about 9:45, and told of a solid sulphur hatch just at dusk, the first of the season, and of five strikes and four good fish.

When should you fish?

The only safe answer, clearly, is "All the time. In season and out. All day. Every day. Even some nights."

But that's only part of the story, isn't it?

31

IN THE CAR

Some of my most pleasant times on fishing trips have been in cars: driving with Les Ackerman the two hours from Big Sky to Island Park Reservoir, chattering without stop about business and being past fifty and fish; in the car with Thom Green, from Denver to Utah, where we intended to pursue rumors of goliath bluegill, listening to him talk about the structure of the earth, the geology of oil exploration; dozens of long trips with Mike Migel, hearing stories about a hundred of his crazy business deals—selling grass-making machines to the Arabs, leaching gold mines in Ghana, peddling cement to Nigeria. None of Mike's deals ever flew. The machines dried up, there was never, anywhere, enough gold, the cement ended at the bottom of a bay after a coup.

The stories went on for years, as we drove to the Catskills or the Connetquot or the Battenkill. Two new ones began before I'd heard the sad end of one I'd been following for two full fishing seasons. Deals came so close to a handshake, there even was a handshake, that I expected our forthcoming trip to the Ausable to be with a multimillionaire. And then they deconstructed. Every last one of them. We'd get into the car in front of my apartment and they'd start at once—interspersed with reports he or I had heard about the river we were going to fish, fish caught or lost ten or thirty years earlier, fly talk, rod talk, family talk, and then more elaborate business schemes and reports.

I loved the man and miss him and wish, somehow, one of those deals had flown, that he had not died dreaming that one last gold mine, with just another few days of search, would reveal its treasure, which Mike proclaimed—almost with his last words—to be there, absolutely.

We had lunch only a few times a year, rarely spoke on the phone, split when we fished; so those hundreds of hours in the close contained box of the speeding car, cigar smoke practically choking us, rocketing toward or from trout country, were (as I think back on those dozen or more years) the heart of our friendship.

And of my many trips with Mari, car time was always best—especially when I was at least an hour from the river, especially when I did not get lost and then come unglued.

We had driven from Bozeman toward the Big Hole, where we were invited to meet some new friends, Dick and Ann. I had left especially early so we could drive to the upper river, near Wise River, where I had once fished. I wanted to show Mari that gorgeous upper valley and then drop down to Glen and meet our friends at their place about 1:00.

At 8:30 we got off the main highway for coffee and, seeing a sign to Twin Bridges, decided we had time to take the long route, through Dillon. We were chattering blissfully, devouring every feature of the moving landscape. We passed through Twin Bridges about 9:45 and I noted that there was a road nearby that led to our friends' ranch. I loved the Big Hole. I had had some spectacular days fishing it with Glen West and Phil Wright. Perhaps we should call and come early. I'd trade a day of even happy sight-seeing for a day of fishing any time.

By 1:30 we'd been upriver and then down, and had barely gotten out of the car. We were already late. I looked at my scribbled notes and saw that Ann had indicated a road half a dozen miles from Glen as the back route to their place. So I got off the main highway, turned left then right onto what had to be old Route One, and headed back toward Dillon. I looked carefully but found nothing that resembled the road she'd described. In fact, when I looked at the mileage gauge, I realized I'd driven eighteen miles already, not the six she'd indicated, so I backtracked, stopped at the Glen Post Office, and asked instructions.

The postmaster did not seem to have talked with anyone for the past six months. He was in no sweat to see me leave. He got out a map. He got out the telephone directory. He laid them on the counter. He had never heard of the road I'd mentioned. "It's only six miles away," I advised him. He had never heard of my friends, though they could not have been ten miles away.

Baffled, tense that I'd miss the afternoon Pale Morning Duns, I called Ann, verified my location, apologized for being so late, listened to my voice—disembodied now— promise to be there in fifteen minutes. It was 2:30 by now and we were clearly very close. "We're very close," I assured Mari. "Very close."

Mari told me, in her great wisdom, that I had been driving too fast and must have missed the road, so I went no more than thirty miles an hour for about ten miles, then picked it up to forty, then fifty-five, then sixty-five. There were no markers or signs on the road. I was now not even sure that we were on old Route One.

Twenty-five miles down the road, my nerves began to race faster than the car and I listened to Mari's third sensible suggestion that we "ask someone."

I had been up and down this road now twice. I was on the verge of heading directly to Dillon and calling Dick and Ann and reporting a seizure, or something.

The only someone I could find was a fellow on a tractor. I jolted the car to a stop at the rim of a side ditch, jumped out, and asked the fellow where our mysterious road was. He shrugged and replied in Spanish. I told Mari I did not think we had gone clear to Mexico but that we were clearly too far and ought to head back to Glen for the third and last time, for one more try.

I raced back at seventy-five miles per hour, decided not to stop at the Glen Post Office again because the fellow might have me arrested for lunacy, and pulled alongside an old fellow in a pickup truck. "Is this old Route One?" I asked, my body pulsing like mad, my foot ready to pounce on the pedal and be off, so we could at least catch a bit of the evening fishing.

"Wal, son," the man said slowly. "What's that you wanted to know?"

I repeated my question.

"I've been driving this road for fifty years," he said.

"Yes," I said.

"No. No, that's not right, son. It's fifty-seven years, exactly fifty-seven years come October since Martha and I came over from Townsend . . ."

"Yes."

". . . and I drove it every day for fifty-seven years. Most every day."

"Is it in fact Route One?" I asked.

"It used to be the only road, of course, until the big superhighway was put in . . ."

"Yes."

". . . and I guess I drove it every day so I ought to know what it's called."

Ten minutes later he admitted it was Route One, I raced back to Glen, barely speaking to Mari—who was the only person I could blame for all this, since she was laughing wildly now—got out, kicked the car, which might be responsible, went into the bar, got the exact mileage from a man I owe my life to, and sure enough found the road and arrived at Dick and Ann's at 5:30, only four and a half hours late. On the way out that evening, I noted to Mari that it took us exactly thirteen minutes to reach Twin Bridges, where we'd been that morning. The fishing had been fair, the driving awful.

The car is not merely the source of good talk and torment, of course. Mari and I once drove with my friend Pierre from Paris to a pike pond near Normandy. It was a long, happy day—but a wet one; and in the evening, having started at 5:00 that morning, Pierre, who has boundless energy, said he wanted me to fish a small chalkstream an hour closer to the city. When we got there it was pouring like mad— steady and very hard. Mari said gently that she'd rather read than have the great honor of watching me catch my first French chalkstream trout. Pierre got out an old blanket and she put it over herself, covering all but her head. She seemed very warm and content as I looked back at her through the wet window.

Then Pierre and I marched a half mile through very wet three-foot-high grasses. I was exhausted from the long day and, without boots, wet to the skin, chest to toes—and cold. The sight of a couple of Green Drakes fluttering above the water and trying to avoid the cold raindrops perked me up a bit. So did the first little slap rise I saw.

Twenty minutes later, fishing to that rise, I caught a happy little seven-incher, got photographed with my first French chalkstream trout, and fled back to the car. I had no itch to glorify or prolong my misery.

Mari was in the backseat, still huddled under the old blanket. She had put down her book.

"You . . . all . . . right?" I asked.

"Fine, fine," she said. "But back so soon? And I thought you boys loved to play in the rain. Isn't the fishing—"

"Had . . . enough," I said.

"Oh, dear. You're chattering," she said.

I grabbed a piece of the blanket for myself and my wife of thirty-five years sat up and hugged me tightly and in a few minutes I felt amiably warm. In a little while my teeth stopped knocking together, I felt no more chills, and was able to talk.

"All these fishing trips," I said. "All these years."

"Yes," she said. "Are you warmer now, dear?"

"Fine, fine," I said, and then feebly: "And I always thought it was so awful for you . . . back in the car."

32

RECORDS

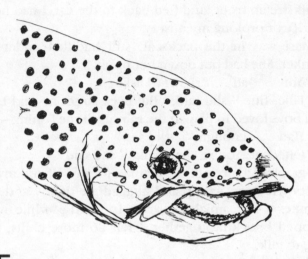

The fact that my old friend Mort recently caught a world-record Atlantic salmon in Norway has got me thinking about records. Mort's fish was fifty-one pounds, fifty-two inches, and not only broke the sixteen-pound-class record handily but bested the biggest salmon taken on a twenty-pound-test leader, too. That's a lot of salmon. Mort is not particularly a pursuer of records but said it did mean more to him than to have caught 113 porgies one day thirty-seven years ago out of Sheepshead Bay—which is a lot of porgy.

Some folks are *only* interested in records—from "trip best" to "river best" on up to the best in the world, ever. Good magazines have, both in the past and today, run whole features on the records by species for a year, for all time, by a particular method—and the great International Game Fish

Association (IGFA) has precise rules and regulations, tests for that rare commodity among fishermen, truth, and accurate record-keeping facilities. For many, getting into the record books for catching the largest of a species ever taken on particular tackle is as important an issue as comes up for a fisherman. You certainly don't forget such a feat.

And such records are of value—both to our knowledge of the species and the limits of its size and to our appreciation of the skills of anglers. Using lighter and lighter leaders successfully has surely shown us what *can* be done, just as the use of smaller, lighter rods (by pioneers like Lee Wulff) has shown us that gamefish can indeed be taken on slighter tools.

Of course the Alta River in Norway, where Mort caught his fifty-pounder, is not your local Little Muddy River, and most of us simply cannot afford to travel to Norway or South America or northern Canada or Africa (where all those giant tarpon are appearing) for our sport. Our records, if we keep them, are more of the homegrown variety—biggest rainbow caught in the Esopus or the Gunnison or the Deschutes, "high hook" for a trip or for a traditional Opening Day gathering, even Smallest Fish or Ugliest Fish or Most Flies Put in the Overhanging Scotch Pine at Mule Bend. My "records" have leaned toward the latter variety: those that reveal not our triumphs but our fallibilities. As such, I have too often come closer to being the house clown than the house hero. This has not troubled me much. Nor has it kept me from striving after that excellence, those honors I value. But a healthy respect for human fallibility and its generally widespread occurrence has kept me from a dozen diseases of the ego, especially that which traps and enslaves some truly superior anglers into entering into the club log dozens of fish that never saw a hook, or abject lies about the size of fish caught—in a manner neither cute nor endemic but like some melanoma on the ego. Catch and release, of course, has generally increased the size of fish by a full 35 percent or more.

I suppose a lot of us just don't go after records. They're ancillary to the chase, and to our memories of days astream. We are as content to catch a four-pound brookie that shocks us in its size and beauty and unexpectedness as we are one over the fourteen-pound Nipigon record. A pleasant afternoon with uncounted bluegill high on the beds and attacking every little popper I pitch to those tan pancakes in the shallow water is enough; I don't need to weigh or measure them. "Big" is big enough; the heavy turn of a buster of a brown I thought by its rise might be a yearling doesn't require a record book to pump blood, make a day, a memory. And if there is simply nothing "big," nothing that approaches "many" about a day on the water? Perhaps there— without being a Pollyanna—we can discover more about why we're fishing in the first place . . . and that "why" is surely less about records than about the nature of the pursuit. Anyway, I generally use the *heaviest* tackle I can because I want what's most effective to cast, most comfortable—and I want my fish in as quickly as possible.

I saw one true record won a couple of years ago on a private stretch of river just crammed with big browns. My son Paul and I were guests of Carl Navarre and the three of us had fished hard for four hours without seeing or moving one of those big browns. It was one of those dead days, or dead mornings. Then Carl, ahead of us, called and pointed: he'd found a batch of feeding fish, with Pale Morning Duns flying. There were three or four, sending up little spurts of water, and with care we might be able to catch a couple of them. The fish in this river got pretty serious about their feeding and would resume if flies were still on the water, even after a fish or two had been caught. We'd rotate, each taking a turn after a fish was caught.

I'd wanted Paul, now his own man, to like this fly fishing, which I loved, but the way the dice fell he'd mostly gone in other directions for the past twenty years and I'd gotten to see that this was all right, too—for we differ in our cells and in our worlds, and though we all overlap (kin or not), only by chance do our passions overlap. I was born to fish. I was born to fish passionately, and with a fly. And he was not. He was born the son of a man born to fish and, happily, he simply had lots of other fish to fry. Still, it would be good if he got a fish here, on this summer visit that he had sought, as he had sought to fish with us that day.

He cast first and promptly rose a fish—a big one that jumped twice, drew shouts from the gallery, and then busted off. Carl and I motioned Paul to try again, so he tied on another Pale Morning Dun and did.

His first cast drew a rise and he promptly broke the second fish off on the strike. Within minutes he'd lost two more, either at the strike or a moment or two later.

I asked to see his leader. It broke too easily and was, perhaps, from one of my old spools that had gotten mixed in with the new ones I bought each season.

"Four fish!" I said, fetching out some new material.

"That must be a record," he said.

I tied on some fresh tippet, dropping to 5X, double-checking the new Surgeon's Knot, pulling on the connection of fly and leader a few times to be sure it was strong. It was. Carl, who had been watching the water, said he'd seen still another spurt rise in the broken water against the far bank. Paul cast there, drew an immediate rise, and had on an even bigger fish than the previous ones he'd raised. It jumped twice and he played it with good care, giving some line, regaining some, keeping his rod high and the fish on the reel, keeping the pressure firm. He'd get this one. It was a big old male but he had it under control. I felt elated. And then I saw the fish steadily angle downstream where the current picked up a chop as it swept to the left and against the far bank and around the bend. Paul took four or five quick steps down toward it. And then, in a rush, the large fish turned the corner and the hook simply pulled out.

Five fish.

I breathed out deeply and had not a word to say.

Then Paul laughed and shrugged and then we all laughed loudly, and then Carl dubbed the spot "Paul's Pool" and that's been its name for the three of us since then, after the record.

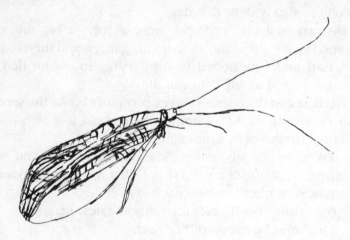

DOG-DAY REDEMPTION

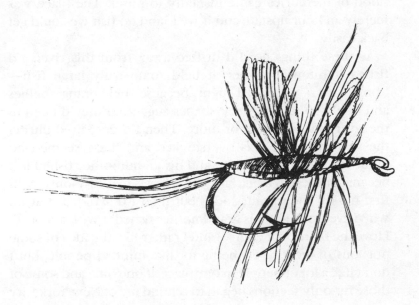

It was high summer and hot and, in the muggy heart of the gray city, I was so restless that when Sandy called and said "Let's go" I agreed before he said "fishing." And I fell over myself, sweating, plucking a day's gear abruptly from my fish closet; I hadn't gone near it in more than a month.

The day was already under way when I got into Sandy's car and we headed upcountry. We were in no hurry. I didn't expect much—certainly not one of the major hatches—but we'd fish the afternoon and on into as much of the evening as looked fruitful. I was so happy to be in a car, heading away from the mean heat, that I didn't ask where we were going until we got to the tollbooths that let you out of the city-trap.

Sandy thought we might make it a short trip to upper Westchester County, where a lot of short rivers run into or out of city reservoirs, and sometimes between two of them. He named a river I'd fished a lot during my teens and a flood of memories came instantly to mind. The place was merely an hour upstate and if we found no fish we could get back easily.

As these things go, I'd drifted away from this river. I'd fished it intensely when it held some truly large fish—"holdovers," we called them, because their orange bellies and bright spots and sleek shapes suggested they'd been in the river at least a year or more. Then I'd despaired during the years when it was overstocked and there seemed no holdover fish and everyone and his grandmother fished it. I became interested in it again when it was made fly-only, with first no-kill then limited kill; but then I'd avoided it again when everyone and his grandmother fished it with a fly rod. I love the fly rod, of course, and I rather like the idea of some portions of most rivers being for like-minded people, but I don't like a lot of people in one place at one time and some of those fly-only sections began to remind me of New York City subways.

That's what we found, even in the middle of the afternoon in the middle of the summer, when you'd have thought everyone would be off playing golf or tossing Frisbees or at the shore or in some sensible place, leaving trout rivers for antisocial types like me. We scouted a couple of places I'd fished successfully before and all of them were occupied.

I asked Sandy if he wanted to try a nearby river we both knew and liked.

He thought that would be just as busy.

Maybe we should just call it a pleasant drive on a hot summer afternoon and head back, I suggested.

"That has a lot to recommend it," he said.

We stood on the bridge and watched a couple of brothers of the angle fishing just below us, rather noisily, surely futilely. Upstream there were three or four others; they were catching a lot of nothing, too—and being none too graceful about it.

I shrugged.

"Ever try the middle section?" he asked.

"It's a swamp up there. I've always avoided it."

"So does everyone else."

So we suited up, rigged our rods, and headed upstream and around the bend. Above a small dam, beyond which I'd never gone, the character of the river changed dramatically. It became a morass of deadfalls in deep slow water with a muddy bottom—difficult or impossible to wade, hard to read unless you saw a trout rise, overhung with a heavy growth of old trees along a sloping hill and walled in by high weed and brambles on the other side. I'd known some places like this. They are moody, strange, trouty waters, taking little of the direct light of the sun, holding mystery— and protecting that mystery. They're never comfortable and you can never fish them out. You half expect a ten-pound brown with an outsized head to show itself some day and scare you out of your waders. Many years ago, I remembered, I'd taken a five-pounder in such water, though not on a fly.

There's hardly room to cast under most circumstances, you can't get far enough out into the river to be clear of the dense foliage on either side, and you have to play Twenty Questions to figure out where the fish will be holding.

I'd come to the tail of this section a dozen times over a period stretching back forty years and had always backed away. It was more trouble, always, than I'd wanted. I'd probably have my fly in the trees all day, if I didn't first slip on the mud bottom and drown.

We tried the sloping side first, where Sandy said he'd taken a few good fish. It was hard going along the base of the hill, a half step at a time, the water three or four feet deep right to the bank, an area filled with deadfalls and odd-shaped rocks that had fallen down the hill and made you stumble or trip every dozen steps.

Sixty yards upstream Sandy spotted a fish rising under the low branches of a heavily slanted maple. The fish was behind one of the largest deadfalls we'd seen and we had to stand helplessly watching it feed, unable to fish over the deadfall, unable to cast around it because we were tight to the bank and the fallen branches stretched out twenty feet.

Maybe upstream from the fish, I suggested.

So we climbed the hill, I ripped my waders and got dirt on my face, and fifteen minutes later we got to a spot sixty feet above the fish. It was still feeding—very gently, just tipping up and sucking down something minute. Sandy made five or six casts, backhand, leaning out as far as he could, but the fish could not be reached.

So we walked all the way downstream to the little dam, crossed to the other side, and worked our way slowly up through a tangle of blackberry bushes and mud and high weed and brambles. It was late afternoon already and I was soaked in sweat. When we finally got parallel to where the fish had been rising, it was no longer having lunch, so Sandy headed upstream. I lingered, found a place where I could wade out gingerly along an underwater bar, selected a position from which I could cast just upstream of the low branches so my fly would float down to where the fish had been feeding, and waited. I waited ten minutes and the water remained quiet. Perhaps it was only a dace, even a small sunfish. I waited a few more minutes and then decided to cast anyway, to see if I *could* get the fly under that branch. I could, which was satisfying. Then I quickly tried a tiny mayfly, a black ant, a black beetle, a jassid, and a leafroller without wrecking the water too badly—and without arousing the fish's interest.

I was rummaging around in one of my fly boxes for a gray midge when I looked up and saw, far upstream, Sandy pumping his arm up and down, like we did in the Army to indicate we wanted someone to come up to where we were.

He was in a difficult place to get to and I took ten minutes busting through the brambles to him. When I got close I could see that he was fishing intently—but not catching anything.

"They're driving me nuts," he whispered.

Five or six fish were in fact rising irregularly, making quiet circles. Sandy had tried four or five flies; he'd put some of the fish down briefly but they'd all come back. They were doing something fussy and hard to decode and they weren't terribly large, but these were clearly trout and we had this stretch to ourselves and we were in no hurry whatsoever.

We might have been in Canada or Montana. We'd seen no one for several hours. We were a half mile back from the section everyone and his grandmother fished, on a river I'd fished for nearly half a century, on a river one hour from New York City, and we'd found some difficult, fussy, interesting trout to fish over on a hot summer afternoon.

We tried for more than an hour to interest those fish. We tried #22 midges, jassids, leafrollers, small ants, even a grasshopper. Not a serious look from any of them. Either we'd put the fish down or fish until we did. Sometimes we'd get one cast, sometimes a dozen. Then two fish made that full smooth arc out of the water and I guessed they were on caddisflies, so we switched to some #18s, elk hair and delta wing, but they wouldn't come to these either.

They may well have been on the nymphs, following them to the surface, either taking them just before they hit the roof of the river or following them out when they flew off. I don't know. It was fun trying. It was fun not finding out this time. Our leaders were light enough, and there couldn't have been a promising dry fly we didn't give a good try. They weren't especially large fish—though a few would have gone 14 inches; and they may well have been stocked at one time, though they didn't act tame.

We left with the fish still rising—a minor reservoir-runoff mystery. But that didn't matter. We'd found a new place where I'd never expected to find one, and we'd fished over some fish too fussy to be caught.

I can make a dog-day afternoon of that any day.

34

ON A SMALL CREEK

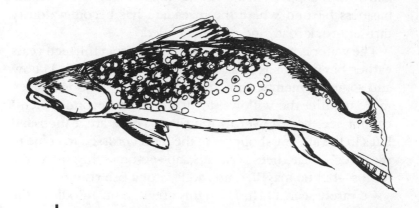

In summer and early fall, when heat and sun have drawn down the great rivers to their best moments in the West and worst in the East, I like to explore little creeks. I like those boulder-strewn, pellucid fingers of water tumbling down a cove or dancing in curves through poplar and birch on a Catskill hillside—quick, bright rivers that look in high summer like the last places on earth in which we might find trout.

The trout are there. You can't often see them, and sometimes they'll only rise in the flat pools in the morning or on a buggy dusk. You can *feel* them, though, in the diminutive eddies where the water grows opaque, in the bubbling water under a dwarf waterfall, under that undercut bank, or in the dark hollow below the boulder.

In the East, the great rush and excitement of the Time of the Hatches is over. I've done my traveling, caught some trout, missed a big one. I've leavened the year with some pleasant bass-bugging—a lazy, intense three hours in a row-boat at dusk. Now, back in trout country for a few days, with other games to play on the long weekend—and a couple of people tugging at me, to get me to swim or wander with them—there is an hour and a half at the end of the afternoon, and I have slipped off by myself to conduct some private business beyond where the macadam has become a dusty dirt-and-rock road, and now has ended.

The water is not quite as I remember it from thirteen years earlier, but it is just as clear, a bit lower, with boulders I know and some I remember not at all. The birch stand is thicker, more mature; the willows, up at the bend beyond which I cannot see, hang lower to the river. There are a thousand bugs in the air, grasshoppers in the field I crossed to come to the river's edge, bees, crickets, no-see-ums, tiny off-white moths—but no mayflies, no caddis, not a fish rising.

I'd rarely seen a fish rise in this creek in the middle of the day—except one, regularly, a long time ago, in a pool a hundred yards beyond the stand of willows and the bend. It was a very large brown in a very shadowed eddy, and it was taking a smorgasbord of minuscule and elephantine insects. Tilting my head low, I could see the eddy laced with a thin embroidery of dust, beetles, grasshoppers, moths, and Chironomids. The big fish, undisturbed all spring and summer beneath the beaver cuttings, had lost all caution and was spending a perfectly splendid afternoon picking daintily at this rich feast.

I hooked it on my first cast, with a foam beetle topped with a bit of white calftail.

It thrashed at the surface once—thunderously in that small space—headed for the crotch of the eddy and the maze of beaver cuttings. And that was that.

Today I have come in my usual high-summer uniform—khaki pants, a light long-sleeved khaki shirt with big chest pockets, a floppy khaki hat, high sneakers (the low ones fall off); no vest, no boots—only a small box of flies and a spool of 6X tippet material. I know this creek well and won't fish much. I might not cast at all. In fly fishing, I think, you get to a stage when your confidence about a few minor patterns grows complete.

It's cool here and the flowing water is cool around my ankles and calves, and the no-see-ums have stayed down-river. This is solo fishing. You don't want to share the few fishable pools or leapfrog with a partner; you don't particularly want to talk. The best of it is to have this happy, bouncing Papageno of a creek to yourself—to kick a bit of dried wood off into the grass, catch a grasshopper and chuck it into the far current near the boulder, learn a new bird or two, watch the water carefully, and perhaps sit on a log and read a book. Now and then you're waked by the whirring rise of grouse—or the quiet circle that marks a feeding trout . . . or a fallen leaf.

Papageno is a skinny, animated fellow Mozart found in himself along with the ogres and dragons. This unnamed creek reminds me of that happy fellow in *The Magic Flute,* who turns scowls to smiles and remains in the world along with the world's liars and poseurs.

I get to the willows without even rigging up, but this seems a true starting place, so I edge back to the woodline, pick a rock, and begin—as I have done a thousand times before—to thread line, tinker with leader, select and tie on a fly. It's a beetle with a tuft of chartreuse poly at the top. I've begun to prefer any specific imitation to an attractor. However loyal that Christmas tree of a Royal Coachman has been to me, I've retired mine. We were great friends once, but we've drifted apart. This trout fishing, I told myself a few years ago, has for me more and more come down to an imitation-of-a-specific-food business. It ain't snobbishness, I now remind myself. I've done all the rest of it and on a given day would no doubt do it again; and I've loved it all hugely. I've caught a whole lot of fish (though it always seems so stupid to brag). I don't have to catch a lot of fish anymore. I don't *need* to catch any fish. So when I go out—especially on a quiet, late-summer afternoon like this—I like to look more, understand a lot more, and fish when there's something to fish for. So I assure myself; and at the same time I know I am becoming too precious.

I turn the bend and walk a hundred yards without spotting fishable water. It's not deep enough here; the water ends too far from the banks (and cover) above me. But I peck my way upstream to the bend and eddy where, once, many years ago, a big trout made short shrift of me. There's no hurry. I've promised to be back at the cabin an hour from now.

The eddy is still there. The river hits a boulder straight on, then sweeps to the right, circumscribing a neat circle along the bank, laced with those fallen willow branches. The pool it forms might, even with this low water, be six or seven feet deep. The logical choice would be a quick-sinking nymph, perhaps one of those with a single- or even double-bead head. I could cast up into the riffle at the head of the eddy, hold my rod high, and let that weighted fly slip into the belly of the pool, flash in the darkness, and then rise as it neared me, like a dozen aquatic foods rising to the surface to hatch. A streamer or Woolly Bugger would work, too.

But I sit down, watch the water, and think of big trout and beetles. I look up ten minutes or more later, and there's a skinny, lanky kid standing in the spot I'd left moments earlier. He holds a fly rod, wears a cheap green vest, carries an aluminum net behind him, in his belt, and wears a five-and-dime creel. He looks at the water hard, lifts a stone, then another, and then clips off what he'd been using and ties on a new leader and fly. He casts quickly, economically, then casts again, then roll casts the line so that the fly lands near the tangle of branches. There is a heavy rise, a sharp strike, a short battle, and no more than a minute later he has the fish on a rock and is summarily bashing its head with another rock before gutting it and putting it into his creel.

I walk over and look at the fish—a brown, probably 20 inches' worth, about the size of the one I'd lost years earlier, brightly colored, with a bead-head nymph still in its mouth. The scene seemed to have been played out for me by a diabolic director.

"Well, that's four," the boy says with a touch of brio. "Enough for dinner and breakfast. Pool's yours if you want it." His hands are covered with blood and bits of guts; his shirt and pants, too.

I say I've just been looking, that I haven't fished and won't this afternoon. It all sounds hollow—or worse.

The boy looks at my graphite rod and Hardy reel, at me—sharply in the eye—smiles, and begins to turn.

He says, over his shoulder, "Yeah, I see." Before I can pontificate about killing trout or bemoan the loss of my own innocence, and while I try to stop shaking, he goes dancing down the little creek that had simply been a good place to spend a summer afternoon and catch breakfast.

35

ENOUGH

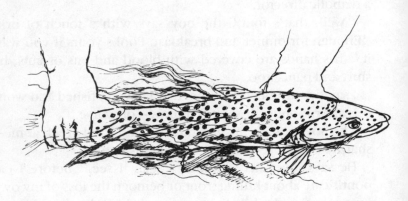

At the Second Bend Pool Dermot Wilson had once
spotted a two-foot brown, plump as a football, lying at the
bottom of a bathtub of an indentation just opposite and
below the spot where I sat when I fished the pool; it was
quite uncatchable. I saw the fish a few times, then it disappeared and I forgot about it. But every time I walked past the
bend, for several years, I looked down for the great fish. I
could not do otherwise.

But big fish and sudden feeding frenzies are rare occur-
rences, triggered by weather, time of day, but mostly the
sudden availability of food. Bluefish blitz when there are
baitfish or bunker available, not because they get a sudden

itch to go nuts now and then, let their hair down. An infestation of grasshoppers one year will make the largest fish and *most* of the fish pushovers for a while, and so, when they occur in sufficient numbers and on a gray day, will lots of aquatic insect hatches.

The salmon fly is notorious, of course, for this, but #18 Pale Morning Duns will bring up great numbers of big fish, too, and so for that matter will #20 Tricos. Like me, a trout can't pass up the chance of a good meal, the unexpected arrival of a plate of chocolate bonbons. So if you knock around rivers and lakes and oceans long enough, when conditions are right you'll be invited to a full-fledged bacchanalian orgy, with birds dipping and darting and screaming overhead, the surface of the water boiling with feeding fish and frantic bait, your quarry so hooked by gluttony they'll lose all wariness of hooks.

Much of our fishing is keyed to such times. We wait for the blitz, the major hatch, the sudden appearance of food, the preoccupation of the fish with belly, not saving their skin. We look for it and often revel in it and boast of it when we've had such moments. I've done so. I once had a ten-fish evening at Henry's Lake; friends speak of sixteen-salmon days in Russia; experts claim sixty-trout afternoons. Numbers impress; a story about having caught three eight-inch trout on a long day of fishing too often—and wrongly—finds no audience.

I can certainly remember the banner days vividly, and those that came to me from the stories of others. How could I forget them? Thirty bluefish in a couple of hours. Ten—or was it twelve?—trout, larger than any trout I'd yet seen, alligators, from Staley Springs, when it was open, in an evening. An afternoon when grasshoppers drew the eyes—and lips—of every trout to the surface and every cast or two drew a strike. Joe's story about bass, Charlie's about silver salmon, Doug's about bonefish—days when the fish were there in numbers and went berserk, when you could not keep fish off your line, when the day provided everything you thought you'd always looked for from fishing, when even the rankest novice would have triumphed.

And perhaps that's the rub.

When fish lose all caution, when there are too many of them available, when anyone can catch them and all those skills you'd prided yourself on having developed over a period of twenty years count for nothing special, is it all as much fun? Or perhaps it's not quite that; perhaps you *have* gained, somehow, after all these years of bumbling, some real degree of skill and even a modest hatch breeds a great triumph.

The question becomes, I think, how much do we need, how much is enough when we go to river or lake in pursuit of sport. Let's assume we're going to kill none, or perhaps just a few fish; let's assume that most of our pleasure is going to be gulling and hooking and capturing the fish. We won't kill any, or many, but we don't get out as much as we'd like and we don't have many moments when the fish are as willing, so we find ourselves removing a fly, cleaning it, and casting again quickly. More hook-ups, we think, are better; anyway, we can't resist casting when the fish are high on the hog. This is our chance. We've made a long trip to get here. The blitz won't last forever. Remember all the days we caught nothing. Better get 'em while they're hot.

Late one morning last summer I fished the Second Bend Pool, which had always been a great challenge for me. A dozen times I'd sent three or four rising trout packing with my heavy-handed doings. On this trip, elsewhere on the river, I'd had four or five very good days of fishing and felt some new impulse stirring in me. With the Green Drakes on, big fish would stir every morning around 11:30, and every day I'd get one or two truly large fish. Oddly, that was usually

enough and thereafter I'd sit down and watch the water or
stalk upstream looking for what I could find. When I saw
other fish rising I'd just sit and watch the spot. Frankly, a
couple of interesting fish were plenty. And on a few days, a
couple of smallish not-so-interesting fish were plenty, too.

Twice Mari had said, with an ironic smile, that I was fished
out. She reminded me that an old fishing pal of mine
had caught a large brown, bigger than any he'd caught before, and had quit fly fishing. He'd said he knew he'd never
get another that size and he'd gotten what he wanted from
the sport.

Was something like that happening to me?

"That'll be the day," I told Mari. I just didn't seem to feel
that I had to stick a hook in every fish I saw.

As I thought of all that while getting my tackle ready at the
Second Bend Pool, that didn't seem a regression, a loss of the
True Spirit. I'd turned sixty; my appetites weren't quite what
they had been; the world wasn't quite what it had been; we
trout fishermen, a small part of the world, had gone in my
lifetime from killing practically everything to killing practically nothing. I had other big and heavy thoughts but I
pushed them away, doubting that any of this would concern
me at the Second Bend Pool, where I'd always been lucky to
raise a fish or two at most. The fish were always cautious here
and I'd never, in six visits, seen a Green Drake in the vicinity.

But I hadn't been seated on my favorite spot on the inside
rim for ten minutes when I heard the unmistakable splash
rise of a huge fish to a large fly. I looked up from my open fly
box but saw no spreading ring; in fact, with my ears growing
duller each year, I could now not tell where such a splash had
come from.

Moments later I saw sparrows swoop, splash rises near the
bend, and drakes everywhere; it looked as if every one of
them was taken with that confident rise of fish who have
seen a week's worth of such flies and trust that none have

nasty hooks in them. I put on a new Sparkle Dun with a bright green body that Craig Mathews had cooked up for me and raised a 19-inch fish on my first cast. By the time I released it, two or three fish were going good again and I hummed and cast back up into the shank of the current and promptly hooked another. It was a little like the fate of Mr. Theodore Castwell, in the Skues story. Would I *have* to go on catching these nineteen-inchers all afternoon, or even forever?

So I stopped and watched and the fish kept coming, and then I heard a gigantic splash, realized it was below me, saw a huge spreading circle in the bathtub hole across the river, back-flipped a Green Drake just above the hole, and the Mother of All Brown Trout came up without hesitation and took the fly, thumped down deep half a dozen times, and broke the 6X tippet. I shook for ten minutes.

Later, Mari asked me how many I'd gotten and I smiled and said merely, "More than enough."

36

DAY OF REST

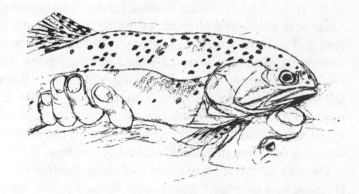

Three days before we headed home, I sat in a log chair on the porch of the sheepherder's cottage and looked down at one of the branches of the river. It was fifty feet below me—cerulean blue, flecked with silver, and I could see a half mile of it in either direction. I had fished it several times, fruitlessly, but I knew from previous years that it held trout. Automatically, from my height, I thought of where the trout might be and why I had not caught any.

The log building was ninety years old, and reportedly the one room had housed a large family right through the winter; I'd have liked it for a writing cottage. I'd put fifty books in it, some fiction, but mostly books that identified plants, birds, minerals, and animals. I'd want a broad strong desk built in, wall to wall, and I'd put the best of my three

Underwood Standard, Model "S," vintage 1945, upright typewriters on it. I'd have plenty of paper and pens, all cheap, and a pot-bellied stove large enough to take foot-long logs and heat the little space in any weather. I'd keep a couple of fully rigged rods on pegs in the inside left wall and all my other gear in a rack in one closet. I'd fish just as often as I pleased, from May through October.

Mari had been painting hard for two weeks. She had painted from the fields, looking off in each of four directions, and she had painted from several spots on this bench. Each year she loved this valley more; she told me that it changed a thousand times, from different motifs and at different times, and it never bored her any more than the fishing ever bored me. On that October afternoon three days before we left, she had gone to the side of the cottage opposite the wind and was painting again. "You sick?" she asked when I said that I'd just like to sit on the porch today and look out over the valley—take a day of rest.

I wasn't sick, but I had stopped fishing for this visit West. Nothing had gone as I'd wanted it to go. On the main river I had not seen a fish rise; they were on the bottom in this bright weather; they had been pursued by too many people in too many boats for too long, and there just weren't enough flies to bring them up. The only way to catch them, I'd been told, was to put on a big Hairwing Coachman and tie on a "trailer"—an eight-inch piece of leader material, tied to the shank of the hook, with a pheasant tail or bead-head nymph on the end. This seemed a clumsy way to fish, and I avoided it for a few hours, during which I fished a hopper and then a Humpy hard, without a touch. But then I tried it for ten minutes and found that it worked as billed—and then I switched back to a hopper, since there were hoppers in the fields, but the trout were restless and sulky and even a good meal wouldn't bring them out to play.

A creek I knew proved not much different—though my rhythm was off the few days I fished it—and there were just no flies. The Tricos had come early and left. Mr. *Baetis* had not yet appeared; one bluebell day followed another, with bright sun in a cloudless sky and heat more appropriate for July than October. The bright days were good for Mari, lousy for *Baetis*.

I had fished the creek hard for three days with a friend; I had tried to find him some fish but proved a miserable guide. Once I insisted he fish up a channel I thought I remembered; I told him it was especially fecund. But the true channel came in thirty-five yards below where I'd pointed, and he advised me that there were no trout in the dry gulch I'd sent him to. I wanted my friend to take some of the pleasure I'd taken from this creek, that I'd told him he could depend upon, but except for his last day, he caught little. Only for an hour on the evening before he left did he see some touch of what the water could provide.

For myself, knowing the creek, I simply kept waiting for the more interesting fishing I knew it held. When you cut a few weeks out of a busy year to do this happy thing, this fly fishing, you plan and pack for months and cannot help but come with bloated expectations. I'd wanted to see flies; there were none. I'd wanted to share a loved piece of water with a friend; he'd been mostly stonewalled. I'd wanted to feel close to the creek in ways that I'd felt many times before and simply did not this time. But why should I? I was different. The season was different. The creek was different.

And then yesterday I had gone to the creek with Mari, and she had set up and launched into a strong day of work. I went up the East Branch and fished it with great care. There were still no flies, and no fish rising, but I took my time, felt all the rush and worry fade, saw that the cottonwoods were beginning to yellow, the aspen go orange, fished the water with deliberation, and had the pleasure of seeing my fly land in the slim dark shadow near the bank most of the time, or in the current lines or the eddies. I raised not a fish at the First Bend Pool, not any at the long back stretch, nor at the Second Bend Pool, nor from any of the undercut banks. But my intensity did not flag.

At the Third Bend Pool most of the water sweeps close to the inside bank, though two or three other tongues of current fold themselves into the flow, too. To the far left the pool is shallow and slack; I'd often raised good fish there and once chased a huge brown a few hundred feet upstream, at a gallop, before I lost it in a tangle of roots near the bank.

I waded to the left shore, to avoid casting across any of the currents, and pitched a #6 hopper with rubber legs up to the head of the slack section. It came down thirty feet dead-drift, then the line picked up a current and the fly began to sweep downstream. Just before I lifted it out, a gigantic brown came at it with open mouth, rushed . . . and missed.

I cast again at once, a little too far right, and the fly dragged. So I breathed deeply a few times, edged toward the bank, leaned there watching the water for ten minutes, saw a couple of smallish grasshoppers leap past me, changed to a #10 Jay-Dave Hopper, and cast away from the main current, smack up into the belly of the bend.

The fly came down a few feet and then the big fish nailed it. The fish jumped twice, bore into the current but did not go far, came down below me a dozen yards, came up, then hovered near the bottom in plain view and would not be budged. For the first few minutes of the fight he was trailed by a female, smaller by six or seven inches but quite large. In five minutes I had the fish near me, turning slightly, and I grasped him under the belly. The hook was tight in the corner of its mouth. My leader was 4X; there was little chance I'd have lost the fish.

He was a ludicrously oversized brown, brilliantly yellow and red, with a great kype and not a blemish from heron or hook. I ran my rod against him, marked his length, and then held the fish's tail for fully ten minutes. Then he moved away, went to the center of the river, and I could see his gills expanding and contracting mightily. I scuffled my feet a few times, and he went upstream and under the far bank; he was all right. He wouldn't look for his lady friend right away, but they'd still get together. Maybe he'd been saving his strength. He hadn't fought that hard.

The fish was longer than 27 inches, perhaps eight pounds, the largest I've ever taken on a floating fly.

I walked back to the car, took down my rod and put it into its tube, watched Mari for an hour, and then we left the creek.

I wasn't sick, I told her the next day while I sat in the log chair on the porch of the old sheepherder's cabin. There just wasn't anything else I wanted from rivers this trip, except to watch them.

37

SEASONS END

It's as easy for a fishing fanatic to let go of a season as it is to let go of a live electric wire. A week ago I tried. I patiently oiled my reels and tucked them into chamois bags, clipped old leader stubs from my flies and placed each fly slowly back into its proper plastic box, packed away my trout rods, looked at it all, sighed, and locked everything safely in my fish closet until spring. I had been to Montana. I had caught more trout than I deserved. I had my memories.

There is a time to fish and a time to live like a normal, rational, civilized adult.

But before I could lose the closet key, Larry Madison insisted we fish a bass lake near his home in Connecticut. He reminded me that the bass were not shrimpy. I thought his offer over sensibly for three seconds. A last day in the country—to gird me for the long gray city winter—sounded harmless. Anyway, we'd be after bass and I'd long ago lost my heart to trout; there was no need to take any of this very seriously.

Larry did. He looked—walking ahead of me to the gray rowboat—loaded for bear. He carried a tiny spin-casting outfit, a bait-casting rig from which hung a five-inch swimming plug, and a gigantic glass fly rod he'd made himself, especially for big bass; it took a #10 or #11 fly line, he didn't remember which. I'd brought only a middling trout rod but I did not intend to fish intently; the day, after all, was an afterthought.

We took turns at the oars, the other casting in against the shore. It was a fishy little lake—maybe a mile around—with long gray trees fallen in from the shoreline, patches of lily pads and pickerelweed, beaver cuttings, stumps, marshes, and coves. The leaves of the maple, beech, and birch were umber, splashed with beige and red; an irregular "V" of wood duck flew overhead. I could see no houses; there were no other boats. We had the lake to ourselves and might have been in Saskatchewan.

Before he'd made a dozen casts, Larry caught a two-pound bass on a bass bug of ridiculous size—perhaps three inches around. The bug was made of deer hair, dyed a dull orange, and had sprouts of hair at either end to make it look like a frog—a bullfrog, I thought—or maybe a duckling. Then he switched to the swimming plug, caught nothing, and then to the little spin-casting outfit and began to catch perch, one after the other, on a Mepps lure with a feather tail. We came

to a spot where the stream entered—sluggish in midautumn—
and he said there would be pickerel near the dropoff of the
sand bar. There were. The man knew everything worth
knowing. I caught one on a popping bug, retrieved as fast as I
could, and then he caught four or five on a spinner and a
plastic-minnow combination. He is a superb fly fisherman
and I advised him that he had sunk very low, indeed, but I
wouldn't tell. "Keep using that silly little rod," he said, "I'd
rather keep catching fish." The pickerel were 14, maybe 16
inches long. They'd take the lure in a lightning lunge and
then, when we brought them in, squiggle like eels. I thought
they'd be too bony to eat.

By five-thirty we'd fished three-quarters around the lake,
had a fish box with twenty or so perch, pickerel, and that
one bass sloshing around, and headed back toward the dock.
The air was brisk. I started to tell Larry about Montana; he
ignored Montana and said that this shore was good for truly
big bass, six pounds or better, and that I ought to switch from
my little toothpick now and fish with a real fly rod. "That
redwood?" I asked. "If you want to catch a really big bass,"
he said. So I tried his rod, with that ridiculous hair bug, but at
first drove it too hard and the line buckled and fell in heavy
loops. "Let the rod do the work," he said. I allowed the fly
line to come back more slowly and then let the bend of the
huge rod push it forward. Miraculously, I got more distance,
great accuracy; I could learn to love a contraption that let me
do that.

We slipped slowly down the shore, Larry rowing now
while I cast in against the deadfalls, the stumps, the lily pads.
I grew curiously more intent about this bass business. My
arm worked in slow rhythms, the heavy yellow line rolled
out, and fifty or sixty feet in against the shore I'd watch
the big hair bug alight and then pop and sputter as I lowered
the rod tip and tugged the line with my left hand. The lake
was perfectly still; reflections of autumn color doubled the

ruddy palette of the place. I felt increasingly mesmerized, intense. I wished Larry would stop alarming me with stories about the big bass he'd caught at night in August; he said he could have promised me a couple of big fish then. There ought to have been a fish there, and there, and near that tree angling into the water. I forgot Montana. I worked the bug with more care, intently.

The trees were dark silhouettes against the ash of the sky; the autumn air was sharp. A bat buzzed us twice and disappeared. Another ten minutes and this second season would be over for me. I did not want to let go of it now. I'd had a perfectly pleasant few hours, in the best of company, but now I was properly stuck on the image of these alleged six-pounders.

And then, not fifty yards upshore from the dock, my bug landed near a lily pad, lay still for a moment, I twitched it twice, three times, and the lake burst up with a great rise and explosion of water and a largemouth bass half-rolled, half-jumped, its great green hump turning, the force of the thing heavy into the butt of the rod. I thought I'd been shot through with electric current. I thought someone had thrown in an anvil or a garbage can. And then it was over. The bug popped out of the water as sweetly as if it were a mayfly emerging from its nymphal shuck.

After a few moments I whispered, "What did I do wrong?"

"Not a thing. He slipped the hook is all. It happens. You look like you're in shock."

I couldn't even nod.

"That was a big bass—a very big bass," he said. "No. Don't cast again. He won't come back. Seasons end."

The great bass, its rise tremendous, its power still raising twitches and trembles in me during the long dark ride back to the city, would cook in my brain all winter.

PART FOUR

Fishing in the head (mostly)

38

FISHING BACKWARD

On a float trip down the Madison one June day some years ago, I got caught in a fierce compulsion to cast and cast again, oblivious to everyone and everything else. The Mckenzie riverboat glided downstream briskly, and my eyes were fixed on the shoreline, which seemed distantly to be careening backward, behind me. I could not cast fast enough; I jerked and rushed my casting to keep my fly—an elk-hair caddis, or a Royal Trude, or a Jay-Dave Hopper—on the water every instant.

My friend Justin spoke to me; my wife, Mari, asked a couple of questions; Glen gave me quiet hints. But I kept fishing silently, compulsively, intent only on the zigzagging shoreline, the pale shapes of rocks beneath thin water, over-hangs, black water, eddies, foam lines, hoping always to see another dark form angle up, the white of its open mouth showing, and to feel the spurt of electricity shoot through me when the fish took or rose short.

As I think of that day, I realize that I was serious about my fly fishing only to the extent that the pursuit of more and bigger fish was my chief goal—just as some people are serious only to the extent that they can beat their neighbor, or a whole field of competitors, or their personal best brown trout. I wanted the intense excitement of the thing itself—of raising, hooking, and playing trout; I wanted as much of it as I could get in the seven or eight hours I'd be on the river. I could dream and read books and talk to my wife and friends at dinner tomorrow, or all winter.

I guess there's nothing too much wrong with some of that . . . for a while. But Walton says, "There is more to fishing than to fish," and increasingly I find myself looking for that *more,* which need never be to the detriment of the thing itself.

One part of the "more" is fishing not in a forward rush, seeing only the water ahead and living in the present and in one's expectations, but fishing backward, into one's memories and into the memories of one's sport.

I've never met a fly fisherman who does not prize his storehouse of memories of first fish, of especially difficult or large fish, of bright days astream and those that chilled the bone, of exotic trips and of nearby waters known as well as one knows one's living room, of funny things said, of sudden revelations of character—good and bad, of great friendships not to be bred other than near rivers, of trout lilies in the spring and the painterly crimsons and yellows of leaves paving the bottom of the Big Bend pool in October, and of leaves floating like little flags of another season done.

How deeply we live in our fishing memories.

We cherish them when we fish old water and at gatherings when the season is long over. We cherish them when we walk gray city streets and when we are tinkering with tackle or tying flies; our memories add texture and dimension to our fishing life, and no two fishermen's memories are quite the same.

The past—in books and as it comes to us from our few museums—is like a larger, collective memory, and perhaps it is just as important: A fly tied by Theodore Gordon or Don Martinez or Preston Jennings; Daniel Webster's fly rod; Charles Ritz's hat; some old Yorkshire wet flies; a Cahill tied by Harry Darbee; an old streamside log by an unknown fly fisherman who lived close to the water and far from fame; the first Orvis reel, a trout reel made by Meek & Milam; a Garrison rod, and one by Ed Payne; an old wicker creel, now a symbol of another time but still so beautiful; gut leaders and silk fly lines; a gadget that never caught the world's eye but was some fellow's stab at fame or fortune or immortality or just something more practical—a better way to keep dry-fly oil or carry a net or house leaders; old words in an old book, still bright with the freshness of hard-won observation.

I find myself more and more attached to this past, which always presses against the present. I watch the catalogs from tackle and book auction houses for fly-fishing antiques; I grow more and more interested in the work of the American Museum of Fly Fishing in Manchester, Vermont, and the Catskill Center for Fly Fishing in Livingston Manor, New York—where I can see these old artifacts of the sport in its various stages of infancy, here and abroad.

Recently I have accelerated my building of a fly-fishing library, not because I want to write a history of the sport or have names to drop at the next meeting of Purely Aesthetic Fly Fishers Anonymous (PAFFA), but because having such a library and reading in it has become a great pleasure. Some of the reading is practical. Some of it, I think, will make me a wiser and more sensible fly fisher. But a whole lot of the reading I've been doing seems unable to make me anything of the sort. I love Percy Nobbs on salmon tactics I may never use, Alfred Ronalds on an entomology that does not apply to the waters I fish, George Kelson on salmon flies I'll never tie, and G. E. M. Skues, Frederic Halford, E. W. Harding, Huish Eddy, J. W. Dunne, Theodore Gordon, John Waller Hills, T. E. Pritt, Martin Mosely, and a raft of others on a whole host of matters piscatorial, only some of which might someday have the slightest practical upshot in my life.

Why?

I'm not quite sure.

I start with the pragmatic: it all is suddenly intensely interesting to me, this reading what serious men thought fifty or one hundred years ago and how they fished. Someone in the *Odyssey* says, "More news about Odysseus is always welcome." I guess I now feel that way about fly fishing, too; it all seems, happily, inexhaustible.

Perhaps, too, it's because no sport lives daily in its heritage more intimately than fly fishing does. When a trout rises to our no-hackle, we are linked instantly to a trout rising to one of Dame Juliana's flies, which also lacked hackle; our concerns for imitation, presentation, approach, trout behavior, propriety, good fellowship, and angling values grow out of and are yet linked to like concerns of fly fishermen who fished fifty, one hundred, and four hundred years ago. There has been change and innovation—and there is a magical constancy.

We love the *thingness* of fly fishing—its exquisite bamboo rods and old reels—even after we have happily taken to using the best new graphite and reels that rival watches in their sweet craftsmanship. We love flies that are minor miniature masterworks, the slightest change in whose architectonics has affected the sport of us all. I've heard a hundred times, as I'm handed a new fly, "This Rat-nosed Skunk will change your life." Museums like the American Museum of Fly Fishing have the ones that did.

We fish more meaningfully in the present if we understand and have protected the past, I guess—and fly fishing has an incomparably textured and richly diverse past. And if we know that past and love it, and the traditions and the breakers of tradition that have grown from its base, we inevitably want to protect them and the waters that make them possible. There is a subtle and seamless web that joins all life in rivers, and there is an equally complex web of relationships in the life and sport and mores of those who protect them.

The past plays not only an indispensable but also a joyous role.

The deeper I've fished backward, the more joyously, fully, I've been able to fish—even now, in the vortex of spring—as I careen downstream into the inescapable future.

39

THE COLLECTOR'S HOOK

Prudently, I've always tried to know my limitations: I'm addictive. I've long known that I shouldn't compound or feed my weakness by flirting either with salmon fishing or collecting. Both are expensive habits. Straight fly fishing, for trout and bass, is a pretty heavy habit the way I practice it. Quite heavy enough for me.

Library-building is different. For ten years I've tried to reconstitute a fly-fishing library that I had to cannibalize in the halcyon middle years of a family's history when there are too many mouths and hands; but I've done that as a reader, not a collector. I wanted a library, cheaply got, that I could use for reference, a group of books that would let me dip into Skues or Halford or Ronalds or Gordon or LaBranche or hundreds of others when fancy struck me; often I bought late reprint editions rather than the high-priced originals; the words were the same. I wasn't especially looking to build something that would appreciate in value, an investment, but something that would give me sustained pleasure. It does. It puts near at hand what I might otherwise need to spend a day or a month finding or borrowing; it expands, in the next room, and quite dramatically, the locus of the intense world of fly fishing in which I always live.

Over the last ten years I've probably acquired a thousand fly-fishing books—some from the mid–nineteenth century, a lot from England, a whole lot more from our time and place, which has spawned as many interesting fly-fishing books as any time in history. I've found them in Salvation Army shops, at garage sales, in the dark corners of junk stores, on book-remainder counters, and of course in the dozens of used-sporting-book catalogs I get each year. I've horse-traded with Ken Callahan and Judith Bowman, both excellent dealers, and I've managed to convert duplicates and books I just would never look at again into bits of gold, books that slowly add more color and texture to some design I'm after.

I've found some gems in the process: *Golden Days,* a perfectly extraordinary account by Romilly Fedden, an English painter, of his days living and fishing in France, just prior to World War I; *Where the Bright Waters Meet,* an ebullient, funny, and memorable account of days on the Bourne and other rivers by the British opera singer Harry Plunket-Greene; and another of those marvelously rich reports on a lifetime of fly fishing, *A Man May Fish,* by T. C.

Kingsmill-Moore, which ranks with Charles Ritz's *A Fly Fisher's Life,* the memoirs of Edward R. Hewitt and F. M. Halford, and a half-dozen other such personal accounts, to which I'm mildly addicted.

I have been after worlds and words, not profits; I'm investing in the fruit of the brain, the invisible coin. I've looked to build something satisfying and useful to me, and it's not at all what would be called a "collection."

Not that I don't admire several great collections by Englishmen and Americans I know: one of only editions of Walton, one of many tens of thousands of volumes that attempts to be complete even unto the multiple printings—first through thirtieth, perhaps—of important (and some much less important) books. But I am cut from coarser stuff—and I don't have the money to collect broadly and well. I acquire what I want to read and what I suspect I'll want to read again some day.

I'm the same with tackle. I want only what I will use, though my eye is still turned by a pretty piece of bamboo. I once had to sell a lot of bamboo and I still feel the pain of that when I remember a specific rod. And I still feel the pain of fly-fishing stuff I missed.

One weekend twenty-five years ago, Mari told me that she'd been browsing in a rummage shop earlier that week and had seen "a dozen tubes, like the ones in which you have your fly rods."

I raced to the shop and learned—of course—that they had been sold in their entirety the day before.

Did they have anything inside them? I asked the proprietor.

"Yeah, a lot of fish poles."

Made of . . . *wood?*

"Sure. Bamboo it's called. The guy bought them real fast."

Paynes? Dickersons? Gillums? Leonards? They could have been anything, or nothing, and periodically over the past couple of decades I've thought about them, and I've spent hundreds upon hundreds of hours at such shops, looking into corners, asking the same innocent question, over and over, "Any fishing stuff—books or rods?"

I often found books—a nice John Taintor Foote *A Wedding Gift;* a first-edition Flick *Streamside Guide* that, as a duplicate, I traded for a first-edition LaBranche and a Halford reprint; a couple of hundred lesser books, which filled in gaps or were fodder for trade; a mint Derrydale hunting book that I sold outright an hour later; dozens of books I skimmed and gave away. Not much. Not an awful lot to show for twenty-five years of odd browsing in musty junk shops in New York, London, New England, and Montana.

In twenty-five years I found not one rod in a tube, not one fly rod that was usable nor any other fly-fishing equipment I'd want to own. I was just beginning to think I'd better stop the whole process and never waste another ten minutes as a scavenger when a ratty guy opened a four-story junk shop in our neighborhood. Four stories' worth is a lot of junk—and each story was crammed to the gills with knick-knacks, household stuff, bric-a-brac, bad paintings, damaged skis, tens of thousands of books, and what-not else. It was the kind of store that looked like it was the final resting place of the lowest junk left from a dozen other junk shops that had sold off all their best wares. And you had to be careful with the proprietor. Nothing was marked for price; he made up numbers as he went along, often gauging the look in your eye, the cut of your clothes. Naturally I asked him, the first time in: "Got any fishing stuff—books perhaps, or rods?"

"You a collector?"

Years of experience dictated my answer. I had once told a street-fair dealer about first editions and the next time I came back, not recognizing me, he'd asked for triple what a common book was worth because: "It's a first edition." It's a cunning game out there. You've got to bargain hard—and dissemble. I told him with a laugh that I was just a guy who did some fishing and liked a good book about it now and then.

"Second floor, left side," he said.

There were some tubes, all right, and a dozen loose rods and reels, but nothing for a fly fisherman; I would have given three bucks for the batch. Mixed in with his tens of thousands of books I found a couple I'd have taken for five dollars; he wanted twenty; for one worth ten dollars he asked thirty-five. Ten times I went to his shop and that's all I found. It was hopeless.

Then one day as I was leaving he said: "I got a fish reel but I got to get a lot of money for it and it's saltwater. It's at my house. I can bring it in but I don't think it's what you're looking for. Made in New England somewhere, I think."

Since I'd turned down books in the twenty-dollar range, as "an awful lot of money," he had me pegged as a looker and niggler. But I said I'd look if he brought it in.

"It's expensive. I need seventy-five dollars for it."

"I'll have to see it first."

Four weeks later, after five or six calls to remind him to bring it in, I called him one morning and he had it there. He said some other guy had asked about it, too, and would be in that evening, so I rushed up during lunch hour and he brought it out.

"No bargaining. It's seventy-five bucks and that's it."

It was a Bogdan salmon reel, with a #9 saltwater taper on it, in a fine leather case, in mint condition, and it made the sweetest music as I turned the handle back and forth and plotted how not to blow the deal as I'd blown so many in the past. I didn't rush. I turned down my lips a little and shook my head slightly. I put it into the case and took it out again. I let him look into my eyes and see me think: "I don't really need this reel and it's not worth much money and it's saltwater, which I don't do much of, and he's asking an awful lot . . ." And then I couldn't stand my bad acting any more and took out the cash and took it off his hands.

I couldn't keep my hands off the reel all day. I kept taking it out of its case all afternoon at work. I loved the delicate jeweled click of it. It would be perfect for salmon. It was made to be fished for salmon. It was as fine a reel as I'd ever want. I *loved* the thing. I wanted to use it that day, as soon as possible. I had a smile on as big as the Ritz.

And then I realized that I'd probably made a tragic mistake.

Hooked again.

I'd condemned myself to a powerful addiction I'd tried for years, desperately, to avoid.

Maybe two.

40

CROWDS

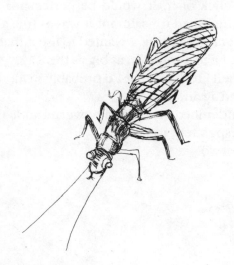

They're wonderful, I suppose, if you're selling something—from snake oil to books to religion to hard rock. And you can't have a political rally for the best—or worst—of causes without them. They are the fodder and the clout of revolutions, the pulse and chorus of great sporting events, comfort and protection for all those who are afraid to act except in concert. But have you ever heard a serious fly fisher sing their glory?

There is a bit of moving water, a few trout rising, and you. That's where all value begins in fly fishing. A bit of moving water, a few rising trout, and ten people are a bad joke.

In the past ten years or so we've seen a huge increase in the number of fly fishers everywhere. A lot of folk refer to ''The Movie'' as the greatest ambassador—or shill—for the sport, and perhaps, if we forget what the book stood for, it has been that. There are lots more books today, too, some of which sell in numbers not previously imagined—while other decent ones vanish simply because there are too many titles vying for attention, crowding the magazine reviews, tackle stores, and patience of anglers.

Fly fishing is also the subject of more and more fashionable ads—and even I (surely the adult with the least possible style or interest in it) have been asked by companies like Ralph Lauren for tips on how the upper end of the fly-fishing world attires itself for sport; I could only laugh uncontrollably and send them elsewhere. Rods and reels and lines are more efficient. Flies are more cunning, making entry-level work more manageable. And a lot of time has been spent to dress the newcomer in a happy uniform (pink waders for new women fly fishers go too far). Schools proliferate and are often filled to capacity. Newspapers like the *New York Times* have run front-page articles on salmon fishing in Russia and the growing number of women fly fishers. The cable television shows take us everywhere and with careful editing can make us think it's heaven on that mosquito-ridden little island . . . and even major news/essay programs think it's all important enough to carry a "segment."

Fly fishing is everywhere—even where we could not have dreamed it would go: parodies—in the *Boston Globe* and the *New Yorker*—of fishing memoirs; and a recent article in a women's magazine showing a batch of young, ruggedly handsome male fly-fishing guides, who are possible "catches" for the young, bright, pretty women who read that rag.

Lots of folks who have loved fly fishing for many years, and have wanted to share it, suddenly discover that the indifferent neighbor now can't get enough of it. And the parameters continue to grow—with the emergence of great travel agencies that explore the world, finding new possibilities in New Zealand, the Pacific, Africa, Russia, and where-not else. "It looks like so much fun," a young friend told me recently. "Will you teach me?" I hesitated.

My friend Steven Meyers, in his *San Juan River Chronicle,* speaks of it as "a river in danger of being loved to death."

And there, on a specific river, is where the problem comes home hardest: will it bear all the love we want to crowd upon it?

Anyone who's fished for a substantial time—I'm beyond fifty years now—continues to feel that steady, inescapable erosion of waters known earlier.

I fished a river two hours from New York a hundred times in my childhood—a back section, meandering from a hillside under a trail trestle, through a broad meadow, making a few sharp turns, and then sliding past a small town. It was a stream uniformly some sixty feet across, with deep water in all but a few spots, soft undercut banks, hundreds of deadfalls. It was never an easy river to fish, because the bordering trees threw a low canopy across it, you could only wade the edges, and it was always slightly discolored from its movements through farm country. But there were five miles of it that I fished, and it always stunned me with its surprises: once, the largest trout I've ever taken in the East—a five- or six-pound brown. Because the water wasn't easy to fish and because it had superb cover with the tangled branches of the deadfalls, the river produced a large number of outsized brooks and browns—and few people fished it after mid-April. I did a number of times and never caught a lot of fish—but I always caught or raised a few tortugas. I went back to it five years ago and found in the meadow no fewer than three or four hundred small houses, all looking pretty much the same. I haven't seen it since.

Mostly it has been the raw need (or greed) for some places to develop, or pollute, that has wrecked the waters I love—but increasingly it's the sheer number of fly fishers.

There is a bridge over a western river near where I used to park some years ago. The water was tough, heavy, but it held very good trout, and a lot of them. I fished it ten or fifteen times when I was the only person in sight, and then, as the years went on, I found other spots. One day recently I went back with Mari, who wanted to paint there, and my son Paul, with whom I wanted to share this exceptional sport, and I could barely control my rage—they thought I'd gone berserk or gotten bitten by a wasp—when I came over the hill and looked down to the bridge: there were no fewer than seventy or eighty cars there. I've never fished it since.

I can remember a dozen places—far back through weed, swamp, bramble patches—where a particular confluence of currents, a bend in the river, and a bottom dug out by the force of the flow combined to create a true "honey hole," a place bound to contain fish—a place that, time after time, *did* hold good fish.

If you fuss around rivers long enough, you find a lot of places like this, often just a bit farther from roads and access points than most folks care to go. You break through the tangle of brush one day by chance—after a dozen fruitless forays, searching—and discover a secret garden that rewards you with remarkable riches. You go back—the same thing. And then, as the entire river gets more pressure, you make the same unpleasant hour-long trek through the swamp that eats waders—get bitten by mosquitos, have your net catch on brush and thorns and then slam into your back, lose a box of your best flies and the whole contraption that holds clippers, fly dope, hemostat—and you find there are four lunatics there. They are fishing hard, wading in the wrong places, shouting over the sound of the water, spooking fish, and pounding the water to a fine frenzy. And you never have the heart to go back.

Or it's a spot to which you must wade through dangerous waters, for half an hour, and when you brave it this time and lift your head, you see that a Mckenzie boat has just lightly deposited two anglers exactly on the bar from which you have always fished.

Home waters become everyone's waters; a favorite spot becomes a public meeting place; and you feel tugged to hunt a receding *new*, or as several old friends have done, just stop. Give it up. Leave the field. One took up golf and loves it. ''The crowds just got to be too much,'' he told me.

Some new people will come into the sport and drift away; a lot will stay. I wish I could see some change in sight—but I'm a Jeremiah about crowds. Look at Cairns Pool on the Beaverkill, Buffalo Ford on the Yellowstone, the traffic at Varney Bridge when Mr. Salmonfly has arrived—any of us could name a couple of dozen more.

The crowds will only increase, I'm afraid. We'll have to start thinking hard about some difficult, unpleasant options: exerting ourselves a lot more to avoid crowds, limiting access, finding or saving more water, and demanding of our new colleagues—before they enter a river—a bit more toilet training.

If you love fly fishing—as I do—we'll do all of the above, and more.

41

MEAN STREAMS

There seems to be a throbbing vein of mean feeling in the body politic of fly fishing these days. Joe doesn't like Yuppies polluting his fly-fishing ambience with too much equipment and ineptitude, too many Porsches and chic-chic buzz words. L. Harry Jones IV resents being called a Yuppie, and he can get along with as little equipment as Joe, catch more fish any day, and talk straight. George doesn't think it's fly fishing if you use a fly larger than a #16, and of course the thing it imitates must be a fly, not a salmon egg or an upstream-swimming mashed potato.

Sperm flies, for some, are definitely out; #22 *Tricorythodes* are definitely in.

Jimmy thinks lead and leadcore line are just peachy and he's not about to let anyone tell *him* how he can or can't fly fish. It's a free country.

Some snicker at graphite. Some snicker at antiquated bamboo—long on tradition, short on practicality.

Some snicker if you don't know Latin. Some snicker if you use very much Latin at all.

Some think a body made of the urine-stained underbelly of a vixen is ridiculous; some think such subtlety is the heart of fly tying.

Sam looks meanly at those who throw back fish and insist that he do so. Walt thinks that Sam isn't just "primitive" in his thinking but Luciferian, bent on destroying our rivers forever.

Frank scowls when I show him the Lyons Super-Flex Leader—one of the more brilliant innovations of the past twenty years—though I am perfectly content that the LSFL is (a) perfectly moral, (b) easy as pie to cast, (c) aesthetically pleasing, and (d) quite capable of making me—justifiably—rich and famous.

So I'm naturally a little miffed that anyone could be so limited in his vision as to find me limited in mine, and to look down at what I consider my obvious genius.

Unrecognized genius, either on the local or national level, always breeds bitterness. We're all quite convinced of our remarkable skills and bewildered that others—who don't know us as intimately as we know ourselves—don't see this. The author of a book that pushed still another new and revolutionary concept of fly fishing was sorely rubbed the wrong way when a reviewer found the book pedestrian, and the innovation less than revolutionary. He challenged the reviewer to a "fish-out" on the OK Madison River—more trout in three hours, or retraction—which the reviewer quietly refused.

I've gone on record myself, a number of times, as disdaining those more formal and public competitions, which continue to proliferate and are as popular as popcorn. Some defenders of these events—of one stripe or another—have thought me a Neanderthal, unable to see the great social, conservation, or other benefits in those events. I'm afraid I don't. I can be quite mean on the subject.

Sometimes the harshness is devoted to the skill—or lack of skill—in competitors, in public or private competitions. Someone who saw himself as Art Flick's rival once asked me—with dead seriousness and a sharp sense of irony—whether I'd actually ever seen Flick catch a trout. Well, yes, I had seen him catch a lot of them, as it happened: big ones, small ones, when everyone else was catching them, when no one else was catching them. Even I get a few fish sometimes.

So long as there are two serious fly fishers in the same room, there will no doubt always be controversy concerning a whole host of matters piscatorial. We fly fishers seem to be the most contentious of anglers, no matter what Izaak Walton observed. Since catching the most fish is generally not the measure of things, we always have lots to contend—including the seventy-three different casting styles, the best knot with which to tie on a fly, the most practical way to spin deer hair, the most effective dry-fly technology for spring creek fishing.

And why not?

Some of it is delightful fun. Some quarrels help us understand the possibilities of the sport better, some quarrels are the flag of our seriousness, and some seem to me merely mean or silly. And still others are exciting exercises in knowledge and logic; I'd have loved to hear G. E. M. Skues and Frederic Halford discuss dry flies *vs.* wet flies—morally, aesthetically, practically.

Usually I bend forward and listen patiently to the worst of the harsh feeling and the most profound of the serious discussion, hoping to improve myself, become a better person and fly fisher. This isn't easy for a flawed specimen: and often I don't even understand the controversy adequately. Sometimes the thicket becomes so tangled and overgrown that I cannot extricate myself, find the positions blurring, want to refer to such authorities as Maimonides' *Guide for the Perplexed* or Walter Hilton's *The Ladder of Perfection,* for counsel, or McClane's encyclopedia or that sage Edward G. Zern. Before long—since I am mercurial and easily persuaded by pitchmen and cold-callers alike—my lower lip trembles in sympathy with one passionate position, my ear twitches in anger at another.

Some of these seem to me important issues. Take this throwing back of fish that seems to anger so many people, who feel their freedom pinched by it. I don't think I'm a higher-type person if I throw back fish; I'm certainly not sanctimonious about my decision to do so. And I know that some of the fish will die, or refuse to take the fly again. But I can't get these simple facts out of my head: there's some awfully good fishing in some rivers, like sections of the Madison, where people have been throwing back fish for a decade—and if I kill a fish it *definitely* won't live. I happen to like to eat trout, and I have no trouble cleaning them; I just like seeing one come to my fly a whole lot better than all of the above. It's that simple.

Certainly it isn't snobbishness. People who like to kill fish ought to be thrilled, in fact, that I throw them back, since this means more trout for them—while their point of view means fewer for both of us.

"Why do you worry about all that stuff?" asks Mari. We're in the off-season and she sees me pacing the living room like a caged panther, stepping lightly amid the chaos of all the equipment I've laid out, some of which I was preparing to unload this year, in deference to some of my new theories.

Well, I don't most of the time; but I've sort of gotten myself into certain preferences when I fly fish, which is mostly because they're more fun for me and because I don't go fly fishing to make it seem too much like KP duty in basic training. Robert Frost, arguing for some discipline and form in poetry, said, "Writing free verse is like playing tennis with the net down." I don't suppose tennis would be much of a challenge that way, even an absurdity. Nor do I think a net that was *too* high would be much fun; you'd never get the ball properly into the playing court. It's the precise balance that we establish which gives us the most pleasure, I think— and since I've finally revealed myself as a shameless hedonist I must admit that "most pleasure" is what I'm usually after, not—as Mari thinks—sunstroke, hypothermia, exhaustion, pneumonia, and endless talk about inconsequential theories.

So I raise and lower the net periodically, fuss with my goals and values as much as I do with my sixty-seven boxes of flies, cut this, add that, learn another kind of cast to enhance my repertoire of three, try to keep learning a bit more, try to keep my windows open to new experience, try not to fall in so often, try not to covet or eschew my neighbor's theory too fiercely, try to keep hooks out of my ears, my neck, and my pride, and not wade too often in mean streams, unless they're directed toward those who would destroy our rivers.

Yeats says, in "A Prayer for My Daughter," that he hopes she won't begin a quarrel *except in merriment*.

Let's have all the quarrels and controversies we can summon—but let's also try, fellas, to keep them merry.

42

MIDSPRING AFTERNOON
DREAMS

John Randolph is telling me, on the telephone, about a theory of matching the fly design to the water type and I am doodling on some company stationery the rough forms of various dry flies. Full-hackled flies for the broken water at the head of the run; thorax flies for the chop that ambles down the middle, as the water flattens a bit; no-hackles, comparaduns, parachutes for the slick slower water in the tail—it all makes sense and I tell John so.

As we talk, I think about some pools and runs I know pretty well, and how the theory has held on them in the past and would hold on other similar pools, and how matching hatches is a great pleasure but how many other factors also come into play, like presentation, knowledge of water, water type.

It's a midspring afternoon and I lean back on my tippy chair, turn from the papers on my desk, and look out toward the looming Empire State Building, a dozen blocks north, and beyond. It is a happy office, I think, filled with good cheer and a whole lot of books and some manuscripts wanting to become books, and mounts of flies by Dick Talleur and Del Mazza and Skip Morris on the walls and shelves, and some new patterns (with a fishy look) by a new young friend named Tatsuhiro Saido, and there are a lot of prints and etchings by Dave Whitlock and Gordon Allen and Joe Fornelli and Bob White, and a rod I just bought by mail and a few books I just traded for, and a lot of light that floods into the big old loft, reminding me now that it is high spring. It's not so tough a place to spend one's days and make one's bread, and I happen to love it here, but I still haven't been out on the water.

John and I talk about some tiers we know and what they've brought to our knowledge of fly design, and how pleasant it is in a world a little too full of madness, avarice, greed, violence, ignorance, disloyalty, and suchlike to worry about the precise architectonics of a fur-and-feathered thing built to gull trout, a thing smaller than an early pea.

But it's too pretty a day to have heavy thoughts so when I hang up I merely remember the fly part of the equation and begin to dream of how I can become a genius and make a major contribution to fly tying myself.

Since I have four thumbs, I dream of founding the Barbershop School of Fly Dressing, members of which can— without damage—have ten thumbs. Only a week ago I was snipping away merrily in my living room on forty or fifty 1930s and 1940s flies tied much too full and with hackle that was far too soft. It wasn't unpleasant work. I had a couple of dozen greenish things, size #14, with a gold-ribbed body and an upswung tail. With the sharp points of a fine pair of surgical scissors I sculpted some really promising Green

Drake designs by clipping most of the under-hackle to expose the body and wing silhouette, leaving a clump for a thorax, thinning some of the hackle above to keep the thing from spinning when it was cast. I felt very proud of the results and went on to some overtied old-style wet flies that I handily converted into decent emergers by clipping the wing and thinning the soft hackle to some evocative strands. I hummed an aria from *The Barber of Seville.* I snipped with a grand bravado. And then I took some newer flies, conventionally hackled, and cut a defined "V" into their underside to expose the body more and create a thorax pattern.

By the time I was done, I realized that Lee Wulff had been talking about such clipping for more than a decade, Vince Marinaro (standing on the shoulders of some earlier guys) had talked about the thorax style I was now "creating," and Len Wright regularly scissor-tinkered with flies he tied himself.

Well, if it wasn't new and wasn't truly a Barbershop School of Fly Dressing (or Un-Dressing), at least the flies I'd barbered (a few looked like they'd been barbecued) looked like they'd catch fish, which was much better than fleeting fame and glory and filthy lucre.

Catching fish seemed to me a better thing to dream about on a bright spring afternoon so I began to think of rivers I knew and, like the young man in Hemingway's "Now I Lay Me," I began to fish them in my mind, all the slicks and runs and riffles of a half-dozen rivers I knew, from places where we usually started to places some varying distances upstream.

Some mail came and I looked at it all eagerly, hoping for a few fishing reports. Craig Mathews always puts weather conditions in the upper right-hand corner of his letters but there was no mail from West Yellowstone this time: just a few complaints, a couple of queries, a batch of bills, and a magazine from West Germany filled with beautiful photographs of trout and salmon.

Looking at one of the trout and the water from which it had come led me to think of a heavy piece of water out West that was all riffle, so I selected a bushy caddis, size #14, and began to fish it in my brain, quartering upstream and then fishing it almost directly upstream, close to the bank I hugged. Having very little imagination, I put fish and rises into my dream that I had once experienced, somewhere, mixing a few from England with a few from Montana, or remembering actual fish from actual runs on that big river I was fishing.

The dream bled over into my arm and I felt myself casting with a ruler, trying to reach ten or fifteen feet farther, where a nice brown was splash-rising. The fishing was quite real to me, full of intensity and clever strategies, and there were no deer flies to peck mercilessly at the backs of my hands.

Fishing up one run on a much smaller river I found that the fish rose more frequently to caddisflies with Mathews' strand of Sparkle Yarn for a tail—or trailing shuck—and I vowed to use that a lot more often this year, if the year ever started. Still, the year had been quite under way when John Randolph told me the fly-design-to-water-type theory, and it had been progressing quite nicely—thank you—since then.

I'd done all the shopping I needed to do—for a dozen seasons—in the madness of March: flies, leaders, new tippet material in all sizes, a new rod, a pair of hippers (in case I didn't lose enough weight to penetrate my old chest waders), a new #5 fly line. I was ready. I had been ready for months. What I was doing now was simply a little vicarious dreaming, and it all made me feel quite awake, though people kept appearing, dreamlike, before my desk with questions or announcements or bearing some kind of printed material that begged for my eye.

Then, outside my window, flush against the huge shape of the Empire State Building, a great hawk caught my eye, circled briefly, and then dropped like lightning toward a flurrying pigeon until the two simply disappeared behind a building.

It was a dramatic, palpable, wild, exciting, unreal thing, the kind of moment I'd had on rivers when a Catskill grouse thunders up suddenly from the underbrush, its wings a-whirr, as I march toward an upstream pool. I stood quickly and scanned the rooftops and above for the hawk. I looked where I had seen it last, below the rim of the building across the street.

Had the hawk caught the other bird?

I'd heard for years that there were hawks in the city but I'd never seen one. And, even along rivers, I'd never seen one swoop like this for a bird, though I'd once mistaken some sparrows that harried a hawk for its prey.

The event, of a stripe that more and more intrigues me near rivers, was gone in a flash—real and unreal—but clung in my memory, like a stark dream.

Two long-distance calls came for me and I slipped out of them deftly. The office day ended and the staff began to leave, one at a time, each checking in and saying good night. Finally, in the late midspring afternoon, the sky just slightly grayer and a touch of breeze feathering my face, I tidied all the remaining papers, breathed deeply, and tilted back in my chair. The windows on the Empire State Building glowed reddish. The air grew cooler. Some pigeons lit on a neighboring windowsill.

And then my brain, crammed to bursting, went back to its simple reveries—for I have never dreamed of exotic places I've never fished; New Zealand and Argentina are Zanzibar to me, and Christmas Island, Antartica. Videos don't help. My mind is not made that way. I was on a Catskill stream now, the intimate upper reaches of a river with a greater destiny ten miles downstream, and I was fishing a certain ledge pool I had not fished in more than half a dozen years. Four or five different flies were on the water—some freshly hatching, some in great swarms of other dancing spinners. The trout had risen high in the water and their dorsals were exposed, like the dorsals of sharks after prey. The fish were slurping steadily.

I chose a parachute for the slick, like John's theory, and put the fly down as I now could cast to such trout, not as I could, so clumsily, when I fished that river. A slurper came readily to the fly, my hand jerked up and knocked over a cup full of pens and pencils, and I went back quickly to the fish, which suddenly rocketed upstream and around a bend. I rushed after it, felt the throbbing pressure still at the end of the line—that telltale sensation we crave when a fish has gone into weed or brush and, for a moment, you've lost contact with it.

The fish was still on.

The line angled upstream perhaps eighty feet and the fish made a curled wake as it plowed through shallow water.

And then suddenly it was gone, all of it was gone.

43

WHAT I DID
LAST SUMMER

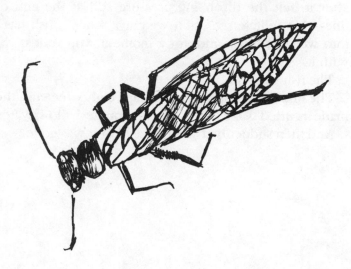

I always wrote best about that topic in high school. Condemned to the concrete of cities, the dust of dirt playgrounds, the fractions of sky and the absence, anywhere, of water, I craved the summer months and crammed them with days on the water. Septembers, with the summer months still fresh in eye and memory, I wrote only about water and fishing—though the eyes of my Brooklyn classmates glossed over when I read them about my pursuit of bluegill and bass, the charge of excitement I felt when a quick pickerel took.

During long summers away from the city, I became a demon rower, a deft caster of plugs and bait for largemouth bass, a hiker, an explorer, a bumbling but enthusiastic fly fisher for bluegill. Trout, in the part of the world where I lived and vacationed, were an early-spring fish. I made long exhausting trips for them in April—by subway, train, and thumb—and rarely thought of them thereafter, though I well remember a day the summer I was fourteen, when I hiked to a place called Bull's Bridge on the Housatonic River in Connecticut, and saw a trout of four or five pounds, in midwater, rise to the surface with amazing grace, take an unseen insect from the roof of its world, and change my life forever. After April, we generally fussed around in the salt water near Sheepshead Bay, for flounder, fluke, and (in the fall) snappers; during the summer we fished for any warm-water fare we could find.

I wrote about that rising trout but everyone's eyes still glazed over. In fact, I used it for the test you had to take to get into the creative writing class at Midwood High School— after all, any rising trout is a remarkable sight and this rising trout was a pivotal moment in my life—and I was one of three people who did not get into the class.

Lately, I have headed west in late June, or as soon thereafter as I could manage, and lingered there as long as I dared, or found ways and reasons to visit in August, September, as far into the fall as mid-October. Summers found me at Henry's Lake or a dozen places within a hundred miles of West Yellowstone—Mecca—growing more and more in love with a world I could not call home, a place I visited, vacationed in, fought to protect at the same time I let more and more people know it was there. We live with such Wildean ironies.

Sometimes, now, in my part of the world, I fish for trout in November, striped bass anytime in the fall, bluegill whenever I'm near them, bass whenever I can slip away to a certain New England lake. Fishing when you can, here and there, summer and increasingly in other seasons too, would not satisfy a lot of people I know. I know those who want to fish all the time, for every species, everywhere, at the expense of work and spouse and kids; those for whom fishing is chiefly a respite from unpleasant work; those for whom fly fishing is indeed a kind of religion, though religion and fly fishing are really two different cats; those who take to rivers to solve midlife crises and, waist deep in some remote waters, do something called "Find themselves." (Their memoirs might well begin, "In our family, there was no clear line between fly fishing and psychotherapy. . . .")

But I now like very much indeed what I do the rest of the year, and though I always think about fly fishing, I generally don't look to my days astream either for a spiritual uplift or psychic cleansing. I like it out there and I love the endlessly interesting and always different pursuit, but I try not to mistake it for something else. "What I did last summer," though, does become a memory that lasts all year, that goes through me like wine in water, coloring every part, that undergoes some sort of metamorphosis in me and becomes words and sentences, that I chew on throughout the winter, that fuels all my new year's hopes.

I took five full weeks of it in the West this past summer, more than I'd had in one dose since I was a kid and time was as inexhaustible as youth. I'd worked for it, my puritan brain advised me—and I was a bit worn and a bit past sixty. I don't need any excuses to go fly fishing but I do to take an extra week or two of it.

Last summer the East sweltered and suffered a lethal heat wave and major drought—and the Midwest nearly drowned. So I'm not complaining when I describe a month in which the Madison was mostly too high (except for the big black weighted nymph, which is always in season there); it rained wherever I traveled, it hailed when I floated, the lakes were roiled and choppy; and my spirits flagged. There were some consolations: a day on a spring creek when the Green Drakes were everywhere; a day when those helicopters, the giant stoneflies, were flying; a grizzly day in Yellowstone Park when the company was good and one of our party caught an outsized brown.

The house we'd rented came with about eighty feet of the headwaters of a spring creek. The water was very thin here, no more than four or five inches deep, and the fish scattered if you blinked; but there were eight or nine of them visible from the rickety bridge, finning restlessly, raising up a few inches now and then, in the morning and then again in the evening, to take some unseen insects from the surface. From our back porch I could see the barn swallows start to dance above the alley of the stream, and then I would leave whatever I was doing, walk down the hill, and watch the show. I watched the show a lot and plotted how to try them the second time, after having spooked them silly the first time I waded quietly upstream, sent waves before me, and scattered all of them into left field.

I remember fish others caught last summer, because I never fished hard: the sight of my son Paul's face when he told me about a twenty-inch brown he'd taken on a small grasshopper from a meadow creek we fished one day; Steve Olsen's big fish on the giant stonefly, which headed directly down the Madison and ran off all the backing before busting off; Craig's big brown on the Madison in the park; Paul's seventeen-incher from the Ruby, after we'd spotted and stalked it, changed flies, and he'd laid down exactly the proper cast; fishing for unbudgeable trout in a crystalline, shallow lake, with Bill and Andy, watching them take at least a trout each. I remember making a few new friends, like

Andy and Bill and Ted, fishing a few new waters, trying a float tube for the second time in ten years.

It was a cold and very wet five weeks, and one took pleasures where one could, while the rest of the country had greater problems. I was grateful when Lester came over from Big Sky with a couple of float tubes, the day before we headed back East. By the time we'd had a long breakfast and then explored here and there and then gotten some stockingfoot waders (because I idiotically thought to bring only those with boots), it was nearly ten o'clock. But the lake was flat as slate and there were fish rising. In fact, they were rising quite prettily, thank you—and close to where we'd parked. So I flip-flopped to the shoreline, backed into the water, sat down in my tube, nearly sank it, and pedaled out a few feet. On my third cast I hooked a good fish on a Parachute Adams, right where it had risen, and had it to the tube five minutes later. "Brown. Nineteen inches," I called to Lester. "Use the ruler on the tube," he called back. The fish was a fraction over seventeen inches.

We had a lovely hour or two and then the winds came up and it rained yet again, and we packed all the rest of the day and the next morning I stopped on the bridge over my spring creek for a last look. The fish were in midwater, making slight wakes as they moved left or right or upstream, taking a nymph or floating fly. I tried again to think of how I could get down there, in position, wave a fly line over that thin water, and take a fish—and came up short.

When I think of what I did last summer I think of my little spring creek, which I never fished a second time, and how I hadn't the slightest idea how those fish could be caught. Some people at least think of fish caught, fish that got away. None of it would have interested my fellow high school students, in the stony heart of Brooklyn—least of all *not* catching any of those fish.

44

RHYTHMS

There is a rhythm to each day we spend on a stream or lake or ocean, and a rhythm to each fishing year. And there is a discrete rhythm to every fly fisher's life—though it's rarely predictable. Mostly we're just too busy to notice all the patterns, though it's well to notice them.

The morning is bleak and barren; the Hendricksons come at 2:00 P.M.; the evening is graced by a short flight of caddisflies. The spring is early or late, wet or dry; the weed growth starts in June or as late as mid-July; the autumn is a gentle extension of summer or a dour early dose of winter. We're rhythmic, too, with our skills, for better or worse: from the backward and forward motions of casting to the three-plus-one-long-pull retrieve of a sunken fly in Henry's Lake to the stuttering stop-and-start action we give to a deer-hair popper, drawing it toward the boat from a shoreline smoky with mist. Our fingers and teeth, in practiced unison, make a barrel knot. Our feet take a measured, rhythmic pace—keyed to the needs of the river—as we shuffle tentatively through the dangerous rush of the Madison, with its rocks like greased bowling balls, or stealthily into the delicate glides of the East Branch.

Take a day in early summer, which I'll take any time I can catch one. I'm up at 7:00, packed and over at Lester's house by 8:00. He's finished his coffee, so we promptly pile all of my gear on top of his, already in his station wagon, and settle into the two-hour drive from Big Sky to Idaho. The time, locked in the car with a good friend, is very satisfying: we talk trout; we talk about our lives; we talk business—talk that has a rhythm of its own.

We're at the Henry's Fork by 10:00, but the flats below Island Park look crowded and unproductive; anyhow, Lester has heard a rumor that the fishing has been poor. Probably because the water looks very low. Low. A sign. This means, Lester tells me, that a stretch of water he knows might, just might, be dynamite.

This seems a slim prospect, but as we drive back upriver toward Montana I feel a certain rhythm developing for the day—and a certain glimmer of expectation, especially when Lester feeds it by telling me the textured details of that day when that upper stretch toward which we're headed *was* indeed dynamite. And Lester never lies. We had expected a certain kind of fishing on the flat water, but low water changed the rhythm. That upper stretch, above the Box Canyon, sounds more and more like the proper bet. We've made a commitment to the Henry's Fork, and the new option is at least worth a try.

Two hours later we realize that it was well worth the try. In fact, we've hit it just right. It's been every bit of the "dynamite" we could have wanted. Better, the fishing continues, only slightly more sporadically, for another couple of hours. And then on the long trip back, tired, faces aglow, we can't stop talking about this fish or that, about numbers of fish caught and their sizes, about entomology, about the possibility of returning the next day. And then we're back. It's dark. We're tired and full of smiles, and the day is done.

The rhythms of our lives and of our fishing lives are infinitely varied—and always tangle and overlap. We come to our water, sometimes from alien lives in cities, offices, classrooms, farms, assembly lines, places where there are other rhythms—not lesser or less important to us but different, as skyscrapers, magnificent as they can be, are different from mountains. Sometimes we come seeking excitement or challenge from the sport, sometimes respite. Often we come to water with what we happen to be at a particular moment in our lives—hurried, harried, patient, still. Or we come with a particular level of skill or development as a fly fisher, or when the river is fecund or barren.

Fresh from spinning, I came to fly fishing in my early twenties with a need to impose my rhythms on the sport. I fished a lot of water as if I were competing in an upstream wading race. Because I fished hard and because I had fished from virtual infancy, I often caught my share of fish. But I missed a lot; I understood very little; and all of the best fish were well beyond my primitive skills and methods.

There seemed at first so much to learn—casting, entomology, fly choice, knots, rod action, wading techniques, even rhythm, even some happy way to fish that would include my wife, a painter who had no interest in fishing.

Then slowly it all began to work. Steadily, I see now, I kept learning and refining my practice of the sport—though punctuated by some minor disasters, for comic relief. And eventually I found that sweet still place which is the thing itself done the way I wanted to do it, mostly alone, with just me and a piece of water and perhaps a good fish rising, with some problems to solve before the fish would come to play, and with more and more skills for my part of the game.

Eight years ago I began to fish a difficult spring creek—a river that baffled, taxed, and then reluctantly began to reward me with some of its most difficult denizens, as my skills grew, my rhythms grew wiser. Last summer, for several weeks, I could do no wrong on it. The Green Drake was on for most of the time and that gave the middle hours of every day a dramatic presence. The Pale Morning Duns were sparse, but the caddis were there—and Craig Mathews' X-Caddis, with mottled deer-hair wings, was exactly the right medicine. And my wife had fallen quite in love with the landscape surrounding the river and could not be pulled away from it, even after I'd had my fill, which was sooner than usual.

One bleak evening I decided to stay up at the ranch, but Mari insisted we head down to the river. It was raining off to the south, quite heavily, and it was cloudy and cold where we were. So I picked an easy place to park and stayed in the car, grateful for the warmth.

"Aren't you going out?" Mari asked. She had already started a watercolor that began, I could see, with the stream at our feet and ended ten miles to the east, with a ragged mountain range.

"It's cold," I said.

"Sissy," she said.

"I'll go out when I see something rise."

"Sure you will," she said.

Rather than contend with all the superior irony, I stepped out, fortified myself with an extra sweater, and waded into the shallows. This was a broad flat stretch, perhaps the toughest on the river, and I'd always been thrilled to move a good fish here. There was nothing moving now—and a steady if modest rain had reached us, blocking most of the light; so I stood quietly, eyes peeled to the surface, and sort of hoped the weather would get better or worse. It was sense-less to cast without seeing a fish, and there was nothing showing on the slate expanse. If the rain got even a bit heavier, I'd have a good excuse to head back to the car. But the weather stayed exactly the same; it was determined to remain cold, wet, grizzly, but not quite impossible.

"Look at that!" I heard Mari call.

I looked out into the flat and saw a snout high above the surface, popping up and then dipping under every few moments. "Muskrat," I called.

"No, *there!*" And I turned to see where she was pointing. It was a rainbow, arced over the mountain range to the east, as sharply defined, complete, and bright as any rainbow I'd ever seen. I nodded but looked back at once to where I'd seen the muskrat. No, it was coming up too regularly in exactly the same spot; it had to be a big brown that had lost all caution. I glanced at the water and saw two spent cad-disflies drift slowly past me.

So I clipped off the hopper I'd been tossing that afternoon, tied on nearly three feet of 6X tippet, slowly added the X-Caddis and tested the knot, and made one cast a couple of feet above the rising trout. It was an easy cast of some fifty feet, but I later realized that it had taken me thirty years to make it—for it was low and accurate, with just enough slack for the fly to float without drag onto the dining table of that trout, and I had positioned myself in exactly the right spot to make it. The fly and the leader and the stiff rod helped, too.

The fish, lost in its bacchanalian feast, took the fly readily, with a smacking of its lips, and ten minutes later I had it on its side, below me. It had not jumped; it had not fought in any spectacular fashion; but it had made heavy deliberate runs, and I had fought it well.

I looked down at the remarkable fish—by far the largest I'd ever caught on a dry fly, in excellent condition, perhaps eight or nine pounds' worth of brown trout—and then held it briefly above my head, between the car and the rainbow, for Mari to see. Usually disinterested in what I catch, she shouted with glee—and then I put the great trout back into its element, held its tail for five minutes, and watched it waver out of sight.

Before we headed back to the ranch I looked at what Mari had caught. She'd had a hot hand: three watercolors and a pencil sketch. We both smiled. She marveled that the rainbow had stayed so long, was so clear. She congratulated me on my great trout. We smiled all the way back to the ranch. It was raining sheets and tracer bullets, and I had to go slowly on the rutted and pitted dirt road, but that didn't matter. I was in no hurry. I was in absolutely no rush to get anywhere at all.

45

THE ANTIC ANGLER

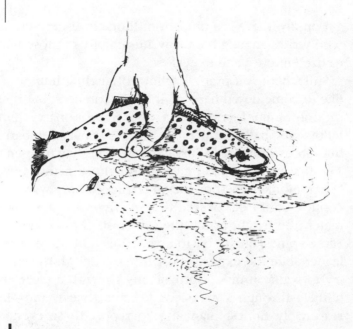

In Ed Zern's "How to Write Funny Stuff About Fishing," an assignment editor at a large general-interest magazine tells him: "I'm not a fisherman myself, but I know that fishing has some very humorous aspects. For example, the fisherman who gets his fly caught in a tree and has to climb up and fetch it down."

Ed says that the business of the fly in the tree has been done before and seems to him rather on the trite side—like the fisherman falling into the stream.

"Wonderful!" says the assignment editor. "By all means, have a fisherman falling into the stream."

Ed asks if the editor has ever himself, in his own person, fallen into an icy-cold river, which ain't funny, and is advised that the magazine has ten million readers and that what is obvious to him, with his specialized experience, is not at all obvious to them—and they'd like flies in the trees and fallings-in.

Happily, there are not ten million fly fishermen, and he who writes angling humor writes chiefly to those with specialized interest and experience.

Still, there *is* a pratfall school of angling humor, and I'd like to come down hard on it for its triteness, but it's about the only humor I write. I am a sober and reasonably humorless fellow who has tried all of his life to stay out of embarrassing, humorous situations at my expense. But they happen to me. The first college class I taught brought so many laughs that for a moment I thought my true calling was stand-up comic—until I discovered that my fly was open. I still mismatch the hatch, botch the backcast, fish for trout in the Scotch pines, fall in, try to invent Roach flies and Super-Flex leaders like the experts, bust things, stick things in myself, try to walk on mud, burn off my fly with a cigar and fish blithely through a manic dusk hatch flyless, and—being a reasonably honest man—try to report these events accurately. I raised, hooked, and caught a big brown on the first cast last summer and my companion told me I'd blown my cover: I was really quite adept. I told him to wait a few minutes, then promptly stepped three feet into a muskrat hole and came up with my face plastered with mud.

Sometimes the humor comes in patches, in otherwise serious books, and is only north-by-northwest hooked to fishing. There's a marvelously funny scene in *A River Runs Through It* where the narrator and his brother come upon a strange sight: two bare asses in the middle of the Big Blackfoot River. They vow never to fish in this area again, it having become a kind of wild game sanctuary. (Sadly, the movie brushes right past this delicious moment.) And there's a hilarious scene in *Fishing Came First* when a teenage John Cole blends the language of a miraculous day fishing, with its sand eels and blowfish, with some heavy necking that evening in a Montauk Point parking lot.

Some angling humor uses inside jokes based on specialized knowledge of everything from road kills to 8X leaders, and in it fly fishermen are often laughing at themselves with a kind of humor that is self-correcting, self-approving, and funny all at once. Only fly fishermen would laugh at images of hatches of upstream-swimming nightcrawlers, mating girdlebugs, girdlebug spinners, the dangers of drag explained in terms of a steak moving unnaturally on a plate, or Sparse fishing with a chunk of rye bread soaked in scotch, and a big brown reeled in, stewed out of its mind. Only fly fishermen could understand the special meanings of words like nymph, fast action, bulging, Bitch Creek, Princess, Nylorfi, riffling hitch, wet fly, butt, tippet, and a thousand other such terms. What lunatics we must sound like to the uninitiated. And we often wonder why the uninitiated don't laugh at our jokes.

Fishing humor exploits laconic wit, buffoonery, slapstick, surprise, the bizarre, satire, the fish tale, and a large measure of hyperbole. Ed Zern, as usual, makes the best sense of hyperbole in angling.

"I make it a rule," he writes in *Are Fishermen Liars?*, "never to weigh or measure a fish I've caught but simply to estimate its dimensions as accurately as possible and then, when telling about it, to improve those figures by roughly 20 percent. I do this mainly because most people believe fishermen exaggerate by at least 20 percent. Thus, if I catch a four-pound brown on a #16 Adams in the Madison, I tell my friend Dubious Dave, 'Dave, I took a five-pound brown on a #18

Adams just below Varney Bridge last week.' Dave thinks to himself, 'In that fast heavy water this klutz couldn't handle a five-pound brown on a #18. It was probably a four-pounder, if that—and like as not it wasn't a #18 but a #16 or a #14.' 'Say, that's great!' Dave says. 'Let me tell you about the 21-inch rainbow I took out of the Big Hole three weeks ago on a 6X leader.' I instantly mark Dave's rainbow down to 18 inches, beef up the leader to 4X, and say, 'Wow! Tell me about it.' Thus we both come away with a fairly accurate understanding of who caught what, nobody is injured, and life goes on.''

"I get all the truth I need from the newspaper every morning," Ed says. "I go fishing to get the taste of it out of my mouth."

There is hyperbole, too, but of a somewhat different order, when a guide tells me that a nice 15-inch rainbow one of his famous fishing-writer clients caught on the Madison, and returned, grew exactly 4½ inches during the trip from Ennis back to West Yellowstone—and is probably still a growing boy.

We laugh at the same time we recognize the depth of his passion when, at eighty-three, Charles Ritz tells me at lunch: "Fly fishing in salt water is for men with hard stomachs—like sex after lunch"—though when, in a recent television documentary, he is reported to have said, "Germans come and go, but fly fishing is forever," we are offended by the trivialization of the Nazi occupation of France. But we recognize the cunning knowledge of the fly-fishing passion in a cartoon by John Troy that depicts a dozen survivors in a lifeboat pleading with the man in the prow, fly casting vigorously into twenty-foot waves: "For the love of God, man, switch to wets, they'll never rise in seas like this."

Brevity, surprise, and impeccable word choices are the heart of fishing wit, much as they are in Thurber, Woody Allen, or S. J. Perelman. Zern says that "Fishermen are born honest, but they get over it." Arnold Gingrich once told me that he had caught 33 inches worth of trout—in six installments.

Sometimes humor becomes an important corrective in that it satirizes that which is pompous, overserious, inept. When Lefty asks if I've heard that a certain fly-fishing writer is in the hospital, and I play straight man and say that I haven't, and he reports that the fellow was walking his dog on the lake and got hit by a motor boat, we get an important brand of ego-puncturing. When Mr. Theodore Castwell, in the G. E. M. Skues story, catches fish after fish, each exactly the same size, on every cast, he (and we) realizes he's not in heaven but in the bad place—and one of our great fly-fishing illusions is punctured, too.

One of the most interesting forms of angling humor is the fish tale, with its complications, surprise reversals, abrupt denouement (like that in Chaucer's "The Miller's Tale"). One of the best—yet again—is Ed Zern's wonderful "Something Was Fishy About Stonehenge," in which Ed discovers that a Mr. Smythe-Preston has been catching hecatombs of trout while everyone else goes fishless. In a moment of desperation, Ed decides to give Smythe-Preston "truth serum" in pill form, and when he does, three pills' worth, the Englishman spills that Stonehenge is really a remarkable fishing calendar, a megalithic solunar table, and that at sunup, by observing where the sun's rays strike, you can tell precisely, "virtually to the split second," when trout will be "voraciously, passionately, uncontrollably on the feed." Ed can't wait to get the precise formula for reading this calendar, which will be revealed to him the next morning. The tale ends when, on the morning he was supposed to meet Smythe-Preston, he learns that the poor man has been killed by his wife that very night—and now will never be able to tell what he has learned about Stonehenge. Zern's last line is: "I suppose I shouldn't have used the third pill."

Ed is in a rest home now and I miss him, and I'm sad to think that there will be no more stories, no more wit from this, the best of angling humorists, ever. Several years ago, in the throes of Parkinson's, he told me that the disease wasn't so bad: "It's improved my 'S' cast." And then, the last time I spoke to him, he mentioned that he was taking some new medicine. When I asked how it worked, he said that it gave him hallucinations. "But that's not so bad," he added. "It's introduced me to a lot of interesting new people."

If angling humor makes us see ourselves and our passion more clearly, if it makes us laugh at our passion and our foibles, it is also, sometimes, a flag of our courage.

46

HUMANITY: A TO ZERN

When Ed Zern died in March, I felt relieved, not shocked—for he'd had a rough couple of years and at a certain time I suppose it's what passes for a blessing, to leave all at once, not inchmeal. Sandra, his longtime companion, told me that when they wheeled him out of the rest home and headed for the hospital, he asked the nurse where he was going; the nurse said, "On a fishing trip, Ed." He slipped into his last coma a short time later.

"Blessing" it may be, but I miss him. Mostly I regret I didn't know him well enough, that I hadn't met him sooner. I didn't see him face-to-face until he was in his seventies, and though we never got anywhere near moving water together, I realized at once that I had been fishing with Ed since I read those first marvelous books of his, *To Hell with Fishing, How to Tell Fish from Fishermen, How to Catch Fishermen,* and *Are Fishermen People?* I trolled a Johnson Silver Minnow down Fifth Avenue with him from one of those old double-decker buses; I learned the "difference between big-game fishing and collecting millstones" (millstones aren't slimy); I recognized the truth in "fishermen are born honest, but they get over it"; and I knew he was right when he jostled the notion of proper imitation of a trout-stream insect by reminding us of that black, curved thing under the artificial's body. I dreamt with him about constructing, in this great dry city, the World's First Indoor Trout Stream—and modified that, *without credit,* when I wrote my first article for *Fly Fisherman,* twenty-five years ago, about stocking the fountains and their pools throughout New York.

He gave me the first alternative slant on Izaak Walton, whom I'd always admired—from a great distance, and predicated on the simple truth that I'd read only some scattered quotes, not all about Piscator, Venator, and the Milkmaids. Ed advises, in "The Truth About Izaak Walton," that the book "has nothing whatsoever to do with fish or fishing. It is, in every detail, a turbidly political allegory intended not for the amusement or instruction of anglers but simply for the advancement of the Caroline cause and the confusion of the forces of Cromwell." His brilliant review of *Lady Chatterley's Lover* taught me that this infamous book was in fact a "fictional account of the day-to-day life of an English gamekeeper" and contained "many passages on pheasant raising, the apprehending of poachers, ways of controlling vermin, and other chores and duties of the professional gamekeeper"—though unfortunately it was filled with "extraneous material" and would never replace J. R. Miller's *Practical Gamekeeping.* Half a dozen readers of *Field & Stream* wrote in that they'd like to know where to buy the Miller book; Admiral Rickover, thinking it was serious, liked to quote it—until told otherwise; and it was reprinted in a half-dozen places, for one purpose or another.

Then, putting together an anthology (*Fisherman's Bounty*) some twenty-five years ago, I met another Zern. I'd wanted to use the delicious "Something Was Fishy About Stonehenge," but Ed said it had first appeared in *Sports Illustrated* and they wanted to see it in an anthology of their own. Why not use "A Day's Fishing, 1948"? he asked me. I'd never heard of it. In fact, its only publication had been in a Theodore Gordon Flyfishers' magazine a few years earlier. Ed said then, and repeated it to me a couple of decades later, that it was his favorite story.

I read it quickly when I opened his letter. It had none of the quick wit, the improbable imagination, the reversals, and the unexpected that I had grown to admire. I put it down and didn't circle back to it for a week.

It was a quiet story about a quiet day's fishing, and its wit was of a different order: that of a wise and gentle human being who loved sport and had the greatest regard for privacy and that connectedness we call friendship.

Ed is fishing in the Adirondacks one summer, and the fishing in the "name" rivers is poor. "There are few things deader," he observes, "than a dead brown-trout stream." So, in that rambling, chancy way in which we sometimes discover the best water—and much else that is important in life—he asks questions, pursues a hint or two, and is led to the place, ninety miles away, of a man named Thompson, "a queer bird" in his seventies, a widower who fishes not at all. "If there's ever an unpopularity contest in this county," his informant tells him, "he'll win it hands down."

Ed meets Thompson and frankly owns up to his informant's description of what will take place: "He told me if you liked my looks, you'd let me go through the place to the river, and if you didn't, you wouldn't." Thompson looks him over with folded arms for a few moments and then curtly says he'll show him the way to the river. Would Thompson like a few trout to eat? Silence—then, a hundred paces later, "I guess I could use some. If they're cleaned."

The two paragraphs of actual fishing bring seven interesting rainbows and brookies and a lost larger fish. It is a day's fishing, what some of us still go to the river for. It is pleasant, rewarding, solitary, unsentimental, with a few happy surprises, and the river itself, with all its life, with no Latin and no tough chances—and it is memorable. It is sport stripped of its pretensions and aggrandizement; it is a simple thing, restorative, continuously interesting, an act caught in its own time; its pace is very different from the pace of the rest of the world.

And then he's back with Thompson, who, though reportedly "well-to-do," lives in a basic, even primitive fashion. Why does he use a dug well instead of a pump? "Had a pump once. It froze. This don't freeze."

Thompson brings out a chocolate cake, says, "There's cake." Ed waits to see if he means to "pursue the subject," then asks directly if he might have a slice of it. Was it cooked by a neighbor? "I do my own cooking," says Thompson. Does he fish? "Don't fish a-tall. Don't see the sense on it." But aren't trout pretty good eating? "Not that good. Not good enough to go traipsing up and down a river all day getting bit by black flies."

He asks if Ed has ever milked a cow, and Ed allows that he has—though poorly. Thompson says he'd known; he could tell a man who'd milked a cow. "Never missed a one."

And then they part, with Ed first asking if he could come back some day and Thompson saying, "I guess so," but it would have to be alone; he didn't want "all creation tramping across them fields." Then, when Ed is turning his car out of the driveway onto the road, Thompson calls, walks over, and says: "You can bring someone, if you want." Ed thanks him and says he'll be back the first chance he gets but will only bring someone who has milked a cow. He means to go back—but never does.

Nor, too often, do we.

We move on. We live in a transitory world. And that day, cut away from the rest, is a special jewel, all too often missed, all too often trivialized. Keeping it, sharing it, conserving it are at the heart of the man, who once said: "When the fishing goes, I'm willing to go, too."

In Ed's wit there is the best corrective lens with which to view our foibles and, by implication, the clearest sense of what our values might be. He anguished over the right word, the exact timing, the just balance, and he became the sharpest wit angling will ever know. There was no self-aggrandizement, and there was never the stasis of mere description. He loved his gear and his many fly boxes—but he did not celebrate them. People—humanity—are at the center of everything he wrote. The fishing gave him great pleasure, but Thompson gave him a connection to an unusual, improbable, uninviting, very human new friend.

When I think of Ed, as I've done a lot this past month or so, I think of that connection to Thompson, of Ed's great love of sport. I think that Ed was the best part of an older generation, now fading, now giving way to new voices—some splendid, some merely loud. We forget him at our peril. I never will. I surely won't see his like again.

A FIERCE PURSUIT BUT
NOT A CIRCUS

I loved nothing better in my teens than the fierce games of half-court basketball with George and Stanley, Ira and Herb at Wingate Field in Brooklyn. Hacked on the arms and neck, eyes dazzled by the sun and motion and the bright pavement, sweat everywhere, picking a guy off on the metal pole that held the basket, bruising a knee, splitting a lip, we used every last scrap of energy when we drove to the hoop. We came not only to play but to win. We loved the intense competition, and we loved to win. In fact, we *had* to win, for there were so many people waiting to play the winner that if we lost a game we could wait until midnight to get back onto the court.

That was a long time ago, more than sixty pounds ago, but even now, when the closest I get to the neighborhood courts are the green benches safely outside the fence, I crave that competitive music. The stately strategies of baseball, the brute force of a pigskin war, the lithe speed and crushing power of a great middleweight championship: I never miss the chance to see a minute of it.

I also fly fish. I always fly fish with passion, often fiercely, often for many more hours at a stretch than ever I played half-court. So I am startled to discover the ferocity of my contempt for fishing derbies, fishing competitions, fishing tournaments (local and international), tagged fish worth fortunes, fishing games of all kinds. There was one aired this morning on a local cable television station, and I sat dumbfounded once again, as I have a dozen times before at such an image, of all these men zooming off in high-speed boats, nose up, zapping bass for a day, and then returning to the mob on shore, weighing in their catch in plastic bags, accepting the honors. Competing with my neighbor (or a stranger, or a hundred strangers) in the pursuit of gamefish offends me to the marrow, and I'm not sure why.

Is there a difference between the football star (who may love to play the game) being well paid for his tackling or tossing and a master bass fisherman earning a couple of hundred grand for a good year's work? Is a day out on a party boat fluke fishing spoiled because someone will win "high hook" in the pool? Does the presence of a $100 or $100,000 or $500,000 bluefish swimming blithely in Long Island Sound contaminate, in some way, my fly rodding for blues or stripers along the shore, or anyone else's pleasure?

Frankly, I'd love to hook and land a fish larger even than my imagination could conjure; and some days, floating a Western river, I'll get so caught up in the movement of a Mckenzie riverboat and the shoreline and the transitoriness of the day that I'll fish monomaniacally, not wanting ever to stop, and friends will wonder if I've gone bats. On a given day, I can be a demon fisherman. On a given day, I can be a frighteningly intense pursuer of fish (usually the kind with spots, those that live in bright rivers). But I have never felt the faintest urge to compete while fishing, and have, in fact, stopped fishing when goaded into competing, or when I'd caught some fish and my partner hadn't. I've done that dozens of times. Even what's called "a little friendly competition" among fishermen interests me not at all. Let the golfers do it.

I find no connection between what those pro anglers do with their superbassboats and jumpsuits and starting guns and what I do when I drift down a weedy shoreline in an old wooden rowboat, Larry on the oars, me casting a big yellow hairbug methodically in against the deadfalls, lily pads, weedbeds, and coves. Maybe a bass will come for it, maybe one won't. Maybe the water will explode with a burst like a cherry bomb; maybe, when I twitch the line, expectantly, I'll just see the bug wiggle and blurp and wait. Maybe. Maybe the "maybes" help make it so enthralling. Or the fact that, with all the clocks in the world, what I do on that lake is at my own sweet pace, lazy or fierce, as I choose.

So long as the competitors release their fish safely, I can't see that much physical damage comes of their onslaught. In fact, some competitions raise money for conservation, which I'm for; and some build up our store of news about the fish we pursue, which is always welcome. But is that enough? As the tournaments grow in prominence and command more and more attention, as the winners become superstars and heroes and models, and the itch of the buck beats the itch to pursue, I keep wondering whether they're trading the quality of the sport for something quite extrinsic to it, whether they're fishing not for the inherent gifts of the activity but for those that come when the business of fishing is over—for winners sell more beer, more books, more subscriptions, more lures, and get well paid for all this.

I keep fearing that something I have always loved about fishing is being crowded out and lost. Bad money drives out the good; bad art drives out Cezanne; and I fear that the idea of these tournaments drives out an idea of fishing that is what first hooked most of us: the sheer love of the chase, coupled with our fascination with the technology of the sport, its gear and practice, the mysterious life of our quarry, the lush happiness of messing around near boats and water. Are we moving to a time when the pursuit of wild game will be a public spectacle or circus, not a private pursuit?

It just ain't why I go fly fishing.

For one thing, all that sounds too much like work. I may fish hard, but I never mistake it for what I do the rest of the time. I fish with Len or Larry or Bill or Sandy or Herb because I like to be with that person, or alone because I feel like simmering in my own juices that day. I may spend as much time looking at the mountain laurel and the rhododendron and the sun and the sunset as I do fishing, for I live where you see none of these things; or I may not, for I have come to fish and fly fishing anchors my eye on water and the life in and around it, and anchors my imagination because the challenge of a fishing problem can be an exquisite kind of pleasure.

Pleasure, fun—that's partly, even mostly, why I fish. Any day on a river is better than a day off the river. I have had days on rivers (many times) when I have caught nothing, and days when the river gods could not have been more generous. Fishing can be easy or frustrating, dumb luck or a game of incisive skill; it is always unpredictable—and the expectation matters. With fly fishing, I can take a plethora of pleasures even if I don't finally catch a fish: in having found and stalked a good trout, chosen the right fly, cast well and accurately, raised it, then possibly hooked but not caught it.

I can't tell someone who loves fishing competition that he doesn't or shouldn't love it. All pleasures are individual, and I don't doubt that he does love it, and that I'd be a smug mandarin to say, "You shouldn't."

But against all the promotion for his game, and others like it, I merely add my voice for something else: I keep coming back, never having got enough of it, because I like the company or the solitude or the chase, because some big fish got away, because I like the chance to use my fierce passions happily, because there are still many skills to learn, mysteries to untangle, because I don't have to win, because I don't have to go but want to go, because of the surprise, the delight, the fun.

I'd hate to go fly fishing if I *had* to catch fish—big ones and a lot of them.

I'd hate to make love, too, by the clock, for a prize, in a public place.

48

A PARLIAMENT
OF SKILLS

In the beginning, I thought that when I could cast an honest thirty feet I'd be a fly fisher. And of course you cannot even begin to play until you can ante up a decent cast of that distance. In some places, under some circumstances, that one skill will get you your first fish—bluegill, bass, even trout, but it won't get you *all* the fish you want, not all the time.

Some of the fish you cannot catch will be another twenty, thirty, or fifty feet distant. Some will be feeding on insects or foods that, on or beneath the surface, haven't yet entered your consciousness. Latin aside, you won't even know the insects are there. Some fish may be feeding in sections of the river that require reach or slack casts, which you don't know exist, or some sophisticated manipulation of the line to avoid drag.

A dozen thwarting errors might have occurred before you're even ready to make your first cast: you might not have seen the bigger fish feeding to the left, nor known from a rise what food a fish might be taking; you might have put your quarry down by clumsy wading, by coming too close to the fish, by standing too tall; you might not have tied your knots with care, or selected the proper fly, or built a long enough leader, or positioned yourself properly to cast to the best advantage.

You might not have known your trout's behavior well enough, or the ecology or hydrology of moving water, or the entomology of the river. You might not have mastered the discrete angling skills needed to gull that particular trout, for it is the compelling fascination of fly fishing that we must constantly bring together many disparate skills and different faculties—even as a parliament does—and that some are learned rather quickly, even in schools and from books, and others require hundreds of hours of actual fishing.

Experience teaches—but only if we encourage it to do so. Without a wiser or more experienced hand nearby we're likely to repeat the same minute—but fatal—casting flaw ad nauseam, or miss the telltale wink of white that indicates a fish's mouth opening to take a nymph in four feet of water.

"Try casting from *here*," the wiser head says, and you shift position, kneel, and the fly no longer drags, and the trout no longer takes you to be a threat. "Don't cast blindly," he says.

"You won't be ready when the fish do rise, or you'll put them down."

Local experience can produce dazzling intimacy with a particular stretch of water, but there is another kind of knowledge that we ought to seek, too: the ability to fish *any* water, under almost any circumstances.

I was fishing a tough little run on the Beaverhead with Al Troth some years ago—well, it was tough for me. The water shot directly above me and the only suitable place to stand was a trifle to the left, directly downstream of the brisk, choppy run, with my left hand required for balance every now and then. I cast upstream and the current tugged the line, which then dragged the fly instantly. I "S"ed the line and it still came down like a shot. I cast hard, stopped the line in the air, and let a whole section of it fall downstream; but the current was too strong, and this induced drag, too. What finally drew a strike, three-quarters of an hour later, was a very long, very supple leader tippet, perhaps thirty-five inches of it, that fell in a near bird's nest on the current and took a few seconds to straighten. Some years later, Lefty Kreh showed me a tower cast that would have worked—and had I asked, Al (who has all the skills) would have shown me what to do at once. I just didn't have the wit to manage that problem yet.

Golf, tennis, baseball, basketball, swimming, and every other sport require unique blends of skills—and some of them are similar, and all powers must exist more or less harmoniously for the thing to get done. Eye, stroke, timing, power—all must work together so that the result is so seamless we think it natural. "A line will take us hours maybe," Yeats says in "Adam's Curse," "yet if it does not seem a moment's thought/Our stitching and unstitching has been naught." That naturalness—in a poem, a golf stroke, the pursuit of a fish with a fly rod—is rarely earned without severe effort. And it's more than synchronized swimming.

isn't it? It is the unique presence of the natural world in the equation, the live unpredictability of the fish and its world, the need to summon the too often forgotten skills of the predator, that makes fly fishing not a sport but a pursuit that engages our total selves.

In fly fishing, when one is learning, it all seems monstrously unnatural: line is always tangling; casts collapse; casts double back upon themselves; we're always a hand and a half short when we're tying knots; the fish fly before us in fright. We guess and we gamble. We're lucky when we succeed. We're clubfooted aliens striving for balletic grace. So we go to schools, read books and magazine articles, seek the help of wiser friends, add more and more time, more and more intensity to our efforts, stretch ourselves toward what we're sure we can be but cannot yet imagine. The confirmation, always, is when the trout takes the fly.

Only much later . . . when in some Zenlike fashion the rod becomes an extension of our arm; when we have tied a knot so often that we can almost do it blindfolded (the way we trained to dismantle and reassemble an M-1 rifle in basic training), using teeth and the feel of the tongue, then pressing the knot against a finger so that the loose strands stand at attention, to be cut; when the stutter flight of an insect instantly says "caddis" or the slow rise says "dun"; when the line is balanced to the rod; when we spot the fish quickly enough, identify its feeding preference, approach carefully to the exactly correct position, make an accurate reach cast (without lining the fish); when the fly is right, the hook properly sharpened; when the leader turns over beautifully and the fly floats with perfect naturalness along the feeding lane . . . it all comes together.

All those minute and differing skills, from the outposts of our existence, meet and find a single order. Eye, ear, foot, fingers—all are there, in concert. You have read the water right, chosen the proper fly, and cast from the proper position. The line has taken wing. The fish has seen the fly, risen, and been tricked. You struck with the deft hand of the young Arthur drawing forth the sword, and it all held.

It happens that way sometimes.

It happens for me more and more lately.

Trust me: it's worth the effort and the wait.

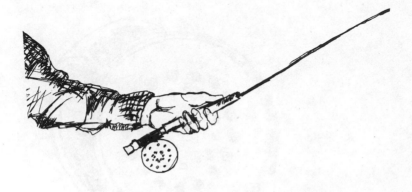

49

THE *THINGS*
OF FLY FISHING

Now and again, after the controversies and the confusions, the remembrances of better rivers past, the good and necessary conservation talk, after the personalities and the skills and the beautiful places where you've been or want to go, after the myriad techniques and strategies, after the gossip and the news and the dreaming of adventures that might or might not occur next summer or in seven years, the new knots, the better tips, the words of it and the images of it and the act of fly fishing itself, I find enjoyment again in the simple things upon which all of fly fishing rests.

Take the dry fly.

There's something to admire for an hour, as it rests on the desk before me, balanced high on its hackles and firm tail, a classic Catskill tie. It took centuries for this fly to be born, from discrete, even minute, changes in its architectonics to the hackle, the winging, the body, the tail. Berners, Cotton, Ogden, Halford, and a dozen (maybe a hundred) others had a hand in it; genetic tinkering gave us that precise shade of blue dun; the great freestone rivers of the Catskills demanded a firm rather than soft tail, crisp rather than limp hackle; Theodore Gordon, Rube Cross, Preston Jennings, Art Flick (who tied this one), and others (known and unknown) fussed with the proportions; and then we got this Dun Variant, perky and brilliant and simple, and (to the right creatures) tasty as blueberry pie.

It took centuries, too, to build the rod and line that would cast such a fly properly—and such rods, dry-fly rods of bamboo, then glass, then graphite, led us to develop these other flies I now lay on the desk beside the first: an elk-hair caddis and a Parachute Adams tied by Al Troth; a Sparkle Dun by Craig Mathews; A.K.'s Baetis; one of Dick Talleur's cut-wings (that goes slant on the table but will float exactly right); a Pale Morning Dun tied for me by Len Wright after Vince Marinaro's thorax-style, with a V at the bottom of the hackle so it will set itself on the film, allowing the body and wings to become visible to the trout, with Len's shrewd body segmentation and the body's precise shade of lemon-yellow chartreuse. I look at a grasshopper tied cunningly with bent turkey-wing legs, a deer-hair head, a yellow body, and at a magisterial Hendrickson, tied by Larry Duckwall, with its pale pink body, blue-dun hackle, and tight head.

The flies are minor monuments, and I touch them lightly and rearrange them, delighted with their ingenuity and with their diversity and with their possibilities. I have a couple of thousand of them in my boxes, and I take *almost* as much pleasure looking at them as in fishing them. But not quite. I'm not a collector but a user, and though I'm mad for them, I only recently allowed myself to be persuaded not to use the flies Art Flick gave me by the handful when we were on the water together. I may not be a collector, but I am a fly fisher who sometimes hoards.

We take special pleasure in all things made well—from a poem to a television set to a dry fly. We like the things in our life that are sweet and useful: color, shape, and form "beautiful" in ways we consider beautiful. And we like the precise taper and action of a rod—in whatever material we love most—such that it becomes an extension of arm and body rhythm. Over the years such tools are different extensions of different arms: how I once loved the soft and the slow; how I insist now on what is firm and fast. I recently lent my friend Knox, an experienced fly fisher, a rod that I had had specially made for me, and on a bonefish flat he found it too stiff to be used for more than half a dozen casts. I had asked the maker to fashion me a "telephone pole," and its authority and power give me great pleasure. With it I can cast more delicately than I can with the most delicate-seeming rods.

Nor is there, objectively, for everyone, the perfect reel, for each person will find most apt the certain sound of a click pawl, the muted hum of another, the absence of sound, the watchlike steadiness of the mechanisms as he turns the handle, its machined brilliance. Len Wright used only Perfects; another friend can afford to choose only Bogdans; I've been in love with my Princess for decades—but have betrayed her lately; and wise fly fishers love the Orvis, the Abel, the durable old Medalist, the Fin-Nor, and a dozen others.

In the beginning we find these *things* of angling bewildering. I once couldn't distinguish between some clunker glass and a Gillum; I scarcely knew the proper fly to choose, what to look for in a fly—and now there are hundreds of patterns and styles I loathe so much that I would drink bile before I'd tie one of them onto a leader.

Experience makes us finicky—but it teaches each of us differently. I like downlocking reel seats to the exclusion of all others, except when a true fighting butt is absolutely needed; perhaps it's my poor casting, which causes line to wrap around even a slightly extended butt—but I eschew butts and rarely use even an uplocking seat.

I look for a certain strength and elasticity in my leaders, looseness in my boot-foot waders, and hundreds of hard-to-define qualities of fishiness in my flies. And the better nipper; there's less to love in a nipper—except when a poor one causes mischief.

Friends say I have betrayed some aesthetic god of fly fishing by abandoning bamboo—but I've found graphite lovable. Still, I've just acquired a bamboo rod from George Maurer that sings, and I may yet convert back, if partly.

I look for the things that are sweet and useful, and when I find them I become an ogler and a hoarder and even a proselytizer . . . until something happens that makes me change completely, and then I see differently and have different loyalties and prefer the opposite of what pleased me last year. "Do I contradict myself?" asks Whitman. "Very well then I contradict myself." And why not? This is not loyalty to a principle that, once seen clearly, might be worth a life or a lifetime; this is the hedonist's search for that "thing" that will give a bit more pleasure on the water, that functions with greater ease, that brings together in a harmonious way the accumulated wisdom of great anglers and persuades because it works.

I never used a Suspender Midge until I sat beside John Goddard as he caught three large trout on his version of this fly—and now I won't go near the water without half a dozen of them. They're beautiful *things* to behold.

In the end, what *works* is what I find most beautiful in fly fishing, and often enough, what works does so because I believe in it and it extends from my discrete skills, at a particular moment in *my* evolution as a fly fisher.

Only at some last moment, on the water, does my attention shift from the lovely *things* of fly fishing to the pursuit, the challenge of the quarry, to the mysterious world of water that it inhabits. Then I want all of my *things*—my playthings and my tools and my weapons—to work seamlessly.

Sometimes, miraculously, they do.

50

FLY FISHING IN BED

For two weeks I lay on my back in the hospital bed, mostly awake and inert, without pain, life coming back into my veins through thin tubes that I knew could be made into splendid sand-eel or minnow imitations. Except for visits, I had not been in a hospital before. I had visited hospitals for births, and twice I had visited them to touch the dying shards of life. I did not especially relish the hospital's odd cross between Chekhov's Ward Six and a daytime soap with its admixture of lives impossible to save, degrees of madness and collapse and loss and pain, lives linked by disease. So I lived mostly in my thoughts, and these were about random moments of my life and whether my current position was the product of poor planning.

I thought a lot about fishing. I was not dying or delirious, nor was I terrified—like Hemingway's Nick Adams in "Now I Lay Me," who fishes every foot of a favorite river as a stay against fear, an exercise in reconstruction. Fishing memories came from times fifty-five years apart, from obscure to popular parts of the Catskills, from creeks fifty miles from New York City to Montana and Idaho and Iceland and England, from places where I'd merely fished for a day, passing through. I let the images appear as they would, a few at a time—some longer, some merely seconds; though I let them play themselves out in my mind, appearing by some happy free association, I found I could hold or dismiss them, too, and I found that they mingled with thoughts of my children and my wife and my little business and what I'd written and things I'd said or done.

There was plenty of time.

I was in no rush whatsoever.

For the first time in forty years, I had no place to go, no work I had to do. Quite selfishly, I had no one to think about but myself. I could take stock or imagine or remember or merely watch the gargoyle on the building out the window and across the street, which, when pigeons flocked to it, appeared to move. I wanted to understand what had happened to me, how I'd gotten here, my role in it. I wanted to walk out, after the operation, with a new plan. I'd had a nasty scare but had been lucky, and the illness had triggered a reset button. I'd been given a chance to head off in another direction, if that's what I chose.

Mostly I thought about fishing—the perch and pumpkinseeds I'd caught almost before memory, a bigmouth bass that wandered off with the three-inch sunny I'd baited for it, a first trout, a ten-pound carp, smallmouth on popping bugs in the Ten Mile River, a first trout ticking a sunken fly on Michigan's Au Sable, a first trout on a dry fly, certain difficult or large or impossible trout, fish caught and fish lost. I thought about a dozen raw Opening Days on the East Branch of the Croton; trips to the St. Lawrence for smallmouth and pike; my first sight of the Rockies, of Henry's Lake, of the Madison River, of a spring creek. It had not been so vast and panoramic and adventuresome a fishing life as many, but I had made the most of what there was, and I had had other business to transact, which I took to be important.

A salmon suddenly took the Hairy Mary, riffle-hitched, at the end of my long line, V-ing its way across a flat slick on the Strengir section of the Grimsa. It was the only time I'd fished for salmon. The fish took in a rush, roiling the surface, and then raced for the far bank and leaped like a rocket. It was the largest fish I'd ever had on a fly rod, and I was sure I'd lose it. Up it leaped, and then again, suspended in the air, shaking. And then, at the end of the long line, two feet from the lip of the pool, it leaped again, and then rolled and slashed at the surface.

Surely it would leave the pool, head into the heavy rapids below, break off. But it turned and sped directly toward me, so I lost contact. I twitched in the hospital bed as I did so, and the arm with the intravenous tubes, my left, moved downward, imping a long stripping tug. And in a few moments we were connected again. While the fish hovered and shook its head, less than half a fly line from me, I got all the slack back onto the reel, raised the rod, and thought I might have a chance. I could see the fish clearly in the clear water— pushing its head down, shaking—and it was surely the largest salmon I'd had on that week, by double.

I kept a wide arc in my rod and pumped and urged the fish closer to me; it came inchmeal—and then it went upstream into heavy current, tired itself, and soon was at hand, bright silver in the auburn shallows, its great jaw hooked, sea lice on its upper flank, gills red and spastic, about eighteen pounds' worth.

I had gotten to this hospital bed through colossal stupidity. I had had what I misdiagnosed and misjudged as flu a full five or six days earlier—and I'd been rocky for several weeks before that. But I never got sick; I was the Lou Gehrig of publishing.

In my teens I'd always been able to hold my head underwater long after thirty competitors had come up for air. I drew liberally on raw will, rarely on good sense, and if challenged, took a few aspirin, slept a bit longer, and made perfectly clear to my body that I would have none of such foolishness. There was always more work to take on, more I *had* to do; there was always a bit more I should do for some good and proper reason. Then after four days of severe intestinal symptoms, chills like the *petit mal,* and increasing weakness, I found myself at a business lunch and took as a poor sign that I could not lift my fork.

And still I persisted, thinking another hour would turn me, until several days later I regained consciousness in an emergency ambulance, oxygen mask on my face, the faces of my wife and two of my children looking down at me with anguished fear—and I was fully dehydrated, yellow with jaundice, high-fevered, with a failing pulse and blood pressure headed south. I might have slipped into shock at any moment, they told me later. For the first time in my life I had not the slightest shred of will to protect myself. I could have danced away without a fight, merely closing my eyes, which wanted to close, and drifting back to where I'd been. I'd have felt no pain.

It was my unconsciousness of my predicament that troubled me most, later, when I lay there, letting whatever was in the tubes do the hard work, quiet the gall bladder that had broadcast such sour news to my liver, bile duct, and other parts of my body that would listen. I had worked too hard, thought too hard about everything and anything and anyone other than myself, and I'd nearly become nothing to anyone.

Many writers have been connecting their psychic lives to fly fishing lately, and the wits have popped out like crab grass and found fly-fishing psychobiography to be the fairest and funniest of game. But if you love and understand the simple magic of water and trout and wilderness and fly imitation, it is not at all far-fetched.

In the bed as I was waiting for the operation, my brain made trips, and the trips had flies in them: the raw strike of big bluefish to a sand-eel fly Lou Tabory had given me; the generous curl on flat water when a parachute Pale Morning Dun slipped over the exact spot where a great trout had just risen; the lumbering bulldog force of a largemouth after it exploded under a hair bug; the rush of a pike and the quick take of mountain brookies; the railroad rush of that first tarpon, at daybreak in the Marquesas; the first sight of Hendricksons, after a long morning's wait with Mike Migel, now gone, on a gray May afternoon. What a glorious sight: the dead water suddenly covered with ten, twenty, then fifty slate-winged flies, like sailboats. Two trout cruising first a few feet from the head of the pool, then drifting back and taking fixed feeding positions. The flies disappearing in silent circles that could quicken the dullest pulse. It was the herald of a new season. The awakening of the dead earth. The return of life when life, in a winter of threats, had not always seemed sustainable.

And then I was home and had days yet to indulge myself in this sweet memory pie. I began to sort and tinker with my scores of fly boxes, and I began to think of my new season.

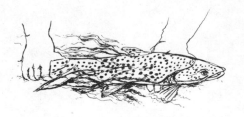